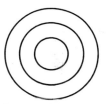

0200 hours, May 17, 1943.
"Goner" is the radio message as a
perfectly placed
Barnes Wallis bouncing bomb
explodes against
the Moehne Dam's inner face.
Painting by Frank Wootton

THE DAM BUSTERS

Paul Brickhill was born in 1916 in Melbourne, Australia, and was educated in Sydney. He volunteered in 1940 and for five years was a fighter pilot in the Royal Australian Air Force. He flew Hurricane bombers at El Alamein, was transferred to Spitfires, and was shot down in Tunisia in 1943. In a German prisoner-of-war camp he worked on "X" Escape Organization. After the war he worked as a journalist in London, Germany, Austria and New York. Brickhill has written several other war books including *Reach for the Sky* in the Bantam War Book series.

THE BANTAM WAR BOOK SERIES

This is a series of books about a world on fire.

These carefully chosen volumes cover the full dramatic sweep of World War II. Many are eyewitness accounts by the men who fought in this global conflict in which the future of the civilized world hung in balance. Fighter pilots, tank commanders and infantry commanders, among others, recount exploits of individual courage in the midst of the large-scale terrors of war. They present portraits of brave men and true stories of gallantry and cowardice in action, moving sagas of survival and tragedies of untimely death. Some of the stories are told from the enemy viewpoint to give the reader an immediate sense of the incredible life and death struggle of both sides of the battle.

Through these books we begin to discover what it was like to be there, a participant in an epic war for freedom.

Each of the books in the Bantam War Book series contains a dramatic color painting and illustrations specially commissioned for each title to give the reader a deeper understanding of the roles played by the men and machines of World War II.

PAUL BRICKHILL

THE DAM BUSTERS

with Foreword by
Marshal of the RAF Lord Tedder GCB
with additional material by
the author

RL 7, IL 8-up

THE DAM BUSTERS
A Bantam Book

PRINTING HISTORY
First published in Great Britain by
Evans Brothers, Ltd. in 1951
Bantam edition / January 1979

Drawings by Tom Beecham.
Maps by Benjamin F. Klaessig.

ISBN 0-553-12571-0

Published simultaneously in the United States and Canada

PRINTED IN THE UNITED STATES OF AMERICA

To the men, living and dead,
who did these things

CONTENTS

FOREWORD

617 SQUADRON, originally formed to carry out one specific operation with a weapon specially designed for that purpose, had, by the end of the war, built up a record of individual and collective courage and skill which is unique. The story which is told in this book cannot but make its readers feel humble in the face of such devotion, such self-sacrifice, and such courage.

Nevertheless this story does more than set out the history of one individual squadron; it throws a spotlight on many of the factors which lay behind the successful and decisive employment of air power. It shows scientist, commander and operator working together as a close-knit team, each contributing towards the common aim of greater efficiency; it shows efficiency interpreted in the short term as "accuracy," and in the long term as "maximum effect with minimum effort." There have been those who allege that the air weapon is necessarily indiscriminate and that the aim of air power is destruction for the sake of destruction. This book is the story of a team that gave the lie to that allegation; a team whose work had a profound influence on the conduct of air operations, a team whose initiative, skill and self-sacrifice on the one hand saved many an air crew who would otherwise have been lost on abortive operations, and on the other hand obviated much useless destruction and pointless loss of life in Europe. Here also is a story of inspired leadership under conditions of almost unbelievable strain, leadership at all levels—within the individual crews, leadership by the Squadron Commander and leadership by the Group Commander—leadership which inspired men to face up to, and overcome, "impossibilities." May their example be an inspiration to us, now and in the future.

TEDDER

BRIEFING

Once I asked an Air Marshal what he thought 617 Squadron was worth, and after a while he said, "Well, one can't really say, but I suppose they were worth ten other squadrons." He pondered a little longer and added: "No, that isn't quite so either. Ten other squadrons couldn't have done what they did, and then of course you've got to consider that inventor chap and the freak weapons he gave them. I suppose 617 was the most effective unit of its size the British ever had."

This is a story of quality as against quantity, demonstrating that exceptional skills and ingenuity can give one man or one unit the effectiveness of ten. It seems that this is a rather British synthesis of talents, and perhaps this story will reassure those who are dismayed by the fact that the British and their allies are outnumbered in this not too amicable world.

What is probably more important, the talents that made 617 what they were evolved a new form of precision bombing which enabled a specific military target to be hit accurately and destroyed. Already this is pointing a way towards the end of "carpet" bombing of cities, that dreadfully inescapable feature of recent war.

Forgive me for cloaking occasional characters in tactful anonymity. They are still alive.

There is so much to tell that some of the "617" men, like David Wilson, Arthur Kell, Bunny Clayton, Bob Knights and many others, cannot be given full credit for their brave competence. Likewise there are too many to name in thanking those who told me about 617. They were too modest to talk about themselves, so I got them to tell me about the others. And vice versa.

The famous dams raid was just the start of it all. Guy Gibson wrote some of the wonderful story of this affair towards the end of his excellent *Enemy Coast Ahead*.* Any full account must draw on this, and I am most grateful for permission to do so, in addition to my own researches. My special gratitude goes to John Pudney, who unselfishly gave me a lot of material he had researched himself and then continued to give wise, professional help. My thanks also to Air Commodore Pat Huskinson for the anecdote from *Vision Ahead;* to Air-Vice Marshal C. N. H. Bilney; John Nerney, Chief of R.A.F. Historical Records; Tom Cochrane, Deputy Chief Information Officer; Mr. A. J. Charge, Keeper of Photographs at the Imperial War Museum; and, by no means least, to Wing Commander Willie Tait for the inspiration of his fine accounts.

PAUL BRICKHILL

---

*Soon to be published as part of the Bantam War Book Series.

Guy Gibson V.C.

1

A WEAPON IS CONCEIVED

The day before the war started Barnes Wallis drove for five hours back to Vickers' works at Weybridge, leaving his wife and family in the quiet Dorset bay where they had pitched tents for a holiday.

He had that morning reluctantly decided that war was not only inevitable but imminent, and he was going to be needed at his drawing-board. No point in bringing the family back yet to a house near an aircraft factory till it became clear what influence the Luftwaffe was going to have on one's expectation of life.

Wallis did not look like a man who was going to have much influence on the war; he looked more like a diffident and gentle cleric. At 53 his face was unlined and composed, the skin smooth and pink and the eyes behind the horn-rimmed glasses mild and grey; crisp white hair like a woolly cap enhanced the effect of benevolence. Many people who stood in his way in the next three years were deceived by this, having failed to note the long upper lip which gave stubbornness to the mouth and was the only visible clue to his persistent refusal to be diverted from his purpose. Even his friends did not quite understand this because Wallis, in a vaguely indefinable way, was a little insulated from the rough and tumble of ordinary life by a mind virtually on another plane, immersed in figures and theories. They knew him as a gentle, if rather detached, aircraft designer, and it was not till later that they began to use the word "genius."

He spent the last night of peace alone in his house

near Effingham, and in the morning, like most people, listened to the oddly inspiring speech of Chamberlain's. Afterwards he sat in silence and misery, not even swearing because the strongest words in his vocabulary were inadequate.

One thought had been haunting him since the previous morning's decision: what could he, as an aircraft designer and engineer, do to shorten the war? The thought stayed with him for a long time and through remarkable events before it was honourably discharged. None of the strange ideas that emerged from it came in a flash of inspiration. There was no one moment in which Barnes Wallis shouted, "Eureka, I have it!" Scientific minds seldom work in that spectacular and convenient fashion. Ideas germinated slowly in his head, a fertile breeding ground, feeding on study and thought, amorphous and unrecognizable at first like any embryo till gradually they took shape and were recognised.

He had been designing for Vickers since before the first world war. When that started he was designing an early British airship, but a potentate in the upper strata of government decided that work on it should stop as the war was not going to last longer than three months; so Wallis enlisted in the Artists' Rifles as a private. As the war, after three months, was disconcertingly remote from ending, the potentate ordered work resumed on the airship, and Wallis was brought back to his drawing-board.

In the twenties he designed the R.100, the most successful British dirigible. In the thirties he invented the geodetic form of aircraft construction and, using this, designed the Wellesley which captured the world's non-stop distance record, and the Wellington, which was the mainstay of Bomber Command for the first three years of the war (and in 1951 was still being used for advanced training).

Vickers' works, nestled in the banked perimeter of the old Brooklands motor-racing track, was turning out Wellingtons as fast as it could, and Wallis was designing their proposed successor, the Warwick. At this

Warwick

time he was on the design of the Warwick's tailplane, which was being troublesome. Clearly any additional work would have to be done in his own spare time and there was, also quite clearly, not going to be much spare time.

Bombers and bombs were the directions in which he was most qualified to help. Bombs, particularly, seemed a fruitful field. He knew something about R.A.F. bombs, their size, shape, weight and so on; the knowledge had been essential when he was designing the Wellington, so that it could carry the required bombs over the required distance. It was not knowledge which, in Wallis, inspired complacency. The heaviest bomb was only 500 lb., and aiming was so unpredictable that the Air Force was forced to indulge in stick bombing—you dropped them one after another in the pious hope that one would hit the target. One hoped then that it would go off. Too many didn't. Years of placid peace and the diffidence of the Treasury had inhibited development of bombs, a natural consequence of a war to end all wars but regrettable in the face of reality. Lack of development had been assisted by the presence here and there in the Services of a few of those officers who thrive only in peacetime, lacking neither in courage nor devotion to Regulations and afternoon tea but lamentably deficient in the vitality and intellectual resilience that lead to actual work being done.

R.A.F. bombs, too, were old, very old. Nearly all were stocks hoarded from 1919. There had been an attempt in 1921 to design a better bomb, and in 1938 they actually started to produce them, but in 1940 there were still very few of them. Both new bombs and old were filled with a mediocre explosive called amatol (and only 25 per cent of the weight consisted of explosive). There *was* a far better explosive called RDX, but production of that had been stopped in 1937. (It was not till 1942 that the R.A.F. was able to use RDX-filled bombs.) Meantime Luftwaffe bombs contained a much more powerful explosive than amatol—and half the weight of the German bomb was explosive.

Wallis knew there had been an attempt in 1926 to make 1,000-lb. bombs for the R.A.F. but they never even got to the testing stage. The Treasury was against them; the Air Staff thought they would never need a bomb larger than 500 lb., and anyway Air Force planes were designed to carry 500-pounders. Thousand-pound bombs would need new and costlier planes for the whole Air Force and the country could not afford it. Not till 1939 did the Air Staff begin to think seriously again of the 1,000-pounder, and six months *after* the war started they placed an order for some.

These shortcomings were not so obvious then, particularly as (as Wallis knew) all air forces favoured small bombs designed to attack surface targets. The blast of bigger bombs was curiously local against buildings, and a lot of little bombs seemed better than an equal weight of larger ones. Even larger bombs needed a direct hit to cause much damage, and there was more chance of a direct hit with a lot of little bombs.

To Wallis's methodically logical mind there was a serious flaw in all this. Factories and transport could be dispersed; in fact *were* dispersed all over Germany.

Bombing (vintage 1939) would not damage enough factories to make much difference.

He started wondering *where* and *how* bombing could hurt Germany most. If one could not hit the dispersed war effort perhaps there were key points. Perhaps the sources of the effort. And there the probing mind was fastening on a new principle.

The sources of Germany's effort, in war or peace, lay in power. Not political power (that was dispersed too, and hidden in deep shelters at the approach of aircraft). Physical power! Great sources of energy too massive to move or hide—coal mines, oil dumps and wells, and "white coal"—hydroelectric power from dams. Without them there could be no production and no transport. No weapons. No war.

But they were too massive to dent by existing bombs. One might as well kick them with a dancing pump! The next step—in theory anyway—was easy. Bigger bombs. Much bigger!

But that meant bigger aircraft; much bigger than existing ones. All right then—bigger aircraft too.

That was the start of it. It sounds simple but it was against the tenets of the experts of every air force in the world.

Wallis started calculating and found the blast of bigger bombs *was* puny against steadfast targets like coal mines, buried oil and dams. Particularly dams, ramparts of ferro-concrete anchored in the earth.

Then perhaps a new *type* of bomb. But there Wallis did not know enough about bombs and the logic stopped short.

The war was a few weeks old when the dogged scientist dived into engineering and scientific libraries, and at lunchtimes, when he pushed the problem of the Warwick's tailplane aside for an hour or so, he sent out for sandwiches, stayed at his desk and started to learn about bombs.

His designing office was evacuated to an old house at Burhill, near Weybridge, which had been built by Wellington, and there he studied the chemistry and behaviour of high explosives, aerodynamic bomb design, the forging, casting and milling, the theories of light and heavy case bombs, the fusing and the aiming. And at night at home he did the same, absorbed and lost to his family for hours. If a bomb had gone off near by he possibly would not have noticed, or if he did his first thought would probably have been to inquire into the chemical nature of its explosive or the type of casing, or the charge/weight ratio. As the hard winter of 1939 arrived he progressed to the study of the sources of power.

Coal mines! Impossible to collapse the galleries and tunnels hundreds of feet underground. Possible, he decided, that a heavy bomb might collapse the winding-shaft so that the lift would not work. No lift. No work. No coal. But that could soon be repaired.

Oil! Rumanian oil-fields were too far for existing bombers, but a possibility for a future bomber. Germany's synthetic refineries were massive and well defended; perhaps a target for bigger bombs.

Dams! Three German dams stood out—the Moehne, the Eder and the Sorpe. All in the Ruhr, they accounted for nearly all the water supply to that monstrous arsenal. Wallis knew that the German method needed eight tons of water to produce a ton of steel. The possibilities were intriguing.

The Moehne dammed Moehne Lake where the Heve flowed into the Ruhr River, maintaining the level so that barges with coal and steel and tanks could go to and from the foundries. Moehne Lake held 134 million tons of water. The Eder dammed the Eder River in Eder Lake, 212 million tons of water. It controlled the level of Germany's second most important waterway, the Mittelland Canal. Even Kassel, forty miles away, got its water from the Eder. The Sorpe dammed another tributary of the Ruhr River in Sorpe Lake.

The Moehne was 112 feet thick at the base, 130 feet high and 25 feet thick at the top where a roadway ran; the Eder was even bigger. Wallis acknowledged that they were formidable. A 500-lb. bomb would hardly scratch the concrete. No less formidable the Sorpe, an earth dam, two sloping mounds of earth sealed and buttressed in the centre by a core of concrete.

In an engineering library Wallis unearthed accounts of their construction compiled by the proud engineers who had built them, and found it hard to discipline his excitement as he read what the effects of breaching the dams could be.

It would not merely destroy hydro-electric power and deprive foundries of essential water, but affect other war factories which needed water for their processes. Disrupting them might cause a dozen critical bottlenecks in the completion of tanks, locomotives, guns, aircraft—almost anything one cared to name. It would deprive the populace of water too, which was no cause for joy in a gentle soul like Wallis but would at least induce in them a lessening of zest for the war as well as some testy sentiments directed not only at the R.A.F. but at Hitler too. Humanity is not inclined to limit its censure for discomfort to the direct cause only. Indirect sources get their share; another and intriguing way, thought Wallis whimsically, of attacking the enemy at the source of power.

There was still more to it. Breaches in the dams would send enormous floods ripping down the valleys, tearing away roads, bridges and railway lines, smashing factories and houses, so that some factories, instead of being deprived of water, would receive somewhat too much.

All this was fine, Wallis thought . . . logical ideas; but again one big flaw. The dams were so colossal that bombs twenty times bigger than existing ones were not going to hurt them.

His figures showed that when a 1,000-pounder exploded the charge expanded as a gas bubble, but at the end the bubble was only 20 feet across. A lot of damage was done beyond this 10-foot radius, however, by flying fragments, by blast and by the pressure pulse, or "shock wave." Wallis well remembered the pedantic description of shock waves: ". . . there is no motion

of the transmitting medium other than the usual oscilla-
tion of particles to and fro about their position of
rest as the wave passes through them." Thin air gave
scope to flying fragments and blast but the shock wave
soon dissipated.

It would vibrate a structure, but not enough. To be
destructive, shock waves had to travel through a more
solid medium than air. And somewhere in Wallis's
brain a little cell awoke and stirred restlessly, an old
memory, locked up and almost forgotten. He felt
there was something he knew about shock waves that
he should remember, tried to think what it was—it
was a long time ago—but the harder he tried the farther
it receded. Memory can be so tantalising. He thought
about it for the rest of the day, trying irritatedly to
isolate it, but it had gone. Memory is like a woman; it
was only when he put it out of his mind that it
sneaked insidiously back to him again.

It was something he had read, something about
concrete. And then it hit him. Waterloo Bridge! Concrete piles being driven into the bed of the Thames!
That was years ago. The piles had kept shattering
mysteriously and there had been an investigation. He
started searching his bookcases and in a quarter of an
hour had found it, an article in a 1935 journal of the
Institution of Civil Engineers. The great drop-hammers
had been slamming the piles into the river-bed and the
tops of the piles had been exploding upwards.

Investigation narrowed the cause to the shock waves.
The sudden blows sent shock waves shivering down the
piles; at the bottom they met the blunt resistance of
the clay and bounced back up the pile at something
like 15,000 feet a second, reaching the top just after
the hammer had bounced off, so there was nothing to
rebound from again and they passed out and away,
and in their wake you got a tension after the compression. A sort of crush and then a sharp stretch, almost in
the same moment: enough to make a structure split—to
shatter it.

Concrete, the article concluded sagely, well resisted

compression but poorly withstood tension. Wallis docketed the fact in his mind, thinking of dams.

You needed a solid medium to get destructive shock waves!

Of course, if you could bury a bomb *deep* in . . . But you couldn't slice a big bomb deep into ferro-concrete. No, but you might be able to inject it deep into some less solid medium before it exploded. You'd get the shock waves then. The expanding gas effects would be greater too; tamped by the encircling solids they would have to burst their way out.

He was aware that bombs and shells often buried themselves 3 or 4 feet in the ground before exploding, but that was so shallow the explosion forced its way easily to the top, causing a small crater, and the shock waves dissipated into the air. It was less effective than a surface explosion because the blast and shock waves went straight up instead of outwards.

But if you could *lock* the explosion underground so it could not break out you would get a sort of seismic disturbance . . . an earthquake! An earthquake bomb!

The idea shaped in his mind while he was sitting in a deep chair in his home at Effingham, an unspectacular setting for the birth of something so powerful.

But how to sink a bomb deeply into a resisting medium? You could not put one deep into a concrete dam. But a dam is set in water!

Water! It might not transmit a shock wave as well as earth but it would do so better than air. The tamping effect of water would produce a concentrated explosion and carry the "shock" punch. Wallis was starting to feel he might be getting somewhere.

And how about sinking the bomb in earth? A schoolboy knew the two principles. The heavier the bomb, the more power and speed it developed in falling. Wallis had learned the classic example in school. Drop a mouse down a well and at the bottom it will be able to get up and run. Drop a horse down and the horse will probably burst. Because it was heavier it would hit *harder*. And the *farther* it fell, the *faster* it would fall!

So there it was: a bomb as heavy as possible (and as slim as possible) dropped from as high as possible.

Wallis looked up more books, studied the propagation of waves in soil, the effects of underground explosions at depth, and even found pages on the penetrative powers into soils of shells and light bombs. There was a piece about an enormous land mine exploded under a German-held hill at Messines Ridge in World War I. A colossal charge sent shock waves ripping into the earth, the hill was destroyed and the shock was felt in Kassel—300 miles away.

Wallis pulled out a pad and pencil and worked for a week, covering sheets with calculations, equations, formulae—accelerations, resistances, kinetic energy, stresses, friction, charge/weight ratios—and came up with a preliminary theoretical answer. A 10-ton bomb, with 7 tons of explosive in an aerodynamically-designed case of special steel, dropped from 40,000 feet, would reach a speed of 1,440 feet per second, or 982 m.p.h. —well over the speed of sound. At that rate it should penetrate an average soil to a depth of 135 feet.

A charge of that size should theoretically "camouflet" (not break the surface) at a depth of 130 feet. What it *would* do was cause a violent earthquake movement on the surface, resulting in a hump forming.

"Such earth movements," said a learned paper, "are capable of doing much damage at great distances."

It looked as though Wallis had found his answer. Or part of it.

2

— AND REJECTED

He worked out theoretical effects, more pages of figures, and decided there was a chance that a 10-ton bomb exploding deep in water by a dam wall would punch out a hole a hundred feet across.

Supposing the bomb did not go as deeply into the earth as the figures predicted? Wallis worked out the effects of a 10-tonner exploding about 40 feet deep. In theory it would throw out the staggering amount of 12,000 tons of earth, leaving a crater 70 feet deep, with lips 250 feet across. He worked out the circumference of the crater and from that the maximum number of men and machines that could gather round the edges. Working day and night they could not fill it in under fourteen days! Supposing one such bomb was dropped accurately in a marshalling yard! Or on a vital railway or canal or road where ground contours prohibited a detour!

Wallis did not get too excited. No bomber in the world would carry a 10-ton bomb. Or for that matter even a 5-ton bomb far enough to get it to a target.

Back to pencil and paper. He knew the limitations of aircraft design in 1940 and in a couple of weeks he knew it was possible to build a 50-ton bomber to carry a 10-ton bomb 4,000 miles at 320 m.p.h. and a height of 45,000 feet. He drew up rough specifications and christened it the "Victory Bomber."

The methodical mind did not overlook anything. At 40,000 feet would constant cloud obscure the targets? Back to the library. The weather should be clear enough on one day in three. That was reasonable.

Could a bomb-aimer pick up a small target from 40,000 feet? Wallis came across a scientific report which showed that a test object a few feet wide could be visible from 35,000 feet.

Winds? Stratospheric winds sometimes reached 200 m.p.h. He set that against bomb-aiming techniques and decided that, whatever the faults of present bomb-aiming, the winds could be allowed for.

And the aiming of bombs—notoriously hit and miss, mostly miss. Wallis found that increasing height did not greatly increase the problems and estimated that new bomb sights being developed and special training could put the bombs near enough to a target to destroy it.

That was the beauty of this 10-ton bomb. It should not have to be a direct hit! The earthquake shock would be so great that a near miss should shake a target to destruction. And another thing—a big bomb exploding 130 feet deep would not crater the surface but cause a huge subterranean cavern. Put such a bomb alongside a bridge or viaduct, and if the shock wave did not shake it to pieces the cavern underneath would knock its support away. An opening trapdoor—a hangman's drop! The bridge would collapse into it.

There was one other possibility—perhaps the greatest of all. A few such bombs, accurately aimed, might shatter the roots of a nation's war effort. That could mean the end of the dreadful "Guernica" carpet bombing, which saturated an area with bombs so limited in effect that the area had to be saturated to make their use militarily worth while. Wiping out cities and civilians at the same time!

But it was only a revolutionary and complicated theory. The Army, Navy and Air Force were deluged with revolutionary, complicated and crackpot theories. The next problem—maybe the biggest—was to get them to listen to this one, to believe and accept it. Wallis spent weeks setting it all out on paper and took it to people he knew in the R.A.F. and the Ministry of Aircraft Production. It was Dunkirk time. A potent new weapon had never been better timed.

Wallis's paper on the "earthquake bomb" roused three main emotions in officials: (1) lukewarm interest; (2) incomprehension; (3) tactful derision.

One man understood and did what he could: Arthur Tedder, a quiet, intensely likeable man smoking a pipe, chained to a desk in Whitehall. But he was only an air vice-marshal then and did not have the influence he acquired later as Eisenhower's deputy in the invasion, and then as Lord Tedder, Marshal of the R.A.F. and Chief of the Air Staff. He brought the bomb and Victory Bomber to the attention of several people in high places but the only result seemed to be a ubiquitous manifestation of courteous but implacable inactivity, often the only defence of hard-working officials plagued by importunate and impractical inventors. Every machine in the country was working overtime on other vital things and the ambitious and excellent four-engined bomber project was just getting under way. It was a fair assumption that it might be disastrous to dislocate that in favour of the Victory Bomber, which would inevitably take much longer to develop. That automatically prejudiced the shock-wave bomb, because there was therefore no aircraft in sight which could drop it from Wallis's prescribed height of 40,000 feet. The new bombers would probably not be able to lift it or, if they could, to carry it far enough to drop it from higher than 20,000 feet, which was not likely to be enough.

And then on July 19, out of the blue, Wallis got an urgent summons to see Lord Beaverbrook, the bright-eyed firecracker who was Minister for Aircraft Production. With "The Beaver" interested anything could happen, and probably at speed. He caught the first train to London, cooled his heels a few minutes in an anteroom and then the big door opened and a young man said: "Lord Beaverbrook will see you now, sir."

Wallis jumped up, cuddling his calculations under his arm, and crossed the threshold, nervous with anticipation; and there was the little man with the wide, mobile mouth, sitting slightly hunched in his chair. It was the speed with which things happened that shook Wallis as much as the things themselves. No gracious, measured preliminaries. He was still in the middle of the floor, walking, when the little man barked:

"Will you go to America for me?"

For a moment Wallis was rattled. He collected himself.

"I'd rather stay here for you, sir."

"What would you do for me here?" Crisply and fast, like repartee.

"Build you a ten-ton bomb and a Victory Bomber to carry it, sir." Wallis was standing his ground better than most. The little man looked at him a moment.

"What good would that do?"

"End the war," Wallis said simply. "An earthquake bomb. I've got it set out here," he touched the papers under his arm.

"All right, never mind that now. Have a look at this," and Beaverbrook tossed over a newspaper clipping. "Look into it and come back and see me to-morrow."

Wallis lost track of the interview after that, probably because there was no more interview. He found himself outside the door; from start to finish it had lasted a bare forty seconds and as his thoughts re-assembled he felt disappointment like a shock. Beaverbrook had never heard of his ideas; it was some other wretched thing he had wanted. Automatically he began to walk away, and it was not till he got to the front door that he began to wonder what the other thing was and remembered the clipping.

It was not in his hand. He searched his pockets. Not there. It was a pretty position; he did not even know what Beaverbrook wanted and he had to advise him to-morrow about it. He could not go back and ask what the subject was . . . he shuddered slightly at the thought. Agitated, he ploughed through his pockets again and in the last one, a fob, when hope had gone, he felt the cutting, drew it out and read it.

It was a report from America about work on pressurised aircraft cabins for high flight. "The Beaver" evidently wanted him to go across and see how it was done.

Very amusing! Wallis had already done experimental work on pressurised cabins and knew how it was done. He went back to Weybridge.

Next day he saw Beaverbrook again, armed this time by experience, and was not rattled. He told the Minister he had all the information needed on pressurising aircraft cabins and there was no need to go to America.

"All right," said Beaverbrook. "What's this about a ten-ton bomb?"

Wallis told him as concisely as he could; difficult for a scientist, who always feels compelled to go into technicalities, but he kept it short and lucid and Beaverbrook was interested.

"You know how short we are of stuff," he said. "This thing's only a theory. We'd have to stop work on other vital things to make it and then it might be a flop."

"It won't be that," Wallis said stubbornly.

"We'd still have to stop work on other things."

"It will be worth it."

"Take too long, wouldn't it?" said "The Beaver." "A ten-ton bomb and a bomber twice the size of anything else sounds like something in the distant future."

"We can do it in stages, sir," Wallis said. "I've got drawings for two-ton and six-ton bombs on the same principle. My Wellingtons can carry the two-tonner all right. The new four-engined ones can carry the six-tonner. They'll be operating in a year."

"Well, I'll see my experts about it," Beaverbrook said. "If it's going to mean diverting too much effort I don't like your chances."

Wallis came out with a sigh of hope and relief, spent some days simplifying his designs and on August 9 took a train to Sheffield to get the advice of steel experts on manufacture of the tempered casings. They would have to be immensely strong to withstand the shock of hitting at 1,000 m.p.h. without breaking, and as light and roomy as possible so the maximum amount of explosive could be crammed into them. Big bomb design

Wellington

is incredibly complicated, but the blitz had started and it was a good time for discussing big bombs to throw back.

Little seemed to happen for a while but behind the scenes things were moving in a ponderous Government way. Little snippets filtered through to Wallis, particularly from that astute ally, Arthur Tedder. Nothing much; just that So-and-so had consented to look into the idea and that So-and-so had expressed mild interest. Out of this came one or two more converts. One was Air Commodore Pat Huskinson, a grey-haired, burly man who was Director of Armament Development for the Ministry of Aircraft Production, renowned for his blunt aggressiveness in forcing new weapons through bottlenecks. But most of Huskinson's time was filled with dozens of other problems, and then a bomb fell on his flat. Huskinson lived but was blinded.

Wallis thought the prospects were still favourable. Sir Charles Craven, managing director of Vickers, was sympathetic and felt confident enough on November 1 to write to Beaverbrook suggesting he gave permission to go ahead on both 10-ton bomb and Victory Bomber.

Then Tedder was posted to take over the R.A.F.

in the Middle East and Wallis had lost his keenest supporter in the sacred and essential precincts of Whitehall. It was soon after that Craven sent for him.

"I'm afraid I haven't very encouraging news for you," Craven said as kindly as he could. "Air Council seem too wary of big bombs. They still believe stick bombing is necessary."

"But can't they *see* what a really big bomb would do?" Wallis said pleadingly.

"Apparently not. They say that from experience they would rather drop four 250-pound bombs than a thousand-pounder. Much less a 22,000-pounder."

"Could they understand my calculations, sir?"

Craven did not comment on their understanding. He said diplomatically that he doubted whether the members would have the *time* to go individually through all the calculations. Which was probably true. And then gently: "They say that anyone who thinks of ten-ton bombs is mad."

Wallis went back to Weybridge in anger, but in the morning the anger had mostly gone and in its place was outraged stubbornness. He started writing a treatise on his 10-ton bomb and called it "A note on a method of attacking the Axis Powers," the kind of obscure title so favoured by scientists; the word "note" being particularly misleading, as such things are often as long as a book.

Wallis's was. He started by outlining his theory of crippling an enemy by destroying the sources of energy, and went on to discuss in exhaustive detail the physical qualities of the targets, shock waves, blast, penetration, bomb design, aircraft design, charge-weight ratios, aiming problems, possible effects, repair potentialities, backed up with pages of graphs and formulae and equations. It was a *tour de force,* explaining step by step so lucidly that a layman could follow it if he took the mathematics for granted.

The "note" took Wallis several months, and then he had it roneoed and bound and posted copies to seventy influential men in science, politics and the Services.

Results were not long coming. A Secret Service man called on him with a copy of the "note" under his arm.

"Did you send this to Mr. ——?" he asked.

"Yes," Wallis said. "Why?"

"I'm afraid you shouldn't have done so, Mr. Wallis."

"Why?"

"It's very secret stuff. This sort of thing must be handled very carefully and only reach authorised persons. Mr. —— was very surprised when this arrived in the post. We were concerned too. I quite realise you didn't mean to be . . ."

"I sent out seventy of them," Wallis said calmly, and the Secret Service was appalled.

"Seventy!" he said. *"Seventy!* Who? To whom? But you shouldn't have. This is vital and very secret!"

"Is it?" said Wallis mildly. "When I showed it to the authorised persons they said I was mad. I'm supposed to be a crackpot and this is regarded by authorised persons as fiddle-faddle."

The Secret Service man said, "Oh!" He asked for the names of the seventy. Wallis read them out and the Secret Service man, who seemed a little uncertain of his ground, went back to London to investigate further.

He appeared again a couple of days later.

"Well, it's all right," he said, "this time. We've decided that as so many were sent out so openly it's actually rather a good form of security. No one will dream it's at all so secret. But please don't do it again."

Wallis bowed gravely. "I hope it will not be necessary again," he said, and the incident was closed.

A few days later there was another result. A copy had reached a Group Captain Winterbotham, who had an office in the City and was used to dealing with unorthodox aspects of the war. He had found it convincing, called on Wallis, and Wallis explained more fully. Winterbotham caught some of his enthusiasm. He knew Sir Henry Tizard, who was scientific adviser to the Ministry of Aircraft Production, and drew his special attention to Wallis's paper.

Tizard read it carefully; as a scientist he could follow the intricate calculations. He went down to see Wallis at Weybridge and was impressed.

"I'd better form a committee to study this more

fully," he said. "It would have to have pretty solid backing from expert opinion. You'll understand, I know. It would divert effort from other important things if we were to go ahead with it and we've got to be reasonably sure it would be worth while."

"Of course," Wallis said. He felt like singing.

Not long after, Wallis met the committee. At the head was Dr. Pye, Director of Scientific Research at the Air Ministry, and the others were scientists too. Wallis explained his ideas and described the probable effect on Germany's war industries if the dams were breached. There was only one really worthwhile time of the year to breach them, and that was in May, when the storage lakes were full after the winter thaw and spring rains, and before the sluice gates were opened to water the country and canals for summer. Then you would get the greatest floods, the most serious loss of water and power. Dr. Pye said the committee would be a few days considering.

A week later Wallis faced the committee to hear their findings. His worst fears were soon over; the report was favourable, but, as they read on, a little disappointingly so. They thought that the dams showed possibilities and the upshot was another committee. This one focused the aim more definitely; it was to be called "The Air Attack on Dams Committee."

The members were again scientists and engineers and in a mood to be interested in something new because even German bombs, though they were more effective than R.A.F. bombs and killed thousands of civilians, had demonstrated the limitations of small bombs. The machine shop in an English factory, for instance, had been hit by seven Nazi 250-lb. bombs and they had damaged only twenty-four out of the 500 machines in the factory. All except two were repairable and the machine shop was running as usual almost immediately. Because aiming was so inaccurate it was obvious that 75 per cent of such bombs were wasted.

"With this big bomb," Wallis earnestly impressed on them, "you don't have to get a direct hit. I think a ten-ton bomb dropped fifty feet away stands a good chance of knocking a hole in a dam like the Moehne. A near miss like that ought to be simple enough to organise."

One of the members, Dr. Glanville of the Road Research Laboratories at Harmondsworth, suggested building a model dam and testing the theories with scaled-down charges of explosive. Wallis accepted delightedly.

Over the next few months, whenever he could spare time from his arduous work at Vickers, Wallis helped Glanville design and painstakingly build a model dam one-fiftieth the size of the Moehne with tiny cubes of concrete, scale models of the huge masonry blocks in the real dam. The model was about 30 feet long, 33 inches high and up to 2 feet thick, a low wall arched between earthen banks, secluded from prying outside eyes in a walled garden.

They flooded the ground at one side to simulate the lake, and Wallis exploded a few ounces of gelignite under the surface 4 feet from the model to give the effect of a 10-tonner going off 200 feet away. There was a commotion on the water and a fountain of muddy water gushed up; on the model a couple of patches of concrete flaked and chipped.

"Not so good there," Wallis said. "Let's try it closer."

He exploded more gelignite 3 feet from the dam, and there was a little more damage. He set off another charge 2 feet away and still found only minor chipping. At a distance of 12 inches (representing a 10-tonner 50 feet from the dam) the gelignite caused a couple of cracks in the outer structure; but they were small cracks, not enough to harm the dam significantly. They tried several more charges, but the cumulative effect was not encouraging.

Months had passed since the first hopeful meeting of the committee, and Wallis could see that their early co-operation was congealing. Glanville built another model, and Wallis tried bigger charges to see what *would* smash the models at a distance. One day a few extra ounces of gelignite a foot away sent a mushroom of water spraying over the wall round the garden and as the spume cleared they saw the water of the little lake gushing through the burst dam. Slabs of concrete had cracked and spilled out and there was the breach that Wallis had been wanting. He calculated the scaled-up charge, which dropped 50 feet away, would smash such a hole in the Moehne. The answer was something like 30,000 lb. of the new explosive RDX, and the gentle scientist did not need pencil and paper to estimate the significance.

Thirty thousand pounds was nearly 14 tons. That was the explosive alone. Add the weight of the thick case of special steel—another 40,000-odd lb. It meant a bomb weighing 70,000 lb.—over 30 tons—and the Victory Bomber, still only on paper and straining the limits of feasible aircraft construction, would carry only a 10-tonner.

The next meeting of the Air Attack on Dams Committee was in a fortnight and it required little thought to foresee it would be the last meeting.

Wallis would not give up.

Supposing, he thought, a bomb could be exploded *against* the dam wall. The shock-wave punch would be much greater. So the explosive needed would be smaller. So would the bomb casing.

"But how to get a big bomb in an exact spot—deep enough for the shock punch and pressed against the wall to make the most of it? Or, as it might require more than one bomb, how could you get them all in the exact spot? A torpedo? But the dams had heavy torpedo netting in front of them and so torpedoes were out. You could drop a bomb from a very low level for accuracy, but bombs don't 'simply drop'. Just after release they carry a lot of forward speed giving them virtually a horizontal trajectory for a while. If you drop a bomb—even a whopper—from very low to get the accuracy, it would simply skid off the water, so that was no good. If you dropped it high enough to enter the water cleanly you had only about one chance in a thousand of putting it right in the exact spot."

Wallis probed at this problem for days and every time he probed he came slap up against the same old problem—the only way would be to drop something from very, very low and somehow make it go and stay where it was supposed to be. But that seemed to be impossible.

Off and on he puzzled about it and then one day out of vague memories he remembered his last holidays with the children just before the war began when they had been skipping stones across the smooth water of a little pond. How on earth, he thought, could I toss a stone low like that and stop it skipping just where I wanted it. Drop any shape of bomb from low at a couple of hundred miles or more an hour and Lord knows where it would skip to.

When dams are full there is practically no space between the level of the water and the top of the dam wall and in his wry imagination he visualised a series of huge grotesque bombs bouncing over the dam wall and flying harmlessly downstream. What a pity, he thought idly, that you can't make a torpedo do a bit of bouncing—over an anti-torpedo net for instance. Hello! that was an idea. If a bomb could hurdle a dam wall it could also hurdle an anti-torpedo net. Such nets were a good 100 yards away from dam walls to keep any explosion at arm's length. But a bomb didn't have to keep skipping farther! Maybe it could be so judged to skip the torpedo net and not skip the dam wall. Hang it all, why not? He felt a little excitement surging inside him. There would probably be three or four feet of dam wall above the water side of the dam. Suppose the skipping of the bomb were timed (if it could be done) so that it was slithering to a stop on the water as it reached the wall—why then the wall would stop it dead and it would simply sink into the water beside the wall as deep as you like. You could have the fuse fixed with a hydrostatic trigger so that the bomb would go off when the water pressure reached the right amount. Set it for 30 feet down or 50 or 100. Please yourself, according to the effect. Hang it, the more he thought

about it the more he liked the idea, even if it did sound
a bit odd.

But the very shape and operation of a torpedo made
that sort of timing virtually impossible. Supposing there
were a missile of a different and more tractable shape
—something that would skip and then be subject to
some form of control or judgement. He began thinking
of those pebbles again and the way they reached the
point where they skipped no longer but sank under the
water.

Wallis went home, dragged a tub into the garden of
his house at Effingham and filled it to the top with water. Then he rigged up a rubber catapult a few feet
away, just a few inches above the level of the water.
A few feet on the other side of the tub he stretched a
string between a couple of sticks so that the string was
also just above the level of the water. Logic told him
that at some time there would be a point where an object might skip the first few times and then slither to a
halt and sink.

He borrowed a marble from his own daughter, Elizabeth, and shot it from the catapult at the water. It
skipped off the surface and cleared the string by several
inches. Elizabeth and the other children looked on
wondering what he was up to. Elizabeth brought the
marble back and Wallis fired it again, this time with a
little less tension on the rubber of the catapult. The
marble slipped off the water and only just cleared the
string. "Ah," thought Wallis, "it *can* be controlled."

He and the youngsters spent the whole morning playing with the marbles on the water and the catapult and
the string, trying different combinations of power and
height while Wallis was finding out how much he could
control the skip. To his deep joy he found that with a
regular shape and weight like a marble, on smooth water he could control it well enough for it to be distinctly
encouraging.

But could he control several skips, which might be
necessary? That remained to be seen. They went in to
lunch eventually, all thoroughly splashed. Wallis was

very cheerful and also, the children thought, very mysterious about it.

Always sensitive to ridicule, Wallis told no one else the details, not even his friend Mutt Summers, chief test pilot for Vickers and the man who had tested his old war-horse, the Wellington bomber. Captain Summers was a hefty extrovert and not inclined to take a freak idea seriously. Unable to keep completely silent, Wallis did say to Summers cagily:

"Mutt—I think I have got an idea about these dams. Something I saw on my last holiday with the youngsters." He would say no more. Summers, looking at him curiously, noted that he was "quite excited."

The day of the meeting of the Air Attack on Dams Committee he went early to London, buttonholed the chairman, Dr. Pye, and privately explained his new theory, so earnestly that Pye did not laugh though he looked a little sideways.

"I'd rather you didn't tell the others yet," Wallis said. "They might think it a bit far-fetched."

"Yes," said Dr. Pye. "I see that. What do you want me to do?"

"Give me time to find out how much RDX will blow a hole in the Moehne Dam if it's pressed up against the wall."

Pye talked eloquently to the committee without giving Wallis's secret away. The members were reluctant when they heard the results of the last model's test and Wallis was like a cat on hot bricks till they consented to one more experiment.

Glanville built him a new model dam, and Wallis started with small charges, sinking them in the water and exploding them when they were lying against the slabs of concrete. The effect was shattering—literally. He smashed wall after wall seeking the smallest charge needed, and soon he knew that in a contact explosion tamped by water a tiny plug of a few ounces of gelignite blasted a satisfying hole through a concrete wall 6 inches thick. From that he calculated he would need only 6,000 lb. of RDX to breach the Moehne Dam. With his new idea he could cut the case weight down to a little over 3,000 lb., making the complete bomb about 9,500 lb. Less than 5 tons. The new four-engined Lancasters would carry that to the Ruhr without trouble.

Lancaster

3

THE GREEN LIGHT

Armed with sums and theories, Wallis faced the task of convincing officials in their brick and stone lairs along Whitehall and other influential thoroughfares that he could put his bomb in the exact spot, an awkward task because they were all allergic to weird inventions. Literally one in a thousand was any good, and that usually not good enough to justify diverting effort. Most were obviously "crackpot," and Wallis's must have looked like one of those. He called on Professor Patrick Blackett, director of an "operational research" branch, and Blackett, a spare, rather intense man, listened to his ideas, carefully examined the calculations, riffled them back into a neat pile and said quietly:

"We've been looking for this for two years."

Wallis was electrified.

"I'd like you to leave these with me for a while," Blackett said. "There are one or two people I know who would be interested."

Blackett moved fast. As soon as Wallis had left he went to see Sir Henry Tizard and told him what he had heard. Tizard also moved with unorthodox haste, driving down to Weybridge next morning, where Wallis eagerly explained it all again.

"It seems," Tizard said when he had finished, "that the main thing to establish is whether this freak of yours will really work, and if so how we go about putting it into practice."

At Teddington, he said, was a huge ship-testing tank which would be ideal for experiments. He also thought there should be more tests to check how much explosive would theoretically punch a hole in a dam.

"I think I know just the thing," said Wallis, whose "damology" researches had been fanatical. "There's a small disused dam in Radnorshire; no earthly use any more as a dam and won't ever be. We could try and knock it down."

"Who owns it?" Tizard asked.

"Birmingham Corporation." Wallis knew all the answers.

"We'll try them," Tizard said, and Birmingham Corporation, with a little prodding, said yes.

It was a nice little dam, about 150 feet long and quite thick, curving gracefully across the mouth of a reach of Rhayader Lake, high in the Welsh hills west of Leominster. The corporation had built a bigger dam across the mouth of the lake to feed a little river that tumbled out of the hills.

Wallis estimated that the old dam should have a fifth of the resistance of the Moehne, an ideal test model. He calculated the smallest charge that should knock it down and set off with a packet of RDX and some explosives engineers. Wrapped against the raw mountain wind, he wasted little time, measured out the charge, tamped it in a sealed casing and lowered it deep into the water against the dam wall. Behind the rocks, his mouth dry with anxiety, he pressed the plunger and the hills echoed with sound. Water spurted a hundred feet high, the lake whipped into fury, and as the water plunged back into the void the concrete crumbled and a hissing flood burst into the main lake. Wallis, pink with glee, saw there was a ragged hole in the dam 15 feet across and about 12 feet deep.

For the next five months he experimented whenever he could in the ship tank at Teddington, an enormous thing hundreds of feet long. He wanted to find out exactly how to control a skipping missile, so that after a given number of bounces over a given distance he could make it reach a certain given point at a particular speed and height. At this ultimate spot the missile

would have to be either slithering across the water or
only, moving slowly, just a fraction above it. He had
to find out the best combinations of weight of missile,
and height, speed and power of release. Using an adjustable spring-loaded catapult so that he could measure the force behind it, he started firing marbles at
first.

Obviously a missile of regular shape, such as a
sphere, was needed so that no matter how it might
flick or spin after the first impact, it would still hit the
water with an identical shape on the next and subsequent bounces. An irregular shape might produce the
same amusingly eccentric hops after it hit, but this
wasn't child's play any more.

But soon he noticed something inconsistent about
the bouncing marbles. More often than not they tended
to dig in and sink after the third bounce or thereabouts.
Maybe it was the small size of the marbles that made
them unstable. Maybe some imperceptible ripple on the
water affected them. The only consistent pattern was
that they never bounced as far as the far end of the
tank—except for one or two strong shots that hit the
end and always bounced back too far. There would
obviously be ripples on the lake's surface held back by
the dams. Something bigger and heavier might not be
so affected. He tried using golf balls, but they were as
unpredictable as the marbles. Then he tried using 2 lb.
spheres of steel, but they were no better either.

Why? He asked himself; and his family could hardly
get a word out of him for days while he cogitated. It
was on a Sunday afternoon that he found what seemed
to be the answer, while he was mulching some spring
daffodils in his garden. Metaphorically (and typically)
he kicked himself for not thinking of it before. It
seemed so simple, really. The first bounce gave the
marble or golf ball or steel sphere a pronounced topspin
and that was why they tended to dig themselves into the
water. Of course one could try a flattish shape like a
disc-type stone but heaven knows how one could control the skips. There was one other answer—just one!
The spherical projectiles must be fired with a pro-

nounced back-spin. Wallis rigged up a cradle for the spring-loaded catapult that allowed him to spin the missile backwards just before release.

He got a double-bonus! For one thing, virtually every shot hit or slithered against the far end of the tank. And even more important—the residual back-spin still on the small projectile made it crawl under the water at the far end, flat against the far wall of the tank. It was exactly what he wanted to happen when the missiles reached a dam wall.

Now another problem cropped up. Wallis had been calculating the size of a sphere that would carry enough RDX explosive inside a steel case strong enough to stand the impact of hitting both the water and the dam wall. Hitting water at something well over 200 m.p.h. would be like hitting concrete.

He started to work out the required diameter of the sphere. He already knew he would have to take both bomb bay doors off the Lancasters and suspend the bombs under the belly with "legs" that stuck down underneath with some sort of belt or chain drive from some power source to get them spinning backwards before the drop.

Finding the necessary size of the sphere wasn't difficult. He soon worked it out, and damn! the sphere was going to be too big. It had to be slung close to the centre of gravity of the aircraft and low enough to clear the tunnel of the fuselage above. And if he slung it low enough for that, the base of the missile was going to be crushed hard against the ground. In fact you could only load the missile in place by jacking the aircraft up till the under-carriage wheels were clear of the tarmac.

Once you took the jacks away either the "legs" would buckle and the missile burst through the fuselage floor, or the aircraft would break its back, or both. And you couldn't sufficiently lift the fuselage floor of a Lancaster (or other suitable aircraft) because the space around the centres of gravity and lift (or balance) was already over-crammed with immovable mainspar (wing), crew and equipment.

Any way you looked at it, neither aircraft nor missile would be getting off the ground. Neither, it seemed, would the entire project. It was pointless making the sphere smaller. That would either weaken the casing too much or cut down the explosive contents too much, and apparently it had to be a sphere. So even if you got it loaded it could not be anything more than a study in still-life until you took the jacks away, and then the scrap metal wouldn't be funny.

It looked like the end of a disappointing (and humiliating) road. But to the stubborn Wallis this was only a challenge—not yet a defeat. Science and stubbornness often produce an answer. He thought constantly about it—and for a few days got nothing out of it except insomnia.

Again he could not pinpoint the exact moment he began thinking about gyroscopic principles. He was only rummaging in his mind and bound to strike it sooner or later.

If you make something spin fast enough around an axis it needs a surprising amount of force to tilt it off that axis. The earth is one example of spinning on an axis. It stays on that same axis (thank God) but it doesn't have to be a sphere. A lot of youngsters have little gyroscopes as toys. Yank hard on a string and a caged disc spins like mad, and people are intrigued at the strength it needs to budge it from its axis. Or take a child's top. It stays upright when it is spinning fast enough and falls over when it isn't. (That's a top secret!) A lot of aircraft blind-flying instruments depend on gyroscopic action, such as an artificial horizon.

Wallis knew that he had to reduce the diameter of his missile. And he knew it still had to hit the water on every bounce with the same shape surface as before. He already knew his missile had to drop with a lot of back-spin on it to control the bounces, and also to make it crawl underwater flat against the dam wall when it hit. So why not a missile shaped like a portly barrel with enough back-spin to keep it gyroscopically on an identical axis all the way? That would reduce the diameter without lengthening the "barrel" shape too much. It seemed all so easy. All one had to do was think it out first.

His assistants carved on lathes a series of fat, barrel-shaped models, each with differing weight-size-shape ratios and all of them with a potential diameter small enough to be carried under a Lancaster.

Wallis tested each repeatedly with varying combinations of back-spin, catapult velocity and height. Consistently they skipped across the water in the tank in little flashes of spray but seldom tilting off their horizontal axis, presenting at each skip the same pot-bellied shape to the water. By trial and error he found at what speeds each model would slither against the far end of the tank and crawl under the water hugging the wall (with the residual back-spin). He filled a notebook with details of each shape, and by simple elimination was able to choose the model with the widest range of reliable performance.

The rest was largely doing sums, such as how fast a five ton "barrel" could be safely spun backwards before release from an aircraft and achieve enough gyroscopic stability for half a mile or more of bouncing bumps. Wallis made it between 450–500 revolutions per minute backwards.

By the middle of 1942 he was satisfied he could make a five tonner do what he wanted it to. The only thing he didn't know was whether to call it a barrel, a bomb, a mine or a missile. Not that it mattered.

Tizard was pleased, but Tizard was an adviser, not all-powerful; the task was to get executive officials keen. Wallis thought he had proved his point, and as an innocent scientist he can perhaps be excused for optimism. In government there are "proper channels" and few short cuts, and the proper channels were preoccupied with other vital work.

Wallis saw several officials, received tea and courtesy, even compliments, but not enough action to please him. Two high executives in particular who could have started things moving seemed irritatingly cautious. They shall be nameless, because they are good men who worked hard and brilliantly in other directions, and no honest man should be censured for failing to understand Wallis any more than he should be condemned for failing to follow Einstein.

But it was so *maddening!* Wallis knew he had proved his theories and still he was up against a barrier that seemed as solid as a dam wall. He got the ear of a great scientist who had access to Churchill, expounded his ideas and showed his calculations. The scientist was not impressed, and said so. Yet there were other officials, like Dr. Pye, who were encouraging him.

The phone rang one day and a man named Lane, speaking from London, said he wanted to talk to Wallis about "a secret matter". He was, he said, from one of the committees dealing with new and secret weapons. Wallis felt his heart skip.

"What's it about?" he asked.

"It's to do with aircraft and water," said the man, "but I mustn't say any more over the phone. Can I come and see you?"

"To-morrow," said Wallis, "as early as you like."

Lane walked into his office in the morning, an alert young man, and Wallis welcomed him warmly. Lane showed his credentials and said:

"Do you remember an idea of yours back in 1941 about putting a smoke screen round a fleet?"

"Smoke screen?" Wallis said, not understanding for a moment; and then he remembered. Many other things besides earthquake bombs had germinated in his fertile mind since 1939, and one of them had been for a radio-controlled pilotless plane which could be catapulted from a cruiser or battleship to lay a smoke screen; cheaper and faster than laying a screen by destroyers.

"Yes," he said heavily. "I remember."

"We're interested in it now," Lane said. "Have been for some time, but we couldn't do everything at once. Can you tell me a little more about it?"

Wallis spent the next hour going into detail, and when he had finished and Lane was thanking him and rising to go Wallis said a little wistfully:

"You know, it's very disappointing. I thought you wanted to see me about my pet idea that nobody seems to want."

"Oh?" said Lane politely, reaching for his hat. "What's that?"

Wallis started to tell him, and as he described his tests the casual attention on Lane's face changed to a look of startled interest. He sat down again and listened for another hour; afterwards, when he rose to go again, he said, "I'll tell my chief about this one. I think he might be interested."

Lane's chief rang Wallis next morning and an hour later he was in Wallis's office in the old house at Burhill, listening. Hours later he went back to London as nearly convinced as a man can be by figures.

He spent just under 48 hours chewing it over and soft-talking one of the two Doubting Thomases. Then he conveniently "forgot" the other Doubter and picked up the phone to call Wallis.

It happened to be lunch-time, when there was a standing order that no calls should be put through to Wallis. That was his sacred hour for dreaming up new ideas while he munched a cheese sandwich and an apple at his desk. Even the gentle Wallis had his limits, and breaking his train of thought at that hour evoked loud protest. Backed by the mystique of Government Authority, the official forced the switch-girl to put him through. Despite her warnings the frustrated protest in his earphone still startled him. When he edged his name audibly into the noise, Wallis subsided into his normal courtesy.

"I thought you might like to know," said the official, "you can go ahead and make six half-size prototypes of your bomb thing. You can convert a Wellington to test-drop them and we'll both keep our fingers crossed. Purely for experiment, you know."

It took a few seconds for it to sink in before Wallis could express his fervent thanks to the official and all concerned. At the end he said, "I'll write a note of thanks to Sir Blank Blank right away."

"Oh my God no!" said the official. "Don't. Don't

make a sound. I'll carry my share of the can if it
doesn't work, but you don't have to throw it at me in
advance."

Converting a Wellington was simple enough. Wallis
had the bomb-doors taken off a production model. Two
sturdy steel struts were bolted in their place so that they
hung down like stiff, short little legs. Each had a bearing
gear at the base so that a "bomb" could be slung between them with freedom to revolve. Wallis was alight
with enthusiasm, anticipating each little problem before it arose. One bearing had a sprocket attachment for
chain drive and twin quick-release shackles were no
problem. Well before this was completed Wallis was
poking around the stores of odd bits of machinery that
accumulate in any large experimental and production
factory. He was looking for a compact, light-weight motor to rotate the bomb and soon found what he wanted
—an electric motor salvaged from the gizzards of an
obsolete Vickers submarine broken up in some marine knacker's yard. He mounted this in the fuselage
of the Wellington. Rigging the chain drive and switches
was no trouble.

By this time the castings of the six half-size 2½-ton
prototype bombs were finished and balanced, then
filled with a harmless substitute the same weight as
RDX. Wallis had been too busy to worry about the
outcome, but suddenly, overnight, it was all ready. The
moment had come!

At 3 p.m. on December 4, 1942, the converted
Wellington took off from Weybridge with the first bomb
slung below and Mutt Summers in the pilot's seat. Wallis, hopeful butterflies fluttering in his stomach,
crouched in the nose as bomb-aimer to test-drop off
Chesil Beach on the south coast.

The strange shape hanging underneath changed the
outline of the plane. Naval gunners at Portland could
not make out the strange aircraft, so they rightly gave
themselves the benefit of the doubt and opened fire, and
the gentle scientist was intrigued to see black puffs of
flak staining the sky. He thought they were tiny clouds

and his scientific mind wondered at the phenomenon until a wingtip flicked up and the Wellington peeled off out of range. Wallis saw Summers muttering explosively, realised what had happened and thought, wryly, the flak was carrying official obstructionism a little too far.

They were not going to worry much this time about precise speed and height. About 200 feet and 200 m.p.h., and for the time being never mind exactly how far the bomb went. It should, however, bounce on cleanly about half a mile. Something near that would do for the first test. The main thing was to see whether a couple of tons of spinning steel *would* bounce according to theory.

Wallis was lying on his stomach in the nose, looking through the bomb-aimer's perspex floor panel for a clear stretch of Chesil Beach water. He sighted one and briefly, over the intercom, guided Summers towards it. As Summers wheeled and then started a shallow dive, Wallis switched on the electric motor just in front of him. It started to whine, louder and louder, and as its speed increased Wallis could feel the growing vibration through the aircraft as the bomb spun backwards, faster and faster towards the 8 revs. a second mark. He couldn't see much of the actual bomb but it wasn't making any nasty thumping noises. Coming up to the clear water, Summers levelled out fairly low and reported briefly, "Speed two-two-zero indicated."

Right! Now! Wallis pressed the button and watched the spinning black thing slip clear of its stowage. It took so long to drop that it seemed like slow-motion, especially as its forward trajectory kept it still under the aircraft, but slowly losing speed and falling behind. Then, quite suddenly, it hit and vanished in a sheet of hissing white spray.

Wallis watched with painful anxiety for it to appear. Just for a moment nothing seemed to happen and then out of the foam lurched the black thing looking vaguely mis-shapen in its aura of spray. It fell back into the water quite quickly, lurched drunkenly up again, hit once more, skipped another short distance, then slith-

ered a few yards and vanished into the green depths.
It didn't seem to have traveled more than about two
hundred yards and Wallis looked down, puzzled, not
quite knowing what to think. It had worked, but not
the way it was supposed to. Something was wrong.
Summers turned the aeroplane back towards Weybridge and Wallis, on the way back, trying to imagine
what could have gone wrong, remembered the mis-
shapen look about the bomb. He decided that the casing
had not been strong enough. It must have crushed a
little under the impact, making the bounces unpredictable and sluggish. When they landed he ordered the
cases of the remaining bombs strengthened.

On December 12 he and Summers took off with a
strengthened bomb, Summers prudently avoiding Portland. Off Chesil Beach, Wallis watched the bomb going
down, holding his breath and feeling his mouth dry
with anxiety. Again the hissing sheet of spray as it hit,
and then, oh the thrill, out of the spray the black barrel came soaring a hundred yards across the water,
hit with another flashing feather of spray and soared
out again, hit again, and again, the distances shortening
every time until at last, after nearly half-a-mile, it slithered to a foaming stop and sank. Summers had banked
the aeroplane round and they could both look down
on that glorious sight of the long necklace of white
foaming scars on the water where the bomb had hit.
Wallis had never known such a moment of triumph.
He crawled half-way out of the nose to look up and
grin at Summers above in the cockpit. The engines were
making too much noise to talk but Summers grinned
down at him, gave him the thumbs-up sign and an
enormous wink.

In the next three days he and Summers dropped
three more bombs and they worked every time. They
took a movie cameraman with them on these flights
and got undeniable evidence that it worked.

On the strength of that Winterbotham arranged an
interview for Wallis with the Ministry of Supply's scientific tribunal to assess new weapons. The tribunal

watched his films and let it be known that the report would be favourable.

After that things happened very quickly. From Somewhere on High Wallis got instructions to try the small prototype bomb in a small Mosquito bomber against a battleship moored in a remote naval station.

This time the aircraft was faster and the bomb bounced further till it hit the side of the battleship virtually amidships and crawled below under the hull (battleships were armoured above the water but not below).

They made several runs and the results were similar in every case—these subsequent runs being filmed by an aircraft flying alongside and following the track of the bouncing bomb.

Next an urgent summons to the Admiralty together with his films and there he found the First Sea Lord, Admiral of the Fleet Sir Dudley Pound, a gaggle of other Admirals, and the Chief of the Air Staff, Marshal of the R.A.F. Lord Portal. In a private cinema the films were run through of the missile hitting the battleship and a startled murmuring burst forth. Wallis did not catch all the conversation but there was one Admiral who remarked audibly, "My God, if we can get a bit of extra range into the Mosquito we can blow that damned *Tirpitz* sky high." (The *Tirpitz* was moored in northern Norway and a constant threat to the convoys carrying war materials to Russia.)

There was another Admiral who said, "So we might, too, but don't forget if the Germans wake up to how it is done we've got a damn sight more big ships to be sunk than they have." Portal did not say very much and the meeting broke up into discussion groups, some apparently in favour and some having distinct qualms.

In the next couple of days Wallis was asked to show his films to the German-born Lord Cherwell, the controversial scientist who had direct access to Churchill over all matters scientific, to the great resentment of a number of distinguished scientists who objected both to his opinions and to his manner. Cherwell saw the

films and indicated in a most lukewarm manner that
he did not think the dams were a very important target
—though he didn't outwardly condemn the idea.

It is unlikely that anyone will ever know the precise
story of the intrigue that went on behind the scenes in
the next couple of days. It is known that the Navy was
in favour of an attack against the *Tirpitz* but apprehen-
sive about the secret leaking out to the Germans. Cherwell was generally recognised as opposed to the whole
proposition, including the dams which he said frankly
did not seem to be a very important target. With
him was Air Marshal Linnell. Undecided was Dr. Pye
of the Attack on Dams Committee. Keen and enthusiastic were Sir Henry Tizard, Prof. Sir Patrick Blackett
and Sir John Merton who also had considerable influence with Churchill. In the end it was apparently
Churchill who made the decision to get the dams project moving. He issued instructions to one of the cautious ones to instruct Wallis to go ahead with the preliminary design of a full-size bomb and Wallis felt the
fierce joy of a front row forward who has heaved man-
fully in the scrum* and gained a couple of inches. The
official tempered his joy by telling him not to expect
too much. Further work would depend on whether it
would dislocate work on a new bomber. It is perhaps
fair to say that the official *had* to be cautious. He
couldn't do everything he wanted to.

This was early February, 1943, and the best time
to smash the dams was in May, when they were full.
To leave it later might annoy the Germans but not
seriously incommode them. There was still just time.
Wallis worked late over his plans and on the eighth day
had them virtually finished when the bomb-shell
dropped. One of the cautious ones phoned, ordering
him to stop work on the big bomb. There was to be no
further action on it.

Wallis went grimly next day to the big tank at
Teddington, sank two glass airtight tanks in the wa-

---

*A part of Rugby football when the play is tough.

ter, put an arc light in one and induced a slight young woman to go into the other with a movie camera. She and the camera could just fit in. He dropped a model bomb into the water and the girl filmed its under-water progress. It was a beautiful film; clearly it showed the bomb plunging under the surface and crawling into position against the side of the tank.

Next he called up Summers and demanded an interview with Air Marshal Sir Arthur Harris, chief of Bomber Command. Summers had known Harris for years, well enough to call him by his first name, which few people dared to do. Harris, it was freely acknowledged, could crush a seaside landlady with a look.

Summers and Wallis drove into the wood outside High Wycombe where Harris had his headquarters, and as Wallis put his foot on the threshold of Harris's office the booming voice hit him like a shock wave:

"What the hell is it you want? I've no time for you damned inventors. My boys' lives are too precious to be wasted by your crazy notions!"

It was enough to strike fear into the heart of the sturdiest inventor. Wallis almost baulked, then pressed on and there was the bulky figure of Harris, grey eyes staring coldly over the half-moon glasses perched on his nose.

"Well?" Harris was a man of few words and forceful ones.

"I have an idea for destroying German dams," Wallis said. "The effects on Germany would be enormous."

"I've heard about it. It's far-fetched."

Wallis said he'd like to explain it, and Harris gave a grunt which Wallis took for yes and went ahead, trying not to be too involved and yet show how he had proved the theory. At the end the bomber chief had absorbed it all. Not that there was any encouraging reaction. Harris said bluntly:

"If you think you're going to walk in and get a squadron of Lancasters out of me you've made a mistake. You're not!"

Wallis started to bristle and Summers, who knew

Wallis's obstinacy and Harris's explosive temperament,
kicked Wallis's shin under the desk. Wallis controlled
himself.

"We don't want a squadron," he said, ". . . yet. We'd
like a chance to prove it in trials with one Lancaster
first."

Harris eyed him stonily. "Maybe," he said. "You
really think you can knock **a** dam down with that
thing?"

"Yes," Wallis said. "Or it may take three or four. We
can put them all in the same place."

Summers said peaceably, "We'll prove it'll work,
Bert."

"Prove it and I'll arrange a squadron," Harris said,
and then with his old fierceness, staring at Wallis, "but
I'm tired of half-baked inventors trying to run things."

Summers kicked Wallis once more under the desk
and broke the tension by saying, "We've got some films
here that show clearly how it works."

"All right. Let's see them." They trooped out to the
Command projection room, picking up Harris's chief
lieutenant, Air Vice-Marshal Saundby, on the way.
Harris curtly told the projectionist to clear out. "If it's
as good as you say," he told Wallis, "there's no point
letting everyone know. Saundby can run the films
through."

Saundby's training had not concentrated much on
film projection work and for a while there was a tangle
of celluloid, but eventually he sorted it out, clicked the
lights off and they watched in silence the antics of the
bombs dropped at Chesil Beach and the tricks of the
model under the water at Teddington.

When the lights went up Harris had his poker face
on. "Very interesting," he grunted. "I'll think it over."

Wallis and Summers went back to Weybridge; Summers, who was a tough customer, amused by the interview, and Wallis with mixed feelings. He did not know
why Harris distrusted inventors so much.

[*It started* (*so the story goes*) *back about 1916,
when Major Arthur Harris led a squadron of fighters*

*in England whose job it was to down German Zep-
pelins. An inventor was sent to him to try out a new
idea, to dangle an explosive charge like a football on
a long line under a fighter, which then flew over a
Zeppelin so that the football grenade hit the Zeppelin, to the mortification of the Germans. Harris, already a firebrand, tried it and found that the long
clothes-line dangling underneath was more of a
menace to the plane.*

*". . . So why not," he said to the inventor, "dis-
pense with the clothes-line and just drop the grenade?"*

*"Ah, that's a good idea," said the inventor. "Let's
try that."*

*"Just a minute," Harris said. "If you're going to
drop it by itself wouldn't it be better to streamline
it so it'll fall faster and more accurately?"*

*"Yes, yes," the inventor said. "Excellent. Let's do
that."*

*"Just a minute," said Harris, and pointed to his
plane standing near by. "What the hell d'you think
those are under the wings?"*

"Those" were little anti-Zeppelin bombs.]

Not long after, Wallis got a summons to a senior
executive whom he knew quite well and who in the
past had encouraged his bomb work.

"Wallis," he said, "I've been asked by ———" (one
of the two cautious ones) "to tell you to stop your
nonsense about destroying dams. He tells me you're
making a nuisance of yourself at the Ministry."

For a moment Wallis was stunned, then recovered
and answered quietly, "If you think I'm not acting in
the best interests of the war effort, I think I should
offer to resign from all my work and try something
else."

For the first and last time he saw the executive lose
his temper. The man shot to his feet, smashed his fist
on the desk and shouted "Mutiny!" Smashed his fist
down again with another "Mutiny!" And again with a
third explosive "Mutiny!" He subsided, red and quivering, and Wallis walked out of the room. He had lunch

somewhere but does not remember where, and afterwards went and told the whole story to Sir Thomas
Merton, one of the Supply Ministry's inventions tribunal. Merton promised support, but Wallis came
away still depressed, knowing of nothing more he could
do; it seemed too late now to organise things for the
coming May, and after a couple of days he was resigned to it.

That was the day, February 26, he got a summons
to the office of one of the cautious ones, and there
he also found the senior executive who had shouted
"Mutiny!" Proceedings opened by the cautious one saying, a little stiffly:

"Mr. Wallis, orders have been received that your
dams project is to go ahead immediately with a view
to an operation at all costs no later than May."

It took some time for Wallis to take it in.

(The Chief of the Air Staff, as it happened, had
sanctioned the project a week before, and Churchill
and Merton were enthusiastic about it.)

4

A SQUADRON IS BORN

After battling for so long, Wallis, in the weeks that followed, sometimes ruefully thought he had got more action than he could stand. Life was work from dawn till midnight, planning, drafting, thinking and discussing, grabbing a sandwich with one hand while the work went on.

He told his workers briefly what he wanted them to do, but not what the bombs were to do, or when, or where. Only he, Harris and a selected few others knew that, and apart from them a curtain of secrecy came down. Each craftsman worked on one part and knew nothing of the others.

The shape of the large bombs, known by the code name of "Upkeep," took a lot of devising. The central core holding the explosive was to be in the form of a cylindrical steel barrel nearly 7 feet long (or rather, *wide*). To fit around that, Wallis had squads of men carving thick staves like the outside of a barrel which were to be clamped around the cylinder with very strong bands of high tensile steel to form his required elongated barrel shape—and then each bomb as it was completed had to be "balanced" so that no single arc was heavier than the others. Rather like balancing a motor car wheel, so that its rotation sets up no vibrations. If one of the bombs had a little "throw" on one segment the whole cumbersome weapon revolving at nearly 500 r.p.m. would tear it out of its cradle and possibly tear the aircraft apart too.

Apart from these demanding details, one of the first things Wallis himself had to do was calculate as closely as possible the speed, height and distance from the dam that the bomb should be released. No good having them bounce over the top or hit the dam wall so hard that the bomb broke open and de-fused itself, or, worse, blew up and wrecked the aircraft without denting the dam. A horrible thought. It was a complex three-way equation, made more difficult by his awareness that pilots were not going to find it easy to fly to precise limits, especially at night. (He already knew it had to be by night. No Lancaster would even reach the low level targets by day, but cover of darkness should protect them well.)

The pilot precision problem was beginning to bother him, and it bothered him still more when he worked out the equation—a speed of 240 miles an hour at 150 feet above the water and 800 yards from the dam wall. The speed was no trouble but the height, at night, was perilously low and the range of 800 yards might be awkward too. He had an uncomfortable feeling that he had concentrated too much on bomb performance and not enough on the human and flight element.

An urgent call brought Mutt Summers to his office and Mutt was stumped for an answer too.

"If I only had more *time*," Wallis said. "I *know* there must be an answer but we've got barely ten weeks to get the whole thing done."

"On these figures, how much margin of error have we got?" Summers asked.

"Just about none," Wallis said. "Not unless we come down lower. A lot lower. And that's too risky for the aircrews."

After a while, Summers said: "I think this is more my department. If there's an answer, we'll find it, and we'll find it in time. You concentrate on getting the bomb ready and I'll pester a few people on the flight problem."

Wallis had no other choice. He still worried, but getting the five-tonners produced and aircraft modifications perfected in the short time allotted kept him busy over 16 hours a day. He was beginning to feel the strain and getting little sleep. Luckily, the teamwork was excellent. By normal standards the task was impossible in the time but people ignored inconvenient regulations and cut whatever corners they safely could. The bombs were on time coming off the production line. Shaped like portly barrels, Wallis had been able to keep the girth at the fattest point well under seven feet in diameter. That was slim enough to fit the barrel shape cross-wise under the aircraft connected by a drive with an electric motor mounted to one side in the belly of the aircraft.

Roy Chadwick, chief Avro designer, fairly soon got the first modified Lancaster converted with the two heavy caliper struts sticking down outside each side of the fuselage like legs and part of the fuselage above cut away to allow for rotation. He had this aircraft test-flown with one of the first bombs rotating at nearly 500 r.p.m. for five minutes and there was no hint of trouble. When the time came the bombs would not have to be rotated for more than a couple of minutes before release.

Explosives experts, tactical authorities, Secret Service men and hundreds of others had a part in it, and over Germany every day a fast Mosquito flew 25,000 feet over the dams taking photographs. Deep in the underground vaults of Bomber Command men studied the photographs through thick magnifying glasses to check the level of the rising water and the defences. If the secret leaked out they would see the extra flak and the raid would have to be called off. It was going to be suicidal enough as it was. There seemed to be at least six gun positions around the Moehne alone, and that was no matter for comfort because the bombs would have to be dropped from very low level, so low that a pilot could lean out and almost dangle his fingers in the water. They would have to fly between two towers on top of the dam, and some of the guns were in these towers.

The Mosquitoes flew a devious way and crossed the dams as though by accident so the Germans would not be suspicious. An ugly sign appeared in the first few days: photographs showed the anti-torpedo boom in

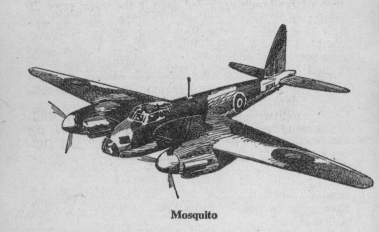

Mosquito

front of the Moehne was being repaired; it had been loose and untidy, and now it was being tightened. Nothing else appeared to be happening though, and after a while it was reasonable to assume that it was only a periodical check. While the work pressed on in England, it seemed that the Germans were doing nothing significant.

And therein lies a story! Barnes Wallis was not the only patriot to find that officialdom can be an immovable object to anything but irresistible force.

On August 29, 1939, a certain Oberburgermeister Dillgardt had written from his office in the Ruhr to the Wehrmacht chiefs in Muenster. "In view of the present military situation," he said delicately, he wanted to raise the question of the defence of large dams like the Moehne and the Eder. Dillgardt was an unusually perspicacious man and it is uncanny how his layman's mind worked along the same path as Wallis's.

Dillgardt said he was worried because he thought that a large bomb exploded deep in the water some 20 metres from the dam might conceivably blow a large hole in it owing to the compressive effects of the water. He admitted humbly that his experts did not agree with him, but he painted an ugly picture of what would happen if the dams were breached—almost identical with Wallis's conclusions. He submitted, with respect, that the dam defences be strengthened.

The military authorities wrote back politely. Dillgardt could "rest assured that the matter will receive the most careful and immediate consideration," and Dillgardt, presumably aware of the real meaning of this fatal phrase, wrote again, drawing their attention to a book called *The Curse of Bombing* in which the author, Camille Rougeron, spoke of the danger of bombing attacks on dams. The authorities thanked him again but the matter stayed "under consideration."

Over the next three years the files between Dillgardt and the Wehrmacht grew to imposing fatness, a series of harrowing appeals sandwiched between dignified and adroit evasions. In a peacetime paper battle civilian officials can usually vanquish military officials, but in wartime the boot is on the other foot, and the military men in Muenster were impregnable.

Dillgardt even predicted that any attack would be made in May, when the dams were full. He pointed out the increasing size and power of British bombs, asked for heavier torpedo nets, for smoke screens, balloon barrages, searchlights and heavy flak, and every time he was fobbed off returned tenaciously to the attack. Now and then he tasted victory; early in 1940 the Wehrmacht posted some heavy flak and searchlights around the Moehne, perhaps to keep Dillgardt quiet, and a few weeks later took them away again.

Twice more, when his persistence exasperated them into some concession, the Wehrmacht posted a little light flak there and then took them away again. And as

Dillgardt pestered them anew a note of asperity crept into the answering letters; the formal politeness deteriorated more and more. Sarcastically the generals expressed their gratitude for having their duty so generously explained to them by a civilian. Uncrushed, the dogged Dillgardt sent fresh reminders until one day a tormented general wrote tersely:

> *"Sir,*
>   *There is no further need for regular reports to be sent in to this office regarding storage level of these dams.*
>
> > *Heil Hitler!"*

Later on they threw him a last crumb by sending some 20-mm. guns.

At his headquarters in the wood Sir Arthur Harris ("Bert" to his friends and "Bomber" to the public) had been pondering how the attack should be made—and who should make it. On March 15 he sent for Air Vice-Marshal the Hon. Ralph Cochrane, who two days before had become Air Officer Commanding No. 5 (Bomber) Group.

"I've got a job for you, Cocky," Harris said and told him about Wallis's weird bomb and what he proposed to do with it. At the end he said: "I know it sounds far-fetched, but I think it has a good chance."

Cochrane said: "Well, sir, I've known Wallis for twenty-five years. He's a wonderful engineer and I've never known him not to produce what he says he will."

"I hope he does it again now," Harris said. "You know how he works. I want you to organise the raid. Ask for anything you want, as long as it's reasonable."

Cochrane thought for a moment.

"It's going to need some good aircrews," he said. "I think I'd better screen one of my squadrons right away and start them on intensive training."

"I don't want to do that," Harris said. "I don't want

to take a single squadron out of the line if I can help it, or interfere with any of the main force. What I have in mind is a new squadron, say, of experienced people who're just finishing a tour. Some of the keen chaps won't mind doing another trip. Can you find enough in your group?"

"Yes, sir." Cochrane asked Harris if he wanted anyone in particular to command the new squadron, and Harris said:

"Yes, Gibson."

Cochrane nodded in satisfaction, and ten minutes later, deep in thought, he was driving back to the old Victorian mansion outside Grantham that was 5 Group Headquarters. There could probably have been no better choice than Cochrane for planning the raid. A spare man with a lean face, his manner was crisp and decisive, perfectly reflecting his mind. The third son of a noble Scottish family, he was climbing to the top on his own ability; he had perhaps the most incisive brain in the R.A.F.—and that is no diplomatic exaggeration. His god was efficiency and he sought it uncompromisingly—almost ruthlessly according to some of his men, who were afraid of him, but his aircrews would do anything he asked, knowing that it would be meticulously planned.

Moreover, Cochrane knew Wallis well; had worked with him in the Royal Naval Air Service in World War I, flying his experimental airships and testing the world's first airship mooring mast, which Wallis had designed. Ever since then Cochrane had had a quick sympathy for the scientific approach.

That night a nuggety little man with a square, handsome face, named Guy Gibson, took off on the last trip of his third tour. If he got back he was due for leave and a rest, having been on ops almost constantly since the war started. The target was Stuttgart and his Lancaster was laden with one of the new 8,000-lb. "blockbusters" (not the penetrating "earthquake" type that Wallis envisaged, but bombs had made startling strides in the past year).

An engine failed on the way to Stuttgart and the aircraft would not hold her height. Gibson eased her out of the stream dropping towards the ground, but headed on. The last trip of a tour is an ordeal with its hopes of a six-months' reprieve. Before take-off the reprieve seems so near and yet so far, and waiting to get it over is not pleasant. Gibson took a chance rather than turn back and go through the waiting again.

Over Stuttgart he had the other three engines shaking the aircraft at full power and managed to drag up to a safe enough height to drop his bomb, then dived to the dark anonymity of earth and hugged the ground all the way back. That was Gibson's 173rd trip. He was a wing commander with the D.S.O. and D.F.C. Aged twenty-five.

He woke late, head still ringing with the engine noise, and lay curled up, half thinking, half dreaming of leave in Cornwall. That morning his leave was cancelled and, to his dismay, he was posted to 5 Group Headquarters.

A day or so later he was shown into Cochrane's office and saluted smartly.

"Ah, Gibson," Cochrane said. "Firstly, my congratulations on the bar to your D.S.O."*

"Thank you, sir."

"Would you like to do one more trip?"

Gibson gulped and said, a little warily:

"What kind of trip, sir?"

"An important one. I can't tell you any more about it now except that you would command the operation."

Gibson said slowly, "Yes, I—I think so, sir," thinking of the flak and the fighters he hoped he had finished with for a time.

"Good; that's fine. I'll let you know more as soon as I can," and a moment later Gibson was outside the door, wondering what it was all about. He waited two days before Cochrane sent for him again, and this time

---

*Distinguished Service Order.

another man was with him, Group Captain "Charles" Whitworth, who commanded the bomber base at Scampton, a stocky, curly-haired man of about thirty, with a long list of operations behind him and a D.S.O. and D.F.C.* on his tunic. Gibson knew him and liked him.

Cochrane was friendly. "Sit down," he said and held out a cigarette. "I asked you the other day if you'd care to do another raid and you said you would, but I want to warn you that this will be no ordinary sortie and it can't be done for at least two months."

Gibson thought: "Hell, it's the *Tirpitz*. Why did I say yes!" The 45,000-ton "unsinkable" battleship was lying in a Norwegian fiord, a permanent menace to the Russian convoys and a lethal target to tackle.

Cochrane was still talking. "Training for this raid is so important that the Commander-in-Chief wants a special squadron formed. I want you to form it. You'd better use Whitworth's main base at Scampton. As far as aircrews are concerned, you'll want good ones; you'd better pick them yourself. I'm telling all the squadrons they'll have to give up some of their best crews. I'm afraid they won't like it, so try and take men who are near the end of their tours. There's a lot of urgency in this because you haven't got very long and training is going to be very important. Go to it as fast as you can and try and get your aircraft flying in four days."

"Well, er . . . what sort of training, sir?" Gibson asked. "And . . . what sort of target?"

"Low flying," Cochrane said. "You've got to be able to low-fly at night till it's second nature. No, I can't tell you the target yet. That's secret, but you've all got to be perfect at low flying. At night. It's going to be the only way, and I think you can do it. You're going to a place where it'd be wrong to send a single squadron at the normal height by itself."

Gibson knew what that meant. Germany! A single

---

*Distinguished Flying Cross.

squadron at 15,000 feet would get all the night fighters. It was not so bad for the main force, the stream of hundreds of bombers; they confused the enemy radar, dispersed the fighters, and there was protection in numbers. Not so with a lone squadron. But low level, "on the deck," yes. Well, maybe! Well, it was going to be low level anyway. Over Germany! He knew a man named Martin who knew all about low flying over Germany. Gibson had met him when Martin was being decorated for it. Cochrane was still talking:

"I'm sorry I can't tell you any more for the moment, Gibson. The immediate problem is to get your crews and get them flying."

"How about aircraft, sir?"

"The equipment staff have that in hand. The first will be flown in to-morrow." The interview was clearly over and Cochrane was already frowning at some papers on his desk. Gibson saluted, and as he turned the door handle Cochrane looked up again.

"One thing more," he said. "You'll have to watch security. As far as others are concerned this is just an ordinary new squadron. We'll think up a cover plan later."

Outside the door Whitworth said, "See you at Scampton in a couple of days. I'll get things fixed up for you. I imagine you'll be having about seven hundred men."

Somewhat bewildered, Gibson went off to the S.O.A. to see how one went about forming a new squadron, and half an hour later he was looking at a long list of things he had to do and people he had to see.

A staff officer helped him pick aircrew from the group lists. Gibson knew most of the pilots—he got the staff man to promise him Martin and help him pick the navigators, engineers, bomb aimers, wireless operators and gunners; when they had finished they had 147 names—twenty-one complete crews, seven to a crew. Gibson had his own crew; they were just finishing their tour too, but they all wanted to come with him.

The Staff Officer Personnel told him how many men of different trades he wanted for his ground crews and

promised to siphon off picked men from other squadrons and post them to Scampton in forty-eight hours.

The equipment officer promised to deliver ten Lancasters to Scampton within two days. Just for a start.
More would follow. With them would come the spare
spark-plugs and tools, starter motors and drip trays,
bomb dollies and winches, dope and paint and chocks
and thermos flasks. Gibson was startled by the unend-
ing list. Another man promised the thousand and one
items for the men: blankets and lorries and bootlaces,
beer and socks, toilet paper and so on. He was two
days on these details, helped by Cochrane's deputy, the
S.A.S.O.*, Group Captain Harry Satterly, a big,
smooth-faced man who was excellent at detail; and
then it was all done—except for one thing.

"What squadron are you?"

"What d'you mean, sir?"

"What number? You've got to have a number."

"Oh," said Gibson, "where d'you get that?"

"Somewhere in Air Ministry," Satterly said, "but
they probably don't work so fast there. I'll get on to
them and fix it up. Meantime you'd better call yourselves 'X Squadron.' "

Just before dinner on March 21, Wing Commander
Guy Gibson, D.S.O., D.F.C., commander of "X", the
paper squadron, arrived at Scampton to take formal
command. In the officers' mess he found some of his
crews already arrived and the mess waiters looking curiously at them as they stood around with pints of beer
in their fists. It was obvious they were not to be an ordinary squadron; the average age was about twenty-
two but they were clearly veterans. D.F.C. ribbons
were everywhere; they had all done at least one tour,
and some had done two.

Gibson moved among them, followed by the faithful
Nigger, his big black Labrador dog, who rarely left his
heels. Someone laid a half pint of beer on the floor for

*Senior Air Staff Officer.

Nigger, who stuck his muzzle noisily into it and did not look up till he had licked it dry.

From his old 106 Squadron, Gibson had brought three crews as well as his own—those of Hopgood, Shannon and Burpee. Hopgood was English, fair and good looking except for a long front tooth that stuck out at an angle. Dave Shannon, D.F.C., was a baby-faced twenty-year-old from Australia, but did not look any more than sixteen, so he was growing a large moustache to look older. He was slender, with long fingers and thick, fair hair, and moved gracefully.

Gibson spotted Micky Martin with satisfaction. They had met at Buckingham Palace when Gibson was getting his D.S.O. and the King was pinning on the first of Martin's D.F.C.s. Though he came from Sydney, Martin was in the R.A.F., slight but good looking, with a wild glint in his eyes and a monstrous moustache that ended raggedly out by his ears. At the Palace they had talked shop and Martin had explained his low-flying system.

He had worked it out that if you flew lower than most bombers you would avoid the fighters; lower still, and the heavy flak would all burst well above. And if you got right down to tree-top height you would be gone before the light flak could draw a bead on you. There was still the risk of balloons, but Martin reasoned there would not be any balloons along main roads or railways, so he followed those. He had had the same two gunners for two years, Toby Foxlee and Tammy Simpson, both fellow Australians, and on their low-level junkets they had become expert at picking off searchlights. Simpson and Foxlee had both come with him; he'd also brought an experienced navigator, a lean, long-chinned Australian called Jack Leggo, and his bomb aimer, Bob Hay, also Australian, had been a bombing expert at Group. Leggo was to be navigation officer of the new squadron, and Hay was to be bombing leader. It is unlikely that there was a finer crew in Bomber Command; hence Gibson's pleasure.

He had chosen "Dinghy" Young as his senior flight

commander. Young had already ditched twice in his two tours, and both times got back home in his rubber dinghy. Bred in California, educated at Cambridge, he was a large, calm man whose favourite trick was to swallow a pint of beer without drawing breath.

Les Munro was a New Zealander, tall, blue-chinned and solemn, a little older than the others. He was standing by the bar looking into space when Gibson located him. "Glad to see you, Les," Gibson said. "I see you're setting a good example already, drinking a little and thinking a lot." Munro up-ended his pint and drained it. "No, sir," he said, "thinking a little and drinking a lot."

The other flight commander was Henry Maudslay, ex-50 Squadron, ex-Eton, an athlete, polished and quiet, not a heavy drinker. Towering above the rest was the blond head of a man who weighed nearly 15 stone*, with a pink face and pale blue eyes; good looking in a rugged way. Joe McCarthy, from Brooklyn, U.S.A., former life-guard at Coney Island, had joined the R.A.F. before America came into the war.

No one knew what they were there for but, looking at the men around them, realised something special was in the wind. Someone finally asked Gibson what "the form" was and Gibson simply said: "I know less than you, old boy, but I'll see you all in the morning to give you what gen I can."

The party broke up late and some of the crews were merry, though none so much as Nigger. Gibson's crew had been shoving cans of beer under Nigger's nose all the time, and Nigger, who had never been known to refuse one, staggered cheerfully out after Gibson, leaving a zigzag liquid trail down the corridor.

In the morning Gibson called all the crews to the long briefing room on top of station headquarters and said:

"I know you're wondering why you're here. Well, you're here as a crack squadron to do a special job

---

*210 pounds, 1 stone = 14 pounds.

which I'm told will have startling results and may short-
en the war. I can't tell you what the target is or where
it is. All I can tell you is you'll have to practise low
flying day and night until you can do it with your eyes
shut. . . ."

There was a little murmuring as they heard "low
flying" and they started making rough guesses. A voice
said distinctly "Christ! The *Tirpitz*!" Gibson said,
"Don't jump to conclusions. Maybe it's the *Tirpitz*,
maybe not. Whatever it is I want you to be ready. If
I tell you to fly to a tree in the middle of England I
want you to be able to do it. If I tell you to fly through
a hangar that isn't wide enough for your wingtips
I want you to have a go at that too. You've got to be
able to do anything you're told without question." And
there was a breathless silence.

"Discipline is going to be essential. So is security.
You're going to be talked about. It's unusual to have
a crowd like you forming a squadron. Rumours are
flying round already, but"—and punching his fist at
the air in emphasis—"you've got to keep your
mouths shut. If you get stuck in a pub on the hops and
someone asks you what it's all about, tell him to mind
his own business. Your lives really depend on secrecy.
If we can surprise them everything'll be fine. If they're
ready for us . . ." He looked at them in silence.

He went on to talk about training and organisation,
and when it was over the crews trooped out with little
flutters in their stomachs, the sort of feeling you get
before a raid. It goes once you get into the air.

Dinghy Young and Maudslay were busy dividing
the crews into flights and Gibson walked over to No. 2
hangar, the great steel shed that was to be squadron
headquarters. Along the sides were the little office
rooms and outside one a queue of "erks."* Inside, a
dapper little man with a toothbrush moustache broke
off his interviewing and saluted smartly; Flight Sergeant "Chiefy" Powell had just arrived to be the

---
*Ground crews.

squadron's disciplinary N.C.O. The ground crews were arriving in scores and Powell already had half of them organised in their billets and sections. Discip. N.C.O.s run a close second to service police for unpopularity, but Chiefy Powell was to become a sort of godfather to the squadron. He knew far more than Gibson about the detail that makes a squadron tick; Gibson had been too busy flying. He gave Powell and Heveron, the orderly room sergeant, a free hand and "X" squadron rapidly took shape but were still only a paper squadron, their entire equipment consisting of one trestle desk, one chair and one phone.

Cochrane rang Gibson: "I'm sending you over a list of lakes in England and Wales that I want photographed. Get someone on to it as soon as you can."

Gibson, who had learned not to ask questions, said, "Yes, sir," wondering when the fog of secrecy was going to lift. Lorries were rolling in with maps and Mae Wests, boots and more "erks" and envelopes and paper clips and spanners* and all the other things.

Then the first crisis. A conscientious service policeman considered that the "erks" arriving for "X" Squadron were inexcusably scruffy and went eagle-eyed round the huts "lumbering" scores of men for dirty boots, tarnished buttons and crooked collars. Zealously he typed all the names on the regulation forms and dumped the wad in front of Chiefy Powell.

"I'm putting seventy-five of your men on a charge, Flight," he said primly. The snorting Powell took the charges into Gibson, and Gibson riffled through them.

"God," he said, "the men didn't look too bad to me."

"They've been travelling to get here and some of them need new uniforms." Powell was like a hen guarding her chicks.

"Fair enough." Gibson ripped the charge forms into shreds and looked round the room. "We need a wastepaper basket."

—————
*Wrenches.

He told Powell to arrange with the station equipment officer for a clothing parade in the morning, and Powell, holding the phone in his hand, called back through the door a couple of minutes later that the equipment officer said it could not be done.

"Give me that bloody phone," Gibson said, and five seconds later on the other end of the line a pilot officer (equipment) jumped with fright as the earphones seemed to erupt against his head. The squadron was re-outfitted next morning.

Gibson spent hours interviewing his aircrews, sizing up the ones he didn't know, and found that some of the squadron commanders, told to send their best men, had played the age-old service game and got rid of a couple they did not want. Gibson told them to pack and go back.

Chiefy Powell found the same thing in the "erks" who were still arriving, among them being two outrageous duds from Gibson's old squadron, 106. A week before Gibson had been trying to get rid of them from 106. Now, with pleasure, he sent them back to 106. Some W.A.A.F. drivers and clerks had arrived and two of them were pregnant; Gibson, more interested in the birth of a squadron, returned them too.

He walked into the mess bar just before dinner, tired but feeling they were getting somewhere, and Charles Whitworth buttonholed him:

"Well, Gibby," he said, "you're going to command 617 Squadron now."

The little man looked thunderstruck. "What the hell!" he exploded. "617? I thought . . . I . . . Who and where the hell are they?"

"Here," said Whitworth peaceably. "You. Your new number. Someone in Air House has moved off his bottom. Your squadron marking letters are AJ."

He called for a pint each and they drank to 617 Squadron.

5

OVER THE HURDLES

Humphries, the new adjutant, arrived next afternoon; a little fair-haired man, only twenty-eight, he was keen on flying but his eyes had stopped him. Gibson told Humphries as much as he knew himself and as Humphries was leaving his office Gibson said:

"I don't know yet what it's all about, but I gather this squadron will either make history or be wiped out."

Humphries looked at him, not knowing whether he was joking.

"I beg your pardon, sir," he said, but Gibson was looking at maps on his desk and didn't answer.

In the morning the curtain lifted a little. Gibson got a call from Satterly, who told him to catch a certain train to Weybridge, where he would be met at the station.

"May I know who I'm meeting, sir?"

"He'll know you," Satterly said.

Gibson walked out of Weybridge Station at half-past two and a big man squeezed behind the wheel of a tiny Fiat said, "Hello, Guy!"

"Mutt," Gibson said, surprised. "God, are you the man I'm looking for?"

"If you're the man I'm waiting for, I am," Summers said. "Jump in." They drove down the winding tree-lined road that leads to Vickers and went past the main gates without turning in. "What's this all about, Mutt?" Gibson said, unable to hold back any longer.

"You'll find out." He turned off up a side road to

the left. "You wanted to be a test pilot for me once. D'you remember?"

"I remember." That was when he had first met Summers. It must have been eight years ago now, back in 1935, when he was eighteen. He had wanted to fly, so he had got an introduction to Summers at Vickers and asked about becoming a Vickers test pilot. "Go and join the Air Force and learn to fly first," Summers had advised.

"You'll be doing some testing soon," Summers said. "Not for me exactly, but quite a test." He turned in some double gates and they pulled up outside the house at Burhill. Summers led the way into a room with windows looking over the golfcourse, and a white-haired man got up from a desk.

"I'm glad you've come," Wallis said. "Now we can get down to it. There isn't a great deal of time left. I don't suppose you know much about the weapon?"

"Weapon?" Gibson said. "I don't know anything about anything. Group Captain Satterly said you'd tell me everything."

Wallis blinked. "Don't you even know the target?"

"Not the faintest idea."

"My dear boy," Wallis said in a sighing and faintly horrified voice. "My dear boy." He wandered over to the window and looked out, pondering. "That makes it very awkward."

"Well," Gibson said, "the S.A.S.O. said . . ."

"I know," said Wallis, "but this is dreadfully secret and I can't tell anyone whose name isn't on this list." He waved a bit of paper in Gibson's direction and Gibson could see there were only about half a dozen names on it.

Summers said, "This is damn silly."

"I know," Wallis said gloomily. "Well, my dear boy . . . I'll tell you as much as I dare and hope the A.O.C.* will tell you the rest when you get back." Gibson waited curiously, and finally Wallis went on:

---

*Air Office Commanding.

"There are certain objects in enemy territory which are very big and quite vital to his war effort. They're so big that ordinary bombs won't hurt them, but I got an idea for a special type of big bomb."

He told Gibson about the shock waves and his weird idea for dropping bombs exactly in the right spot. Gibson was looking baffled trying to follow the shock-wave theory.

"You've seen it working in pubs, Guy," Summers said. "A dozen times. The shove-ha'penny board. Remember how you get two or three discs lying touching and flick another one in behind them. The shock waves go right through them but they all stay where they are except the front one, and that goes skidding off. That's the shock wave."

"Ah, now I get it."

"I thought you would."

"Come and I'll show you," Wallis said and led Gibson into a tiny projection room. Wallis thumbed the switches and a flickering screen lit up with the title "Most Secret Trial No. 1." A Wellington dived into view over water and what looked like a black barrel fell from it, seemed to drop slowly and then was hidden in spray as it hit. Gibson started in amazement as out of the spray the black thing shot, bounced a hundred yards, bounced again in a cloud of spray and went on bouncing for what seemed an incredibly long time before it vanished. He was still staring at the screen when the lights went up again and he heard Wallis's voice.

"Well, that's my secret bomb," Wallis said. "That's how we . . . how *you're* going to put it in the right place."

"Over water?" Gibson said, fishing for a clue.

"Yes," but Wallis avoided the subject of the target. "Over water at night or in the early morning when it's very flat, and maybe there will be fog. Now, can you fly to the limits I want, roughly a speed of two hundred and forty miles per hour, at 150 feet over smooth water, and be able to bomb accurately?"

"It's terribly hard to judge height over water," Gibson said, "especially at night. Not too bad in moonlight if there's a chop on the water. You know, a few white horses. But smooth water?" He wrinkled his brow. "A bit dicey. It's like a mirror. How much margin of error?"

"Very little, I'm afraid. Almost none. Otherwise . . ." Wallis hesitated, frustrated by security. "It's got to reach the right spot at the right speed and the right height—150 feet. If one of the factors is wrong, the sum doesn't add up."

"Well . . ." Gibson was thinking about echo altimeters—bouncing an electric signal down and back off the water again—but decided (correctly) that they wouldn't be fast or sensitive enough. He said hopefully: "We can try a couple of things. I suppose we can find some way." He sounded a little dubious and Wallis sighed.

"Oh, I hope so. There isn't much time and there's an awful lot to do."

On the way back to Scampton, Gibson puzzled over the target. The only likely ones, he decided, were either the *Tirpitz* or the U-boat pens, and he shuddered a little at the thought. They would be smothered in guns. At Scampton he found some Lancasters had arrived and ground crews checking them over. In the morning he told his senior men what height they would have to bomb at but nothing about the bomb itself.

Dinghy Young said: "We'll have to do all the training we can by moonlight, and you don't get much reliable moonlight in this country."

"Could we fly around with dark glasses on?" Maudslay asked.

"No, that's no good. You can't see your instruments properly."

Gibson said he'd heard of a new type of synthetic night training. They put transparent amber screens round the perspex and the pilot wore blue glasses; it was like looking out on moonlight but you could still see your instruments. He would see if Satterly could get them some.

Leggo was worried about navigation. Low-flying navigation is different. You don't see much of the area when you're low, so they were going to need large-scale maps with plenty of detail. Large-scale maps meant constant changing and awkward unfolding. He suggested they use strip maps wound on rollers; navigators could prepare their own. And if they were flying low, radio was not going to be much use for navigation. It would be mostly map reading.

Bill Astell, deputy A Flight commander, took off the first Lancaster and was away five hours, coming back with photographs of lakes all over the North Country. Gibson laid out ten separate routes for the crews to practise over, and in the days that followed the Lancasters were nosing thunderously into the air all day and cruising at 100 feet over the flat fens of Lincolnshire, Suffolk and Norfolk.

Flying low seems faster and is more exciting, also more dangerous. There is the temptation to slip between chimneys or lift a wingtip just over a tree, and the R.A.F. was losing a lot of aircraft every month from fatal low-flying accidents. It was (naturally) strictly forbidden, and the pilots were delighted to be ordered to do it. Across several counties outraged service police reached for notebooks and took the big AJ aircraft letters as they roared over their heads; the complaints came flooding into Gibson's office, and with smug rectitude he tore them up.

After a few days they came down to 50 feet and flew longer routes, stretching out to the north country, threading through the valleys of the Pennines, climbing and diving over the Welsh mountains, then down to Cornwall and up to Scotland, eventually as far as the Hebrides, winging low over the white horses while the pilots flew steady courses and the rest of the crews gave a hand with the map reading.

Gibson took his own Lancaster, "G for George," and flew over to a lake in the Pennines to test the business of flying accurately at 150 feet over water. Diving over the hills he throttled back and flattened out over the lake, but it took him time, busily juggling control column, trimmers and throttles, to get the needle fairly steady within a few feet of the 150 ft. mark. He just had time to note that the speed was still too high when the hills at the far end loomed ahead and he had to ease the stick back quickly and slam on throttle. "G for George" lifted noisily and cleared the crest with an adequate margin but not a generous one. Gibson's chunky bomb-aimer, Spam Spafford, had a front-row view in the nose and said conversationally over the intercom: "That was interesting, Skipper. About fifty feet, I'd say."

Gibson didn't answer at first. He was thinking how much difference the weight of a heavy bomb load on board would have had. Then he said, "Keep interested, Spam. I'm doing a one-armed fiddler act up here. Next time, *you* watch the hills in front and say 'When,' loud and clear." Spafford agreed to give it his urgent and immediate consideration.

Gibson made another run, but slower this time. He had both height and speed needles closer to the mark by the time Spafford yelled in his ear. They tried it several times more and Gibson was getting his approach drill into a fairly consistent groove, not spot on but not far off, apart from one run when he hit a thermal over the approach crest and had to abort early. It was promising, but only in a limited way. Over Germany, barometric pressures would be unpredictable, and altimeters work off (adjustable) barometric pressure. Gibson knew he still had to be able to do it at night, without relying too much on the altimeter, unless Intelligence could find some kind and courageous soul in the target area who could radio target area pressure at the right time.

His limited hope did not last long. They tried it again at dusk that evening, with fog drifting over the lake. Spafford couldn't see the hills and Gibson couldn't see the water until, on the second run, cutting the corners a bit, he hit a slight down-draft, presumably from the last ridge on the run-in. Gibson reacted fast but they

near as dammit went in. He heard a grunt over the
intercom as Trevor-Roper, in the rear turret, saw ripples on the water from the slipstream. Even Spafford
was shaken. He had had a brief close-up of the looming
water from the nose perspex, and as Gibson hauled her
up, Spafford muttered, for all to hear: "Christ! This is
bloody dangerous!" (The only one not perturbed was
Nigger, dozing by the G-box. Nigger often flew with
Gibson—though not on ops—and went everywhere
with him on the ground.)

Gibson flew back and told Cochrane that if he could
not find some way of judging height accurately there
would be no chance of doing the raid.

"There's still time to worry about that," Cochrane
said. "Just now I want you to have a look at models of
your targets." He waved a hand at three packing-cases
in a corner of his office and Gibson eyed them curiously. "You can't train your men properly unless you
know what they are, so I'm letting you know now, but
you'll be the only man in the squadron to know. Keep
it that way."

A corporal brought in a hammer, and Cochrane sent
him out of the room while Gibson gently pried the lids
loose and lifted the battens. He stood looking down at
the models, and his first reaction was a feeling of tremendous relief. Thank God, it wasn't the *Tirpitz*! It
took him a couple of seconds after that to realise they
were dams. One was the Moehne, and the other two
were the Eder and the Sorpe, handsome models that
showed not only the dams but the countryside in detail
for miles around, as though photographs had taken on a
third dimension. There were the flat surfaces of the
lakes, the hills, winding rivers and the mosaic of fields
and hedges. And in the middle the dams. Gibson
stood looking for a long time and then Cochrane laid
the lids back over them.

"Now you've seen what you've got to attack," he
said. "Go and see Wallis again and come and see me
when you get back."

The first thing Wallis said, eagerly, was:

"How did you get on?"

"Only fair by day," Gibson said, "but pretty awful at night. In fact, flying level at night over water at 150 feet seems plain impossible."

Wallis sighed and looked anxious—then his stubborn lips compressed. "We still have some time to work out some way of doing it. We have to. Now I'll tell you more about this Downwood business."

"Downwood?"

"The code name for the raid." Wallis explained how the bombs were to explode deep against the dam walls.

"I've calculated that the first one ought at least to crack them, and then more bombs in the same place should shift the cracked wall back till it topples over . . . helped, of course, by the water pressure. The best times, of course, are when the dams are full. That will be in May. You'll need moonlight, and there's a full moon from the thirteenth to the nineteenth of May."

"About six weeks."

"Yes. You've *got* to be accurate or you might overshoot and the bomb will hit the parapet and go off there. That won't hurt the dam."

"Hurt us though," Gibson said as it dawned on him. "The aircraft would be just above it."

"Yes it would."

"Oh," Gibson said and went back thoughtfully to Scampton.

The synthetic night-flying gear arrived, transparent amber screens and blue glasses; "two-stage amber," it was called. The screens were fitted in the cockpits, pilots donned the glasses and flying by day was exactly like flying in moonlight. They flew thousands of miles with them, first at 150 feet and then, as Gibson decided they were good enough, at 50 feet, the bomb aimers looking through the nose to warn of trees and hills.

Micky Martin lectured them on night low flying and there was little he had not learned about the pitfalls. One night he had hit a balloon cable low over Kassel, flying a Hampden, and should have crashed, but the cable carried away and they saw it in the moonlight dangling from the wing; not a comforting sight, because when they had to come in slow to land at base with flaps and wheels down the cable would drag on the ground and almost surely catch in a hedge or fence and spin the Hampden in. On the way back Martin was wondering what to do about it when, to make things worse, a fighter jumped them. He dived to 50 feet to lose it and the cable caught on a tree and at diving speed it pulled itself free and they were all right—even lost the fighter.

Gibson took the screens and blue lenses away and sent the crews on low-level night cross-countries, first aircraft singly, and then, when the moon was right, in loose formations. Two crews were too keen and came back with branches and leaves in their radiators.

So far only Gibson knew what it was all about, but the rest of the people at Scampton were mighty curious. A pretty little W.A.A.F. driver called Doris Leeman summed up the general feeling when she entered in her diary: "Everyone speculating on the reason for the new gen squadron. So far nothing but training—most unusual as the crews have already done a tremendous amount of ops. They're evidently specially chosen." And a day or so later: "Have never seen Lancs fly so low as these boys fly them!"

The squadron did not know it, but security men were in the district to make sure that nothing leaked out. Phones were tapped and all mail censored. Security, as it happened, was good, though an "erk" said in a letter home: "The aircraft have been flying low with special night aids for some special op," and the letter was intercepted.

"Who is this fool?" Gibson asked Chiefy Powell. He always asked Powell about any ground crew up on a charge. Powell knew them all, and Gibson knew Powell and trusted his opinions. "He's a good type, sir," Powell said, "and a good fitter."

Gibson had him brought to his office and tore a ferocious "strip" off him. All the ruthless side of his manner came out and the fitter broke down and cried. Gibson let him go with a reprimand.

One of the aircrews rang his girl friend, and told her he could not see her that night because he was flying on special training. The phone had been tapped. Gibson called the whole squadron together and ordered the offender up on a table in the middle of them. He stood there miserable and pale.

"Look at him!" Gibson bawled. "Look at the fool. Hundreds of men's lives in danger because one bloody fool can't keep his trap shut." And more in the same strain.

There were no more lapses.

Gibson was on the move from dawn to midnight every day, usually careering about on a little auto-bike from flights to armoury, to orderly room and so on. When he flew he kept his auto-bike in the hangar, apparently against some fiddling regulation because Scampton's zealous service policemen told Chiefy Powell the auto-bike would have to be moved.

Powell eyed him flintily. "You'd better see the owner," he said. "I don't think he'll move it."

"I'll see him all right," said the sergeant, "and he'll move it too."

So Chiefy took him in to see Gibson and shut the door behind him. There was a violent roaring behind the door and a white-faced sergeant came out.

The bike stayed where it was.

The crews were getting good at low night cross-countries and extended their trips out over the North Sea. Two of them were coming back in formation over Grimsby when the gunners of a couple of naval ships (who have itchy trigger fingers at sea) opened up on them, and as they darted in over the land the shore-based flak had a go too. They landed with little holes punched in the fuselage, complained to Martin and the wiry and diabolical Martin grinned and said, "Bloody good training. Make you flak-happy!"

They practised low-level bombing on the range at Wainfleet, diving over the sand dropping 11½-lb. practice bombs with the low-level bombsight. The drops were not nearly accurate enough and Bob Hay said so disgustedly. Gibson took the problem to Cochrane.

Two days later a Wing Commander Dann, from the Ministry of Aircraft Production, called on Gibson.

"I hear you're having bombsight trouble for the dams raid."

"How the hell do you know about this?" Gibson said.

"I've been let into it because I'm supposed to be a sighting expert," Dann explained. "I think I can solve your troubles. You may have noticed there are a couple of towers on top of each dam wall. We've measured them from the air and they're six hundred feet apart. Now this"—and he produced some drawings of a very elementary gadget—"is how we do it."

It was laughably simple: a carpenter ran up one of the gadgets in five minutes out of bits of spare wood. The base was a small triangle of plywood with a peephole at one angle and two nails stuck in the other corners. "You look through the peephole," Dann said, "and when the two towers on the dams are in line with the nails, you press the tit. You'll find it'll drop in the right spot but you'll have to stick right on the speed."

Gibson shook his head in wonder. Workmen put two dummy towers on the dam across the neck of a midland lake, the bomb aimers knocked up their own sights and on his first try one of them dropped eight practice bombs with an average error of only four yards.

Still the problem of the height. Gibson tried repeatedly to see if practice made perfect, but it didn't. After his fifth try Dinghy Young landed and said, "It's no use. I can't see how we're going to do it. Why can't we use radio altimeters?"

Gibson said he had thought of them a long time ago but they were not sensitive enough.

Time was getting short. Gibson got a call from Satterly. "They've finished the first two prototypes of the new bomb," Satterly said. "Fly down to Herne Bay tomorrow and watch the test drops. Take your bombing leader with you."

That was April 15.

Wallis met them and next morning they drove out
to a bare beach near Reculver. Half a mile back from
the sea M.I.5* had cordoned the area off.

"I'm sorry to get you up so early," said the ever-
courteous Wallis, "but the tide is up and that is the right
time. We want to walk out at low tide and see how the
bomb stands up to the shock of the dropping."

He pointed to two white buoys bobbing on the water about 100 yards apart. "The idea is to drop the
thing about half a mile short of those markers and if it
works all right it should bounce the rest of the way
and go right between them."

"Like goal posts," Gibson said, and Wallis smiled.

"Yes, but there won't be any goalkeeper."

In the east came two specks which grew into Lancasters, heading low over the shallows towards the two
buoys bobbing on the water. "The other one's the camera aircraft," Wallis said as they watched them, and
as the noise of engines filled the air Wallis was shouting
above the roar, "He's high. He's too high." He sounded
agitated. They swept up side by side and a great black
thing dropped slowly away under the nearer one. It hit
and vanished in a sheet of spray that hissed up towards
the plane. For a moment there was nothing but the
spray, and then out of it the fragments came flying.

"Broken," Wallis said and stood there very still. He
took a deep breath. "They said it wouldn't work. Too
big and heavy and the case too light. We've got another
in the hangars. We'll try it this afternoon. The aircraft
was too high."

Men worked hard that afternoon to strengthen the
case of the second bomb while Wallis stripped to his
underpants and waded to his neck in the freezing water, feeling with his feet for the fragments of the broken
one. A launch took the broken bits on board and Wallis
climbed in shivering, oblivious to everything but the
ragged edges where the metal had burst.

They were on the dunes again as the sun was go-

*British Intelligence.

ing down and the two aircraft came in sight, lower this time. Mutt Summers in the bomb plane was holding her steady at about 150 feet. The suspense was painful. The black monster dropped away below, and again the water gushed skywards as it hit and out of the foaming cloud came the flying fragments as it broke.

Wallis said, "Oh, my God!" and then out of the spray the twisted bulk of the main body of the bomb lurched spinning into the air and skipped erratically for 100 yards or so before it rolled under the water. Wallis stared in silence for a few seconds with the look of a man who had lost a shilling and found three pence. He sighed and said "Well, it's a bit better than this morning."

(In the Lancaster, Summers was not happy. A lump of the casing had hit the elevators and one of them had jammed. The plane could just hold its height while Summers was holding his breath. He did a wide gentle turn and made a heart-stopping landing on the long runway at Manston with the trimmers.)

Wallis told Gibson: "We've still got a lot of work to do on the bomb; but don't worry, it's going to be all right." Gibson and Hay took off in a little plane for Scampton and a few hundred feet up the engine coughed and died. There was only one way to go and that was down, but all the good fields were still covered with poles so the Germans could not land troops in an invasion. Gibson did his best to steer between them but a wingtip hit a pole, and as the aircraft slewed, the other wing hit and they finished up sitting in a ball of crumpled duralumin, but were able to climb out and stand up, slightly bloody but unbowed.

A man came haring across the field, and when he saw they were not badly hurt he said severely, "I think they teach you young fellows to fly too early"; and then a policeman arrived and said unemotionally, "I'm glad to see our landing devices work."

Gibson and Hay went back to Scampton by train, and on the way Gibson thought up a scheme to overcome the height problem: to dangle a long wire under

the aircraft with a weight on it so that it would skim the
water when the aircraft was at exactly 150 feet. Full of
hope he tried it in "G for George" but it didn't work.
At speed the line trailed out almost straight behind.

Cochrane set the "back-room" boys to work on the
problem and a day later Ben Lockspeiser, of the Ministry of Aircraft Production, arrived at Grantham with
an idea. It was absurd to think how simple it was and
how effective. "Put a spotlight under the nose," he said,
"and another one under the belly, both pointing down
and inwards so they converge at 150 feet. When the
two spots come together on the water, there you
are!" Gibson cheerfully told the crews and when he had
finished Spafford said casually "I could have told you
that. Last night Terry Taerum and I went to see the
E.N.S.A. show and when the girl was doing her strip-
tease, there were these two spotlights shining on
her and the idea crossed my mind then and I was going
to tell you."

Gibson just looked at him.

Maudslay flew a Lancaster down to Farnborough and
they fitted two spotlights on it the same day. Coming
back he made test runs across the airfield and it worked
beautifully. Maudslay said it was easy to get the circles of light together and keep them there. The idea was
that their circumferences should touch each other,
forming a figure "eight." He had Urquhart, his navigator, leaning his head out of the perspex observation blister behind the pilot, looking down at the ground and
saying, "Down, down, down . . . up a bit . . . O.K." and
that was the procedure they adopted.

They all tried it over Derwentwater using the same
drill and could fly to within two feet of the prescribed
height with wonderful consistency. Everyone got a tremendous kick out of it. That was a very major problem
solved.

Down at Weybridge Wallis was still trying to
strengthen the bomb and things were not going well.
One of his experiments was to get his technicians working overtime to put a hard steel skin flush around the
barrel shape without upsetting the balance.

On April 22, Wallis and Gibson, plus the usual gaggle of Air Ministry officials, watched as this first new model was dropped over Reculver. It hit and rose briefly from the water and then again fragments flew off it and it didn't work, or skip. The tormented scientist groaned in his anguish. He had been getting little sleep for weeks. Three weeks now to the time for the raid and if they couldn't make it then it would have to be put off for another year; probably, in view of official scepticism, for ever. The water in the dams was rising.

Wallis became aware of the Air Ministry officials wandering wordlessly away to their cars and it was not hard to guess what they were thinking.

He became aware of Gibson beside him. "They left you a bit short of time."

Wallis turned wryly: "Not really, I suppose. I got my sums wrong. Tried to put in enough RDX to make sure." He looked at the water where the bomb had sunk. It was smooth and unruffled again. "Time and tide for nae man bide," he quoted. "It's the first impact that does the damage. I'd allowed for the extra weight that quadruples the blow but a five tonner drops just that much faster."

Gibson said, "You didn't miss by much." More of a question than an observation.

"Marginal, but enough." Wallis sighed. "A bit slower, a bit lower—say 60 feet—and I'd bet my life on it."

A silence fell between the two and Gibson could feel his scalp crawling a little. He had an unpleasant feeling that he was going to break the first rule of the service —"Never volunteer for anything!" He said quietly, "You really think 60 feet would do it, Sir?"

Wallis said absently, "Yes, I'm certain. The initial impact would be so much less."

Gibson said hesitantly, "Maybe we could have a crack at that, Sir."

Wallis put his mental slide-rule away and smiled his wan appreciation. "It's good of you to suggest it, Gibbie, but I said *my* life, not yours. Sixty feet against a defended target—and it *is* defended—wouldn't give you much chance, would it!"

Gibson was thinking of his 173 missions and he still had a whole skin. Just one more to do. Did he have the guts to do it and did he have the right to ask the others? He said to Wallis: "Maybe we'd have a little more chance now than you realise, Sir. I didn't have time to tell you before but we have solved the height problem. I mean *really* solved it. Down to inches. Foolproof."

Wallis looked at him in mild surprise, changing to excitement as Gibson explained about the fore and aft lights. At the end, all Wallis could say for a while was "Good heavens," in an astonished sort of way. The two stood in silence while Wallis creased his brow in thought. Gibson thought he could practically hear the computer mind ticking over. Wallis started spelling it out so to speak, talking half to himself . . . "Yes, you could alter the angle of the lights for 60 feet . . . I can calculate a new speed and range—from-target for bomb release . . ."

He broke off and looked directly at Gibson:

"You know you and your chaps would not only have to fly much lower into the defences . . . you'd have to delay the drop until you were much nearer the dams, all of you. Isn't that too risky?"

"No Sir," Gibson lied, and added, more truthfully or more hopefully, "They won't be expecting us."

"Oh heavens, I hope not," Wallis said. "I've been working on that hypothesis."

(Gibson thought privately, "Hell! Me too!")

Wallis looked at him thoughtfully before he spoke again, rather gently. "Look, Gibbie, would you and your boys really be game to have a go from 60 feet? I'm not going to pretend it's not going to be more dangerous but we don't seem to have much alternative."

Gibson said simply, "Yes. We'll have a go if it will work."

Wallis said, his voice a little unsteady with emotion, "Thanks, Gibbie, and to all your boys. I don't know what else to say. I wish it were my life in the balance and not yours."

Gibson said with forced cheerfulness, "I wouldn't worry too much about it, Sir. They won't be expecting us at 60 feet at night."

"Not even showing your height lights," said Wallis painfully.

Gibson said, "If the bomb works at 60 feet we'll give it a go and that's that, Sir." Wallis seemed to find it a little difficult to speak for a moment and then he said cautiously, "Well, we're not there yet—first we have to make sure. Test another strengthened bomb from 60 feet and we haven't got much time."

They turned towards the waiting cars. Wallis went back to Weybridge and Gibson arrived a few hours later at Scampton. He called the pilots, bomb-aimers and navigators together and told them that the arrival of the modified Lancasters might be delayed a day or two as technicians from Farnborough and Avro would be adjusting the height lights to converge at 60 feet. That was the new height for dropping the bomb! He said it calmly without histrionics and there was hardly even a gasp. (As one of them said, years later, "You have to be breathing to gasp.")

Gibson finished on a lighter note. "You had better sharpen your night low-flying reflexes. We can't afford to waste a single bomb."

No one complained. Likewise no one cried "Hurrah!"

On April 29, Wallis finished another strengthened bomb and Vickers test pilot Shorty Longbottom (a name he never lived down) flew it to Reculver for the drop. Only two Air Ministry Officials were there this time. Rain was pouring down but Wallis, out on the dunes, did not even notice it as he watched the Lancaster charging out of the east towards the markers. Shorty had her tucked down neatly to 60 feet at just under 250 indicated air speed, squinting through the rain squalls to hold his height and see the markers. The bomb fell slowly, hit cleanly—and worked. From the first creamy splash of impact the bomb soared up and away, splashed down again without any distortion a couple of hundred yards farther on and then on and on till she slid through the marker buoys.

Banking round after the drop, Longbottom saw a white-haired figure bobbing about down on the dunes. Wallis had taken his hat off and was waving it in the air, dancing and shouting while the rain ran down his face.

6

TAKE-OFF

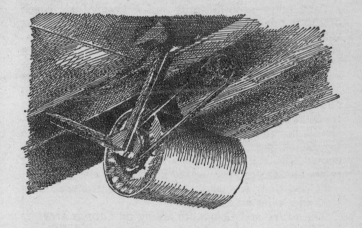

Early in May a strange-looking aircraft flew over Scampton. "God," Martin said, squinting up at it, "is that a Lanc, or isn't it? What a monstrosity!"

The aircraft dropped its wheels, landed and taxied to a hardstanding by 617's hangar, the first of the modified aircraft. It looked like a designer's nightmare; the bomb doors were gone and the mid-upper turret and some of the armour, and there was a lot of queer junk sticking out underneath. It looked better for walking than flying. Avro's had done an unusually difficult and complicated job very quickly and quite brilliantly and the rest of the modified aircraft arrived in the next few days. "Capable" Caple, 617's "plumber," or engineering officer, checked them and the pilots found they flew all right, though they had lost a little performance.

A couple of days later, on May 8, Gibson, Martin and Hopgood flew three of them down to Manston and Martin and Hopgood watched goggle-eyed while a bomb was loaded into each. Two larger dummy towers had been anchored in the water at Reculver. Wallis had already worked out a new drop-range and the quaint, plywood bombsights had been adjusted accordingly for a risky range of 600 yards and a lowered air speed of 230 m.p.h. (The fore and aft height lights on all the squadron aircraft incidentally had been adjusted to converge at 60 feet.) All three aircraft and crews had a run at the towers and it was beautiful to watch. Three enchanting direct hits. Three times in a row the great black barrels skipped and skipped over the water until they ploughed between the dummy towers. Micky Martin came in a little low on his run and the spouting water hit his elevators and tore one of them loose. The big plane dipped towards the grey water but he had just enough control to get the nose up again and landed safely at Manston, where they fitted a new elevator.

"Good thing to check on," he said, unruffled. "Now we know what we *can't* do."

The worry and rush were telling on Gibson now; he was irritable and a carbuncle was forming painfully on his face so that he could not get his oxygen mask on. Not that he was going to need oxygen on a low-level raid, but his microphone was in the mask. He went to the doctor, and in his detached professional way the doctor said, "This means you're over-worked. I'm afraid you'll have to take a couple of weeks off"; and Gibson stared at him ludicrously and laughed in his face.

He planned to control the raid by plain-language radio, and Cochrane got them VHF fighter sets. Hutchison, squadron signals leader, wanted to set them up

first in the crew room so they could have dummy prac-
tices on R/T procedure, and he and Chiefy Powell went
to work on the sergeant carpenter to make screened
benches for this, but the carpenter said he could not
find any wood and was adamant till Gibson delivered
him one of his blistering monologues over the phone,
and the benches arrived that afternoon.

The stage was nearly set, but at Bomber Command
and at Grantham there was secret dismay. For three
days the Mosquito had been bringing back photographs
that showed mysterious activity on top of the Moehne
Dam. The dark shapes of some new structures had
been appearing, growing from day to day. There were
about five sets of them, visible as short black rectangles.
The interpretive experts puzzled over them for hours,
blowing up the photos as large as the grain would
take, examining them under strong light and through
magnifying glasses nearly as strong as microscopes.
The structures threw shadows across the dam top, and
they measured the shadows but still were baffled.
There seemed to be only one answer—new gun positions. There must have been a security leak somewhere.

At midnight on May 13 a convoy of covered lorries
rolled round the perimeter track to the bomb dump at
Scampton; a cordon of guards gathered round and the
bombs were trolleyed into the dump and hidden under
tarpaulins. They had only just been filled and were
still warm to the touch.

Gibson drove off to see Satterly and plan the routes
for the raid, taking with him Group Captain Pickard
(of "F for Freddy" fame) because he was a "gen"
man on German flak positions, and on a low-level raid
there is nothing more important than plotting a track
between the known flak. They spread their maps out on
the floor and carefully pencilled in two separate tracks
that wound in and out of the red blotches of the known
flak.

The first one sneaked in between Walcheren and
Schouwen, cut across Holland, delicately threaded be-

tween the night-fighter aerodromes at Gilze-Rijen and
Eindhoven, snaked round the crimson blotches of the
Ruhr, round Hamm, and south to the Moehne. The
second one cut in up north over Vlieland, came in over
the flak-free Zuyder Zee, and joined route one north-
west of Wesel. They plotted two more widely differing
routes for the trip home so that any flak aroused on the
way in would watch out in vain for the return.

The attack would be in three waves, Gibson leading
nine aircraft on the southern route, Munro leading others on the northern, and five aircraft taking off a couple
of hours later to act as a reserve. If the Moehne,
Eder and Sorpe were not smashed up by the first two
waves, Gibson would call up the reserves. If they
were smashed the reserves would bomb three smaller
dams in the same area, the Schwelm, Ennerpe and
Dieml.

Accurate navigation was going to be vital or there
were going to be sudden deaths. The pencilled tracks
had to go perilously near some of the red flak areas.

"Doc" Watson and his armourers were loading the
bombs into the Lancasters. Martin watched Watson
winching the bomb up into his aircraft, "P for Peter"
(or, as Martin always insisted with a leer, "P for Popsie"). "Just exactly how *do* these bombs work, Doc?"
he asked.

"I know as much as you do, Micky," Watson said
busily. "Sweet Fanny Adams."

"Ar, what do they pay you for?" Half an hour later
the bomb was in position and he and Bob Hay, Leggo, Foxlee, Simpson and Whittaker were crawling about
inside the aircraft seeing that everything was in order
when a fault developed in the bomb release circuit, the
release snapped back and there was a crunch as the
giant black thing fell and crashed through the concrete
hardstanding, embedding itself 4 inches into the earth
below. Relieved of the weight, "P for Popsie" kicked a
little from the expanding oleo legs of the under-carriage.

Martin said, "Hell! What's that?" There was a startled yell from an armourer outside and Martin yelled,
"Hey, the bloody thing's fallen off!"

"Release wiring must be faulty," Hay said professionally, and then it dawned on him and he said in a shocked voice, "It might have fused itself." He ran, yelling madly, out of the nose. "Get out of here. She'll go off in less than a minute." Bodies came tumbling out of the escape hatches, saw the tails of the armourers vanishing in the distance and set off after them. Martin jumped into the flight van near by and, with a grinding of gears, roared off to get Doc Watson. He had his foot hard down on the accelerator and swears that a terrified armourer passed him on a push-bike. He ran into Watson's office and panted out the news and Watson said philosophically, "Well, if she was going off she'd have gone off by this."

He got into the flight van and drove over to the deserted plane. Pale faces peeped out, watching him from the deep shelters round the perimeter track hundreds of yards away, and Watson turned and bellowed, "O.K. Flap's over. It's not fused."

The squadron was fused though; painfully aware that something tremendous was about to happen. The aircraft were there, the bombs were there, both had been put together and crews were trained to the last gasp. Now was the time, Gibson knew, nerves would be tautening as they wondered whether there was going to be a reasonable chance of coming back or whether they would be dead in forty-eight hours. (And it was not only the aircrews who were tensed. Anne Fowler was too; she was a dark, slim W.A.A.F. officer at Scampton, and in the past few weeks she and the boyish David Shannon had become a most noticeable twosome.)

Perhaps the least affected was the wiry and rambunctious Martin. Aged twenty-four, he had already decided that he was going to die, if not on this raid then on some other. Before the war was over anyway. During his first few "ops" he had often had sleepless nights or dreamed of burning aircraft. He saw all his friends on his squadron get "the chop" one after the other till they were all gone and knew it would only be a question of time before he would probably join them. So finally he had accepted the fact that in a fairly short time, barring miracles, he was going to die, not pleasantly. That was his strength and largely why he was so boisterous. Having accepted that, the next step was automatic: to fill every day with as many of the fruits of life as possible. He did so with vigour.

It was a corollary, more than a paradox, that he was not suicidal in the air but audacious in a calculating way, measuring every risk and if it were worth while, taking it, spinning it out as long as he could, but making every bomb tell. He did not believe in miracles.

One of the New Zealanders, painfully aware he might well be dead in forty-eight hours, had been getting his mind off it in the bar during the last few evenings, and after a few cans he always got a little homesick. He was only about twenty and home for him was about as far away as it was possible to get round the globe. He'd got into the habit, when the bar closed, of weaving over to the phone and saying gravely:

"Get me New Zealand."

The switch girl got to know the form well and she would answer, equally gravely:

"I'm sorry, sir, but the line to New Zealand is out of order. You'd better go to bed and I'll try in the morning."

"Oh! Where's bed? Give me course to steer to bed."

"You'd better get your batman to give you a course, sir. He'll show you where bed is."

"Oh, thank you very much." He was very young and always polite.

On the morning of May 15, you could clearly sense the tension, more so when word spread that the A.O.C. had arrived. Cochrane saw Gibson and Whitworth alone and was brief and businesslike.

"If the weather's right you go to-morrow night. Start briefing your crews this afternoon and see that your security is foolproof."

After lunch a little aeroplane landed and Wallis and Mutt Summers climbed out; ten minutes later they were with Gibson and Whitworth with a guard on the door. Gibson could not take his beloved Nigger on the raid but could not bear to leave him out altogether, so he gave him the greatest honour he could think of . . . when (or if) the Moehne Dam was breached he would radio back the one code word "Nigger."

In the hangars, messes and barracks the Tannoy came loudly and dramatically to life: "All pilots, navigators and bomb aimers of 617 report to the briefing room immediately." At three o'clock there were some sixty of them in the briefing room on the upper floor of the grey-and-black camouflaged station headquarters. They sat silently on the benches, eyeing the familiar maps, aircraft identification and air-sea rescue posters on the walls, waiting. Whitworth, Gibson and Wallis filed down the centre to the dais and Whitworth nodded to Gibson: "Go ahead, Guy." The room was still.

Gibson faced them, feet braced apart, flushed a little. He had a ruler in one hand, the other in his pocket, and his eyes were bright. He cleared his throat and said:

"You're going to have a chance to clobber the Hun harder than a small force has ever done before." Outside his voice, no sound. "Very soon we are going to attack the major dams in Western Germany." A rustle and murmuring broke the silence—and some deep breaths. They were going to have a sporting chance. Gibson turned to the map and pointed with his ruler.

"Here they are," he said. "Here is the Moehne, here the Eder and here is the Sorpe. As you can see, they are all just east of the Ruhr." He went on to explain the tactics, told each crew what wave they would be on and what dam they were to attack.

Wallis took over and described the dams and what the queer bombs were supposed to do, how success would cripple the Ruhr steel industry, how other factories would be affected and bridges and roads washed away.

Gibson stood up. "Any questions?"

Hopgood said: "I notice, sir, that our route takes us pretty near a synthetic rubber factory at Huls. It's a hot spot. I nearly got the hammer there three months ago. If we go over there low I think it might . . . er . . . upset things."

Gibson looked thoughtfully at the map. Huls was a few miles north of the Ruhr. Satterly and he had known about the Huls flak when they were planning the route but had taken the track as far away from the Ruhr as they could. Better the flak at Huls than the Ruhr.

"If you think it's a bit too close to Huls we'll bring it down a bit," and he pencilled in a wider curve round the little dot. "You'd better all be bloody careful here. The gap isn't too wide. Err on the Huls side if you have to, but watch it, you navigators."

Maltby got up. "What are the dams' defences like, sir?"

"We've had extensive photo-recce over them for some time now," Gibson said, "and the defences seem to be confined to light flak. You'll be shown their position." He was uneasily wondering about those mysterious new structures on the top of the Moehne.

"Any balloons, sir?" That was Maudslay.

"Up till yesterday the nearest ones were round a small factory twelve miles away. We don't expect any."

Someone asked if there were any nets on the lake and Gibson described the torpedo booms in front of the dam walls.

Leggo wanted to know how effective they would be against the bomb, and Gibson, with a sidelong glance at Wallis and a fierce grin, said:

"Not a sausage!"

He crossed the room to a couple of trestle tables where three dust covers were hiding something, pulled the covers off, and there were the models of the dams.

"All of you come over and have a look at these," he commanded, and there was a scraping of forms as sixty young men got up and crowded round.

"Look at these till your eyes stick out and you've got every detail photographed on your minds, then go away and draw them from memory, come back and check

your drawings, correct them, then go away and draw
them again till you're perfect."

They were two hours doing that; each crew concentrated on its own target, working out the best ways in
and the best ways out. The known flak guns were
marked and they took *very* special note of them. Martin's crew were down for the Moehne with Gibson and
Hopgood, and they stood gazing down at the model.

"What d'you reckon's the best way in?" Leggo asked.

"First thing is to get the final line of attack," Martin
said. "There's the spot!" He put his finger on the tip
of a spit of land running out into the Moehne Lake
and ran his finger-tip in a straight line to the middle of
the dam wall, right between the two towers. It met the
wall at right angles. "A low wide circuit," he said;
"come in over the spit and we're jake."

It was eight o'clock before Gibson was satisfied they
knew it all and said, "Now buzz off and get some grub.
But keep your mouths shut. Not even a whisper to
your own crews. They'll find out to-morrow. If
there's one slip and the Hun gets an inkling you won't
be coming back to-morrow night."

Back at the mess the gunners, engineers and wireless
operators, who'd been waiting in a fever of speculation
for five hours, were a little hard to convince.

"Well," demanded Toby Foxlee, Martin's gunner,
his eager nose sniffing at the prospect, "what is it?"

"Nothing," Martin said airily. "More training. That's
all. You'll hear about it to-morrow."

"Training?" Foxlee almost wailed. "I don't believe
it. It can't be."

"It's true."

"Will you swear it?"

"I swear it," Martin lied piously.

"Christ!" Foxlee said. "I need a drink. What're you
having?"

"Shandy," said Martin, who drank little before a raid,
and Foxlee gave him a long, cold look.

"Martin," he said, "you're a horrible bloody liar."

They all drank shandy and went to bed, taking little
white pills that the doctor had doled out so they would

sleep well. As Gibson was going along to his room Charles Whitworth came in looking worried and but-tonholed him quietly.

"Guy," he said, "I'm awfully sorry, but Nigger's just been run over by a car outside the camp. He was killed instantaneously."

The car had not even bothered to stop.

Gibson sat a long time on his bed looking at the scratch marks that Nigger used to make on his door. Nigger and he had been together since before the war; it seemed to be an omen.

The morning of May 16 was sunny. Considering the scurry that went on all day it was remarkable that so few people at Scampton realised what was happening. Even after the aircraft took off hours later the people watching nearly all thought it was a special training flight.

It was just after 9 a.m. that Gibson bounced into his office and told Humphries to draw up the flying pro-gramme.

"Training, sir?"—more of a statement than a ques-tion.

"No. That is yes—to everyone else," and as Hum-phries looked bewildered he said quietly: "We're go-ing to war tonight, but I don't want the world to know. Mark the list 'Night flying programme,' and don't men-tion the words 'battle order'."

Watson, the armament chief, was dashing around busily, and so was Caple. The pilots were swinging their compasses. Trevor-Roper was seeing that all guns were loaded with full tracer that shot out of the guns at night like angry meteors and to people on the receiving end looked like cannon shells. That was the idea, to fright-en the flak gunners and put them off their aim. Each aircraft had two .303 Brownings in the front turret, and four in the tail turret. Each gun fired something like twelve rounds a *second;* each rear turret alone could pump out what looked like forty-eight flaming cannon shells a second; 96,000 rounds lay in the am-munition trays.

Towards noon a Mosquito touched down with the last photos of the dams. The water in the Moehne was 4 feet from the top. After lunch "Gremlin" Matthews, meteorological officer at Grantham, spoke to all the other group met. officers on a locked circuit of trunk lines for half an hour. Such conferences rarely found agreement but this time they did. The lively bespectacled figure of "The Gremlin" walked into Cochrane's office as soon as he had put the receiver down.

"It's all right for to-night, sir." He gave a definite prediction of clear weather over Germany.

"What?" said Cochrane. "No ifs, buts and probables?" and "The Gremlin" looked mildly cautious just for a moment and took the plunge. "No, sir. It's going to be all right."

Cochrane went out to his car and drove off towards Scampton.

The Tannoy sounded about four o'clock, ordering *all* 617 crews to the briefing room, and soon there were 133 hushed young men sitting on the benches (two crews were out because of illness).

Gibson repeated what he had told the others the previous night, and Wallis, in his earnest, slightly pedantic way, told them about the dams and what their destruction would do. Cochrane finished with a short, crisp talk.

The final line-up was:

Formation 1: Nine aircraft in three waves, taking off with ten minutes between waves:

> Gibson,
> Hopgood,
> Martin.
>
> Young,
> Astell,
> Maltby.
>
> Maudslay,
> Knight,
> Shannon.

They were to attack the Moehne, and after the Moehne was breached those who had not bombed would go on to the Eder.

Formation 2: One wave in loose formation:

> McCarthy,
> Byers,
> Barlow,
> Rice,
> Munro.

They were to attack the Sorpe, crossing the coast by the northern route as a diversion to split the German defences.

Formation 3:

> Townsend,
> Brown,
> Anderson,
> Ottley,
> Burpee.

They would take off later as the mobile reserve.

Supper in the mess was quiet, the calm before the storm. No one said much. The non-flying people thought it was to be a training flight, but the crews, who knew it was going to be business—probably sticky—could not say so and there was a faint atmosphere of strain.

With a woman's wit Anne Fowler realised it was to be the real thing. She noticed the crews were having eggs. They often had an egg before a raid, and always after they landed. Most of the others did not notice it, but she started worrying about Shannon.

Dinghy Young said to Gibson, "Can I have your next egg if you don't come back?" But that was the usual chestnut before an "op" and Gibson brushed it aside with a few amiably insulting remarks.

In twos and threes they drifted down to the hangar and started to change. It was not eight o'clock yet; still an hour to take-off and still broad daylight. Martin stuffed his little koala bear into a pocket of his battle-dress jacket and buttoned the flap. It was a grey furry thing about 4 inches high with black button eyes, given to him by his mother as a mascot when the war started. It had as many operational hours as he had.

They drifted over to the grass by the apron and lay in the sun, smoking and quietly talking, waiting. Anne was with Shannon. Fay, the other W.A.A.F. officer, was talking to Martin's crew. Dinghy Young was tidying up his office, just as a matter of course. He had no pre-monition. Munro seemed half asleep in a deck chair.

Gibson drove up and walked over to Powell.

"Chiefy, I want you to bury Nigger outside my office at midnight. Will you do that?"

"Of course, sir." Powell was startled at the gesture from the hard-bitten Gibson. Gibson did not tell him that he would be about 50 feet over Germany then, not far from the Ruhr. He had it in his mind that he and Nigger might be going into the ground about the same time. He said to Hopgood: "Tomorrow we get drunk, Hoppy."

Gibson found himself wishing to God it were time to go and knew they were all wishing the same. It would be all right once they were in the air. It always was. At ten to nine he said clearly, "Well, chaps, my watch says time to go." Bodies stirred on the grass with elaborate casualness, tossed their parachutes into the flight trucks, climbed in after them, and the trucks moved off round the perimeter track to the hard-standings. Shannon had gone back to the locker room for a moment and when he came out his crew, the only ones left, were waiting impatiently.

The bald-headed Yorkshireman, Jack Buckley, said like a father to his small son, "Have you cleaned your teeth, David?" Shannon grinned, hoisted himself ele-gantly into the flight truck and then they had all gone. Shannon had one of the best crews. Buckley, older than most, of a wealthy family, was his rear gun-ner and a wild Yorkshireman. Danny Walker was an infallible navigator, a Canadian, dark, quiet and im-mensely likeable. Sumpter, the bomb aimer, had been a guardsman and was tougher than a prize-fighter. Brian Goodale, the wireless op., was so tall and thin and bent he was known universally as "Concave." And in the air the babyish Shannon was the absolute master, with a scorching tongue when he felt like it.

At exactly ten past nine a red Véry light curled up from Gibson's aircraft, the signal for McCarthy's five aircraft to start; the northern route was longer and they were taking off ten minutes early. Seconds later there was a spurt of blue smoke behind Munro's aircraft as his port inner engine started. One by one the engines came to life. Geoff Rice's engines were turning; Barlow's, then Byers'. The knot of people by the hangar saw a truck rushing at them across the field, and before it came to a stop big McCarthy jumped out and ran at them, roaring like a bull, his red face sweaty, the

sandy hair falling over his forehead. In a murderous
rage he yelled:

"Those sons of bitches. My aircraft's u/s and there's
no deviation card in the spare. Where are those useless bloody instrument jerks?"

The 15-stone Yank had found his own Lancaster,
"Q for Queenie," out of action with leaking hydraulics,
rushed his crew over to the spare plane, "T for Tom,"
and found the little card giving the compass deviations
missing from it. No hope of accurate flying without it.
If McCarthy had met one of the instrument people
then he would probably have strangled him.

Chiefy Powell had gone running into the instrument
section and found the missing card. He dashed up to
McCarthy shouting, "Here it is, sir," and McCarthy
grabbed it, well behind schedule now, and, turning to
run back to the truck, scooped up his parachute from

the tarmac where he'd thrown it, but his hand missed
the canvas loop handle and he yanked it up by the D-
ring of the rip-cord. The pack flaps sprang back in a
white blossom as the silk billowed out and trailed
after him, and he let out a roar of unbearable fury.

Powell was running for the crew room, but McCarthy snarled, "Goddammit, I'll go without one." He
jumped into the truck but before the driver could move
off Powell came running up with another parachute,
and McCarthy grabbed it through the cabin and shot
off across the field. There was a swelling roar from the
south side; Munro's Lancaster was rolling, picking up
speed, and then it was low in the air, sliding over the
north boundary, tucking its wheels up into the big in-
board nacelles. Less than a minute later, as McCarthy
got to his aircraft, Rice was rolling too, followed by
Barlow and Byers.

At precisely 9.25, Gibson, in "G for George," Martin, in "P for Popsie," and Hopgood, in "M for Mother," punched the buttons of the booster coils and the
wisps of blue smoke spurted as the engines whined and
spun explosively, first the port inners, the starboard
inners, the port outers and the starboard outers. They
were going through their cockpit drill while the crews
settled at take-off stations, running the engines up to
zero boost and testing the magnetos. A photographer's
flash-bulb went off by Gibson's aircraft; Cochrane was
there too, standing clear of the slipstream. Fay stood
by "P Popsie," waggling her fingers encouragingly at
the crew.

"G for George" waddled forward with the shapeless bulk under its belly ("like a pregnant duck," Gibson had said), taxied to the south fence, swung its long
snout to the north and waited, engines turning quietly.
"P Popsie" turned slowly in on the left, and "M Mother" on the right. Gibson rattled out the monotonous orders of his final check.

"Flaps thirty."

Pulford, the engineer, pumped down 30 degrees of
flap and repeated, "Flaps thirty."

"Radiators open."

"Radiators open."

"Throttles firm."

Pulford checked the nut on the throttle quadrant.

"Throttles firm."

"Prepare to take off," Gibson said and checked through to all the crew on the intercom. "O.K., rear gunner?" "O.K." And then all the others. He leaned forward with his thumb up, looking to left and then to right, and Martin and Hopgood raised their thumbs back. Pulford closed his hand over the four throttles and pushed till the engines deepened their note and the aircraft was throbbing . . . straining; then Gibson flicked his brakes off, there was the hiss of compressed air and they were rolling, all three of them, engineers sliding the throttles right forward.

The blare of twelve engines slammed over the field and echoed in the hangar, the tails slowly came up as they picked up speed in a loose vic, ungainly with nearly 5 tons of bomb and over 5 tons of petrol each. Gibson held her down for a long time and the a.s.i.* was flicking on 110 m.p.h. before he tightened back on the wheel and let her come unstuck after a long, slow bounce. At 200 feet they turned slowly on course with the sun low behind.

McCarthy eased "T for Tom" off the runway twenty minutes late and set course on his own. At 9.47 Dinghy Young led Astell and Maltby off. Eight minutes after that Maudslay, Shannon and Knight were in the air. Anne waved them off. The final five, the reserve aircraft, did not take off till two hours later. By the time they arrived in the target area Gibson, if still alive, would know where to send them.

---

*Air speed indicator.

7

ATTACK

Gibson slid over the Wash at a hundred feet. The cockpit was hot and he was flying in his shirtsleeves with Mae West over the top; after a while he yelled, "Hey, Hutch, turn the heat off."

"Thank God for that," the wireless operator said, screwing the valve shut. The heat in a Lancaster runs down the fuselage but comes out round the wireless operator's seat, so he is always too hot, while the rear gunner is always too cold.

The sun astern on the quarter threw long shadows on fields peaceful and fresh with spring crops; dead ahead the moon was swimming out of the ground haze like a bull's-eye. Gibson flew automatically, eyes flicking from the horizon to the a.s.i., to the repeater compass in its rubber suspension.

The haze of Norfolk passed a few miles to port. In the nose, Spafford said, "There's the sea," and a minute later they were low over Southwold, the shingle was beneath them, and then they were over the water, flat and grey in the evening light. England faded behind. "G George" dropped down to 50 feet, and on each side Martin and Hopgood came down too, putting off the evil moment when German radar would pick them up. You couldn't put it off indefinitely; about twenty miles from the Dutch coast the blips would be flicking on the radar screens and the orders would be going out to the flak batteries and fighter fields.

Martin ranged up alongside and there was a light winking as he flashed his Aldis lamp at them.

"What's he saying, Hutch?" Gibson asked.

"We're going to get screechers to-morrow night."
Hutchison picked up his own Aldis and winked back,
"You're damn right. Biggest binge of all time." Hutchison didn't drink.

Taerum spoke: "Our ground speed is exactly 203½
miles an hour. We will be there in exactly one hour, ten
minutes and thirty seconds. We ought to cross the coast
dead on track. Incidentally, you're one degree off
course." The last part was the standing joke. The pilot
who can fly without sometimes yawing a degree or so
off course has yet to be born.

In the ops. room at 5 Group H.Q. at Grantham,
Cochrane was walking Barnes Wallis up and down,
trying to comfort him. Wallis was like an expectant father, fidgety and jittery, and Cochrane was talking of
anything but the bomb, trying to get Wallis's mind off
it, but Wallis could think of nothing else.

"Just think what a wonderful job you made of the
Wellington," Cochrane said encouragingly. "It's a magnificent machine; been our mainstay for over three
years."

"Oh dear, no," lamented the disconcerting scientist.
"Do you know, every time I pass one I wonder how
I could ever have designed anything so crude."

A black Bentley rushed up the gravelled drive outside, pulled up by the door and the sentries snapped
rigidly to attention as Harris himself jumped briskly
out. He came into the ops. room. "How's it going,
Cocky?"

"All right so far, sir," Cochrane said. "Nothing to
report yet." They walked up and down the long room
between the wall where the aircraft blackboards were
and the long desk that ran down the other side, where
men were sitting. Satterly was there, "The Gremlin," the
intelligence man and Dunn, chief signals officer, sitting
by a telephone plugged in to the radio in the signals
cabin outside. He would get all the Morse from the
aircraft there; it was too far for low-flying planes to
get through by ordinary speech.

Harris and Cochrane talked quietly, and Wallis was

The DAM BUSTERS

SQUADRON 617 R.A.F

walking miserably with them but not talking, breaking
away every now and then to look at the big operations
map on the end wall. The track lines had been pencilled in and he was counting off the miles they should
be travelling. It was 10.35 when Cochrane looked at his
watch and said, "They ought to be coming up to the
Dutch coast now."

The sun had gone and the moon was inching higher
into the dusk, lighting a road ahead across the water;
outside the dancing road the water was hardly visible,
a dark mass with a couple of little flecks.

Taerum said, "Five minutes to the Dutch coast,"
and the crew snapped out of the wordless lull of the
past half hour. "Good," Gibson said. Martin and Hopgood eased their aircraft forward till the black snouts
nosed alongside Gibson and veered out to make a wider
target, their engines snarling thinly in gusts above the
monotonous roar in "G George." Flying so low, just
off the water, they seemed to be sliding very fast along
the moonpath towards the waiting flak.

Spafford said, "There's the coast." It was a black line
lying dim and low on the water, and then from a couple
of miles out on the port side a chain of glowing little
balls was climbing into the sky. "Flak ship," said Martin laconically. The shells were away off and he ignored them. The sparkling moonpath ended abruptly,
they tore across the white line of surf and were over
enemy territory. "New course 105 magnetic," Taerum called, and the three aircraft swung gently to the
left as they started the game of threading their way
through the flak.

The northern wave made landfall about the same
time, sighting Vlieland and turning south-east to cut
across the narrow part and down over the Zuyder Zee.
Munro led them across the dark spit; it was so narrow they would see the water again in about thirty
seconds and have another 70 miles of comparatively
safe water, but without warning there were flashes
below and up came the fiery little balls. Munro felt the
shock as they hit the aircraft, and then they were past

and over the water again. Munro called on the intercom,
to see if the crew were all right, but the earphones were
dead.

Pigeon, the wireless op., was standing by his shoulder shouting into his ear, "No radio. No intercom.
Flak's smashed it. I think everyone's O.K." Munro
flew on several miles, trying to fool himself they
could still carry on, but it was no good and he knew it.
Without radio he could not direct the attack on Sorpe;
could not even direct his own crew or get bombing instructions. Swearing, he turned for home.

Inside the Zuyder the water was dark and quite flat,
treacherously deceptive for judging height. Geoff Rice
slipped down a little to level at 60 feet by his belly
lights, but the lights were not working properly and
lured him lower as he tried to get a fix. A hammer
seemed to hit the aircraft like a bolt and there was a
tearing roar above the engines. Rice dragged her off
the water, but the belly was torn out of her and the
bomb had gone with it. The gutted fuselage had
scooped up a couple of tons of water; it was pouring out
of her and the rear gunner was nearly drowning in his
turret. Marvellously she still flew but was dropping
back, and when they found the bomb was gone Rice
turned her heavily back towards England.

The remaining two, Barlow and Byers, skirted their
pinpoint on the cape at Stavoren and ten minutes later
crossed to the enemy land again at Harderwijk. No
one knows exactly how soon it was that the flak came
curling up at them again, but there is a report that as
Barlow's aircraft hit the ground the bomb went off with
a blinding flash, lighting the countryside like a rising sun
for ten seconds before it died and left nothing. It was
either then or soon after that Byers and his crew died
too. Nothing more was heard from him. Only McCarthy
was left of the Sorpe team, flying 60 miles behind,
and perhaps that is what saved him.

Over Holland, Gibson, Martin and Hopgood were
down as low as 40 feet, playing hide-and-seek with the
ground, the bomb aimers calling terse warnings as
houses and trees loomed up, and the aircraft skimmed

over them. They were cruising fast and under the
cowlings the exhaust manifolds were glowing. Once the
three pulled up fast as the pylons of a power line
rushed at them, and they just cleared the wires.

Four miles to port they saw the flare-path of Gilze-
Rijen, German night-fighter field, and a few miles farther on they passed just to the left of the night-fighter
aerodrome at Eindhoven. They could expect night
fighters now; the ops. rooms for miles around must be
buzzing. Martin and Hopgood closed in on each side of
Gibson for mutual protection. They should be able to
see any fighter coming in because he would be
higher, while they, low against the dark ground, would
be hard to see, and that was their strength. Also their
weakness, where the flak was concerned. Their aircraft
were higher, outlined. Just past Eindhoven, Gibson led
them in a gentle turn to the north-east on the new
course that would take them round the bristling guns of
the Ruhr.

A few miles back the other two vics of three were on
course too. Dinghy Young pin-pointed over the canal
at Rosendaal and turned delicately to take them between the fighter fields, but Bill Astell did not seem
sure this was the exact turning point. He bore off a
little to the south for a minute and then turned back,
but had fallen half a mile behind and was a fraction
off track. They did not see him again, and it must
have been quite soon after that the flak or fighter, whatever it was, got him.

Fourteen left.

The leading three slid across the border into Germany and saw no light or movement anywhere, only
darkness filled with the beat of engines. Taerum thought
they were south of track, so they edged to the north,
a little nervily because this was the treacherous leg; they
were coming up to the Rhine to sneak between the
forewarned guns of Huls and the Ruhr. Just short of the
river some twelve light flak guns opened up without
warning; the aircraft gunners squirted back at the roots
of the tracer and then they were out of range. No one
badly hit. The Rhine was rushing at them and up from

a barge spat a thin line of tracer, but they were past before the bullets found them.

Two minutes later more guns opened up, and this time three searchlights lit on Gibson. Foxlee and Deering were shooting at the searchlights. One of them popped out but the two others held, and the air was full of tracer. The rear gunners came into action, the searchlights switched to Martin, blinding him, and Gibson could read the big P on the side of the Lancaster. Every gun was firing, the aircraft juddering with the recoil, and then they were through with throttles wide.

Ahead and just to the left another searchlight sprang into life and caught Gibson. Foxlee was firing instantly, holding his triggers in a long burst, his tracer whipping into the light. It flicked out, and as they went over in the dying glow they saw the gunners scattering. Tammy Simpson opened up from the rear turret till they were out of range. You can't take prisoners in an aircraft.

They were past and shook themselves back into formation. Hutchison tapped out a flak warning, giving the exact position, and way back in Grantham Dunn picked it up and the powerful group radio re-broadcast it at full strength to all other aircraft.

Gibson swung them north around Hamm, whose marshalling yards will for years be notorious. Taerum said, "New course, skipper, 165 magnetic," and then they were hugging ground on the last leg, slicing between Soest and Werl. Now the moon was high enough to light the ground and ahead loomed the dark hills that cradled the water. They climbed to the ridge that rimmed the horizon, crossed into the valley, and down below lay the flat sheet of Moehne Lake.

It was like looking down on the model; the same saucer of water, the same dim fields and across the neck of the lake the squat rampart hugging the water, crowned by the towers. In the half-light it looked like a battleship, but more impregnable. Reinforced concrete a hundred feet thick.

"God," Bob Hay said, "can *we* break that?"

The dam came suddenly to life, prickling with sharp flashes, and the lines of angry red meteors were streaming into the sky and moving about blindly as the gunners hosed the area.

"Bit aggressive, aren't they?" said Trevor-Roper. The pilots swung the aircraft away and headed in wide circles round the lake, keeping out of range and waiting for the others. There seemed to be about ten guns, some in the fields on each side of the lake near the dam, and some—a lot—in the towers on the dam.

Gibson started calling the other aircraft, and one by one they reported, except Astell. He called Astell again at the end, but Astell had been dead for an hour. After a while Gibson gave up and said soberly over the intercom, "Well, boys, I suppose we'd better start the ball rolling." It was the end of the waiting and the start of action, when thought is submerged. He flicked his transmitter switch:

"Hello, all Cooler aircraft, I am going in to attack. Stand by to come in in your order when I tell you. Hello, 'M Mother.' Stand by to take over if anything happens."

"O.K., Leader. Good luck." Hopgood's voice was a careful monotone.

Gibson turned wide, hugging the hills at the eastern end of the lake. Pulford had eased the throttles on and she was roaring harshly, picking up speed and quivering, the nose slowly coming round till three miles ahead they saw the towers and the rampart of the dam, and in between, the flat dark water. Spafford said, "Good show. This is wizard. I can see everything." They came out of the hills and slammed across the water, touching 240 now, and Gibson rattled off the last orders:

"Check height, Terry! Speed control, Pulford! Gunners ready! Coming up, Spam!" Taerum flicked the belly lights on and, peering down from the blister, started droning: "Down . . . down . . . down . . . up a bit . . . steady, stead-y-y." The lights were touching each other, "G George" was exactly at 60 feet and the flak gunners had seen the lights. The streams of glowing shells were swivelling and lowering, and then the shells were whipping towards them, seeming to move slowly at first like all flak, and then rushing madly at their eyes as the aircraft plunged into them.

Gibson said tersely: "Bomb on!"

Spafford flicked the switch and heard the whine of the electric motor starting back in the fuselage. He could hear it winding up speed and a vibration grew through the aircraft as the black barrel underneath stirred out of its inertia and started revolving backwards, faster and faster, building up to optimum revs, until "G George" was thrumming like a live thing.

Gibson held her steady, pointing between the towers. Taerum was watching out of the blister, Pulford had a hand on the throttles and his eyes on the a.s.i., Spafford held the plywood sight to his eye and the towers were closing in on the nails. Gibson shouted to Pulford, "Stand by to pull me out of the seat if I get hit!" There was a sudden snarling clatter up in the nose; Deering had opened up, his tracer spitting at the towers.

The dam was a rushing giant, darkness split with flashes, the cockpit stank of cordite and thought was nothing but a cold alarm shouting, "In another minute we shall be dead," and then Spafford screamed, "Bomb gone!" loud and sharp, and they rocketed over the dam between the towers. A red Véry light soared up as Hutchison pulled the trigger to let the others know, and then the deeper snarling chatter as Trevor-Roper opened up on the towers from the rear.

It was over and memory was confusion as they corkscrewed down the valley, hugging the dark earth sightless to the flak. They were out of range and Gibson lifted her out of the hills, turning steeply, and looked back. A voice in his earphones said, "Good show, Leader. Nice work."

The black water between the towers suddenly rose and split and a huge white core erupted through the middle and climbed towards the sky. The lake was writhing, and as the white column reached its peak and hung a thousand feet high like a ghost against the moon, the heavy explosion reached the aircraft. They looked in awe as they flew back to one side and saw sheets of water spilling over the dam and thought for a

wild moment it had burst. The fury of the water passed
and the dam was still there, the white column slowly
dying.

Round the lake they flew while Hutchison tapped
out in code to base. In a few minutes Gibson thought
the lake was calm enough for the next bomb and called:

"Hello, 'M Mother.' You may attack now. Good
luck."

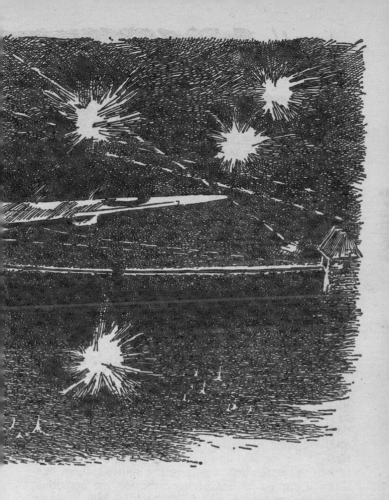

"O.K., Leader. Attacking." Hopgood was still carefully laconic. He was lost in the darkness over the
hills at the end of the lake while the others waited. They
saw his belly-lights flick on and the two little yellow
pools sliding over the water closing and joining as he
found his height. He was straight and level on his run;
the flak saw him and the venomous fireflies were darting at him. He plunged on; the gap was closing fast

when the shells found him and someone said, "Hell, he's been hit!"

A red glow was blossoming round the inner port wing tank, and then a long, long ribbon of flame trailed behind "M Mother." The bomb aimer must have been hit, because the bomb overshot the parapet on to the power-house below.

"M Mother" was past the dam, nose up, straining for height so the crew could bale out, when the tanks blew up with an orange flare, a wing ripped away and the bomber spun to the ground in burning, bouncing pieces. The bomb went off near the power-house like a brilliant sun. It was all over in seconds.

A voice said over the R/T, "Poor old Hoppy."

Gibson called up: "Hello, 'P Popsie.' Are you ready?"

"O.K., Leader. Going in."

"I'll fly across the dam as you make your run and try and draw the flak off you."

"O.K. Thanks, Leader."

Martin was turning in from the hills and Gibson headed across the lake, parallel to the dam and just out of effective range of the guns. As Martin's spotlights merged and sped across the water Gibson back-tracked and Deering and Trevor-Roper opened up; six lines of tracer converged on the towers, drawing their attention, so that for some seconds most of the guns did not notice Martin rocketing over the water. He held his height and Whittaker had the speed right. They were tracking straight for the middle of the dam between the moon-bathed towers when the gunners spotted them and threw a curtain of fire between the towers, spreading like a fan so they would fly through it. Martin drove straight ahead. Two guns swung at them, and as the shells whipped across the water sharp-eyed little Foxlee was yelling as he squirted back, his tracer lacing and tangling with the flak.

A sharp "Bomb gone!" from Bob Hay, and in the same instant a shudder as two shells smacked into the starboard wing, one of them exploding in the inner petrol tank. A split second of flashes as they shot through the barrage. Tammy Simpson opened up from the rear turret, Chambers shot the Véry light and they were down the valley. Whittaker was looking fearfully at the hole in the starboard wing, but no fire was coming. He suddenly realised why and nudged Martin, yelling in his ear, "Thank Christ, the bloody starboard tank was empty!"

Martin shouted, "Bomb gone, Leader."

"O.K., 'P Popsie.' Let me know when you're out of the flak. Hello, 'A Apple.' Are you ready?"

"O.K., Leader."

"Right. Go ahead. Let me know when you're in position and I'll draw the flak for you."

Martin called again, " 'P Popsie' clear now, Leader."

"O.K. Are you hit?"

"Yeah. Starboard wing, but we're all right. We can make it."

The lake suddenly boiled again by the dam and spewed out the great white column that climbed again to a thousand feet. More water was cascading over the dam, but it cleared soon and the dam was still there.

Dinghy Young was on the air again. " 'A Apple' making bombing run."

Gibson headed back over the lake where his gunners could play with fire, and this time Martin did the same. As Young came plunging across the lake Gibson and Martin came in on each side, higher up, and the flak did not know where to shoot. Young swept past the dam and reported he was all right. The great explosion was up against the dam wall again, beautifully accurate, but the dam was still there, and again Gibson waited till the plume of spray had cleared and the water was calm.

He called Maltby and ordered him in, and as Maltby came across the water Gibson and Martin came in with him, firing with every gun that could bear and flicking their navigation lights on this time to help the flak gunners shoot at the wrong target. The red cartridge soared up from Maltby's aircraft to signal "Attack successful."

In a few moments the mountain of water erupted

skyward again under the dam wall. It was uncanny how
accurate the bomb was. The spray from the explosion
was misting up the whole valley now and it was hard to
see what was happening by the dam. Gibson called
Shannon to make his attack, and the words were barely
out of his mouth when a sharp voice filled his
earphones:

"Hell, it's gone! It's gone! Look at it for Christ's
sake!" Wheeling round the valley side Martin had seen
the concrete face abruptly split and crumble under the
weight of water. Gibson swung in close and was staggered. A ragged hole 100 yards across and 100 feet
deep split the dam and the lake was pouring out of it,
134 million tons of water crashing into the valley in a jet
200 feet long, smooth on top, foaming at the sides
where it tore at the rough edges of the breach and boiling over the scarred earth where the power-house had
been.

Gibson told Shannon to "skip it."

The others flew over and were awed into silence. In
the moon glow they watched a wall of water rolling
down the valley, 25 feet high, moving 20 feet a second.
A gunner still on his feet in one of the towers opened
up at them until lines of tracer converged on the root
of the flak and it stopped abruptly. The awed silence
was broken by a babble of intercom chatter as they
went mad with excitement; the only man not looking
being Hutchison, sitting at his keyboard tapping out
"Nigger."

Soon the hissing steam and spray blurred the valley. Gibson called Martin and Maltby to set course for
home, and told Young, Shannon, Maudslay and Knight
to follow him east to the Eder. Young was to control
if Gibson was shot down.

8

THE WRITHING LAKE

At Grantham a long silence had followed the flak
warning at Huls, and then Dunn's phone rang sharply,
and in the dead silence they all heard the Morse crack-
ling in the receiver. It was quite slow and Cochrane,
bending near, could read it. "Goner," he said. "From
'G George.' " "Goner" was the code word that meant
Gibson had exploded his bomb in the right place.

"I'd hoped one bomb might do it," Wallis said
gloomily.

"It's probably weakened it," Cochrane soothed him.
Harris looked non-committal. There was no more from
"G George," and they went on waiting. A long silence.
Nothing came through when Hopgood crashed. The
phone rang. "Goner" from "P Popsie." Another dragging silence. "Goner" from "A Apple." Wallis swears
even to-day that there was half an hour between each
signal, but the log shows only about five minutes.
"Goner" from "J Johnny." That was Maltby, and the
aura of gloom settled deeper over Wallis.

A minute later the phone rang again and the Morse
crackled so fast the others could not read it. Dunn
printed it letter by letter on a signals pad and let out a
cry, "Nigger. It's Nigger. It's gone."

Wallis threw his arms over his head and went dancing round the room. The austere face of Cochrane
cracked into a grin, he grabbed one of Wallis's hands
and started congratulating him. Harris, with the first
grin on his face that Wallis had ever seen, grabbed the
other hand and said:

"Wallis, I didn't believe a word you said about this

damn bomb, but you could sell me a pink elephant now."

He said, a little later when some of the excitement had died down: "I must tell Portal immediately." Sir Charles Portal, Chief of the R.A.F., was in Washington that night on a mission, actually at that moment dining with Roosevelt. Harris picked up the nearest phone and said, "Get me the White House."

The little W.A.A.F. on the switchboard knew nothing of the highly secret raid. Even at Grantham, Cochrane's security had been perfect. She did not realise the importance of it all, or the identity of the great man who was speaking, and was caught off guard. "Yes, sir," she said automatically and, so they say, dialled the only White House she knew, a jolly little roadhouse a few miles out of Grantham.

Harris must have thought she was a very smart operator when the White House answered so quickly, and there are reported to have been moments of incredible and indescribable comedy as Harris asked for Portal, and the drowsy landlord, testy at being hauled out of bed after midnight, told him in well-chosen words he didn't have anyone called Portal staying at the place; in fact, he didn't have anyone staying at all, because he didn't have room, and if he did have room he would not have anyone staying there who had people who called him up at that time of night. Not for long anyway.

Harris went red, and there were some explosive exchanges before one of them slammed the receiver down. Someone slipped down and had a word with the little W.A.A.F., and she tried in terror for the next hour to raise Washington, but without success.

Three kilometres down the valley from the Moehne lay the sleeping village of Himmelpforten, which means Gates of Heaven. The explosion had wakened the village priest, Father Berkenkopf, and he guessed instantly what was happening; he had been afraid of it for three years. He ran to his small stone church, Porta Coeli (which also means Gate of Heaven—in Latin), and began tugging grimly on the bellrope, the signal he had arranged with his villagers. It is not certain how many were warned in time. In the darkness the clanging of the bell rolled ominously round the valley and then it was muffled in the thunder moving nearer. Berkenkopf must have heard it and known what it meant, but it seems that he was still pulling at the bell when the flood crushed the church and the village of the Gates of Heaven and rolled them down the valley.

It went for many miles and took more villages, a tumbling maelstrom of water and splintered houses, beds and frying-pans, the chalice from Porta Coeli and the bell, the bodies of cattle and horses, pigs and dogs, and the bodies of Father Berkenkopf and other human beings.

War, as someone said, is a great leveller, but he did not mean it quite as literally or as bitterly as this.

The Eder was hard to find because fog was filling the valley. Gibson circled it for some time before he was certain he was there. One by one the others found it and soon they were all in a left-hand circuit round the lake. There was no flak; probably the Germans thought the Eder did not need it. It lay deep in a fold of the hills; the ridges around were a thousand feet high and it was no place to dive a heavy aircraft at night.

Gibson said, "O.K., Dave. Start your attack."

Shannon flew a wide circuit over the ridges and then put his nose right down, but the dive was not steep enough and he overshot. Sergeant Henderson slammed on full throttle, and Shannon hauled back on the stick and they just cleared the mountain on the far side.

"Sorry, Leader," Shannon said a little breathlessly. "Made a mess of that. I'll try it again."

Five times more he dived into the dark valley but he failed every time to get into position and nearly stood the Lancaster on her tail to get out of the hills again. He called up finally, "I think I'd better circle and try to get to know this place."

"O.K., Dave. You hang around a bit and let someone

else have a crack. Hullo, 'Z Zebra.' You have a go now."

Maudslay acknowledged and a minute later was diving down the contour of the hills, only to overshoot and go rocketing up again like Shannon. He tried again but the same thing happened. Maudslay said he was going to try once more. He came slowly over the ridges, turned in the last moment and the nose dropped sharply into the gloom as he forced her down into the valley. They saw him level out very fast, and then the spotlights flicked on to the water and closed quickly and he was tracking for the dam.

His red Véry light curled up as Fuller called "Bombs gone!" but they must have been going too fast. The bomb hit the parapet of the dam and blew up on impact with a tremendous flash; in the glare they saw "Z Zebra" for a moment just above the explosion. Then only blackness.

Gibson said painfully, knowing it was useless:

"Henry, Henry—hullo, 'Z Zebra,' are you all right?"

There was no answer. He called again and, incredibly, out of the darkness a very faint voice said, "I think so . . . stand by." They all heard it, Gibson and Shannon and Knight, and wondered that it was possible. After a while Gibson called again but there was no answer. Maudslay never came back.

Gibson called, "O.K., David, will you attack now?"

Shannon tried and missed again; came round once more, plunged into the darkness and this time made it, curling out of the dive at the foot of the lake and tracking for the dam. He found his height quickly, the bomb dropped clear and Shannon roughly pulled his plane over the shoulder of the mountain. Under the parapet the bomb spewed up the familiar plume of white water and as it drifted down Gibson, diving over the lake, saw that the dam was still there. There was only Knight left. He had the last bomb. Gibson ordered him in.

Knight tried once and couldn't make it. He tried again. Failed. "Come in down moon and dive for the point, Les," Shannon said. He gave more advice over the R/T, and Knight listened quietly. He was a young Australian who did not drink, his idea of a riotous evening being to write letters home and go to the pictures. He dived to try again, made a perfect run and they saw the splash as his bomb dropped in the right spot. Seconds later the water erupted, and as Gibson slanted down to have a look he saw the wall of the dam burst open and the torrent come crashing out.

Knight, more excited than he had ever been, was yelling over the R/T, and when he stopped he left his transmitter on for a few seconds by mistake; the crew's remarks on the intercom were broadcast, and they were very spectacular remarks indeed.

This was even more fantastic than the Moehne. The breach in the dam was as big and there were over 200 million tons of water pouring through. The Eder Valley was steeper and they watched speechlessly as the flood foamed and tossed down the valley, lengthening like a snake. It must have been rolling at 30 feet a second. They saw a car in front racing to get clear; only the lights they saw, like two frightened eyes spearing the dark, and the car was not fast enough. The foam crawled up on it, the headlights turned opalescent green as the water rolled over, and suddenly they flicked out.

Hutchison was tapping "Dinghy" in Morse; that was the code to say that the Eder was destroyed. When he had finished Gibson called, "O.K., all Cooler aircraft. You've had your look. Let's go home," and the sound of their engines died over the hills as they flew west to fight their way back.

McCarthy had fought a lone way through to the Sorpe, tucked down in rolling hills south of the Moehne. The valleys were full of mist, so it was a long time before he pin-pointed himself over the lake, dimly seeing through the haze a shape he recognised from the model.

He tried a dummy run and found, as the others found before at the Eder, that there was a hill at each end so that he would have to dive steeply, find his aim-

Moehne Dam

ing point quickly and pull up in a hurry. He tried twice more but was not satisfied and came in a third time, plunging through the mist trying to see through the suffused moonlight. He nearly hit the water and levelled out very low. Johnson picked up the aiming point and seconds later yelled, "Bomb gone!" and they were climbing up over the far hills when the bomb exploded by the dam wall. McCarthy dived back over the dam and they saw that the crest had crumbled for 50 yards. As they turned on course for England, Eaton tapped out the code word that told of their successful drop.

Wallis's joy was complete. Cochrane radioed "G George," asking if he had any aircraft left to divert to the Sorpe, and Hutchison answered, "None." Satterly, who had been plotting the path of the reserve force by dead reckoning, radioed orders to them.

Burpee, in "S Sugar," was directed to the Sorpe, but he did not answer. They called again and again, but there was only silence. He was dead.

Brown, in "F Freddy," was sent to the Sorpe and reached it after McCarthy had left; the mist was swirling thicker and, though he dived low over the dam, Oancia, the bomb aimer, could not pick it up in time.

Brown dived back on a second run but Oancia still found the mist foiled him. They tried eight times, and then Brown pulled up and they had a conference over the intercom. On the next run Oancia dropped a cluster of incendiaries in the woods to the side of the dam. They burned dazzlingly and the trees caught too, so that on the tenth run Oancia picked up the glare a long way back, knew exactly where the target was and dropped his load accurately.

They pulled round in a climbing turn and a jet of water and rubble climbed out of the mist and hung against the moon; down in the mist itself they saw a shock wave of air like a giant smoke ring circling the base of the spout.

Anderson, in "Y Yorker," was also sent to the Sorpe, but he was still later than Brown, and now the valley was completely under mist so that the lake and dam were hidden and he had to turn back with his bomb.

Ottley, in "C Charlie," was ordered to the Lister Dam, one of the secondary targets. He acknowledged "Message received," but that was the last anyone ever heard from him.

The last man was Townsend, in "O Orange," and his target was the Ennerpe. He searched a long time before he found it in the mist, and made three runs before he was satisfied and dropped the bomb. It was accurate.

Ten out of the nineteen were coming home, hugging the ground, 8 tons lighter now in bomb and petrol load and travelling at maximum cruising, about 245, not worrying about petrol; only about getting home. The coast was an hour away and the sun less than that. They knew the fighters were overhead waiting for a lightening sky in the east.

Harris had driven Cochrane and Wallis to Scampton to meet the survivors, and in the ops. room at Scampton he picked up the phone to try and get Portal again. This time he prepared the ground for smart service by telling the girl that the speaker was Air Chief Marshal Sir Arthur Harris, Commander-in-Chief of Bomber Command.

"Yes, of course," said the indulgent girl, who knew the absurd things that plastered New Zealand flight lieutenants were liable to say, "you've been on it again, sir. Now you go and get your batman to put you to bed. He'll give you your course to steer."

There was an explosion in the ops. room and an unusually intelligent intelligence officer hared down the stairs and told the girl the frightful thing she had done. Someone soothed the irate man in the ops. room while the girl beseeched the G.P.O. to get Washington faster than ever before. This time the lines were clear and before long a mollified Harris had the pleasure of telling Portal, "Operation Downwood successful . . . yes, successful!"

Gibson saw the dark blotch of Hamm ahead and swung to the east. To the left he saw another aircraft; it was going too near Hamm, he thought, whoever it was, and then the flak came and something was burning in the sky where the aircraft had been. It was falling, hit like a shooting star and blew up. It may have been Burpee. Or Ottley.

Townsend was the last away from the dams area. He flew back over the Moehne and could not recognise it at first; the lake had changed shape. Already there were mudbanks with little boats stranded on them, and bridges stood long-legged out of the shrinking water. The torpedo net had vanished, and below the dam the country was different. There was a new lake where no lake had been; a strange lake, writhing down the valley.

Miraculously most of them dodged the flak on the way back; lucky this, because dawn was coming, the sky was paler in the east and at 50 feet the aircraft were sitting ducks. In Gibson's aircraft Trevor-Roper called on the intercom, "Unidentified enemy aircraft behind."

"O.K., Trev." "G George" sank till it was scraping the fields and they could see the startled cattle running in panic. Trevor-Roper said, "O.K., we've lost him," but Gibson still kept down on the deck.

Over Holland he called Dinghy Young, but there was no answer and he wondered what had happened to him. (Group knew! They had got a brief message from Young. He had come over the coast a little high and the last squirts of flak had hit him. He had struggled on a few more miles, losing height, and then ditched in the water.)

Coming to the West Wall, Gibson climbed to about 300 feet, Pulford slid the throttles right forward and they dived to the ground again, picking up speed, and at 270 m.p.h. they roared over the tank traps and the naked sand and then they were over the grey morning water and beyond the flak.

Ten minutes later it was daylight over Holland, and Townsend was still picking his way out. He was lucky and went between the guns.

Maltby was first back, landing in the dawn and finding the whole station had been waiting up since dusk. Harris, Cochrane and Wallis met him at the hardstanding and he told them what he had seen. Martin landed. Mutt Summers went out to meet him and found Martin under the aircraft looking at a ragged hole in his wing. "Hullo, Mutt," he said. "Look what some bastard's done to Popsie."

One by one they landed and were driven to the ops. room, where Harris, Cochrane and Wallis listened intently. Gibson came in, his hair pressed flat from eight hours under his helmet. "It was a wizard party, sir," he said. "Went like a bomb, but we couldn't quieten some of the flak. I'm afraid some of the boys got the ham-

mer. Don't know how many yet. Hopgood and Maudslay for certain."

They had bacon and egg and stood round the bar
with pints, drinking and waiting for the others. It was
an hour since the last aircraft had landed. Shannon and
Dinghy Young had ditched, and someone said, "What,
is the old soak going to paddle back again? That's the
third time he's done it. He'll do it once too often."
Young *had* done it once too often. He was not in his
dinghy this time.

Wallis was asking anxiously, "Where are they?
Where are all the others?"

Summers said, "Oh, they'll be along. Give 'em time.
They've probably landed somewhere else"; but after a
while it was impossible to cover up any longer and
Wallis knew they were all standing round getting drunk
for the ones who were not coming back. Except himself;
he didn't drink. Martin made him take a half pint but
he only held it and stood there blinking back tears and
said, "Oh, if I'd only known, I'd never have started
this!" Mutt and Charles Whitworth tried to take his
mind off it.

The party was getting wound up. Someone said,
"This shouldn't be only a stag show," and a couple of
minutes later an Australian and three others were in-
vading the sacrosanct W.A.A.F. officers' room. One
girl sat up in bed and pulled the clothes high over her.

"You can't come in here!" she shrieked.

"Yes, I can," one of them said, grabbing up two
tennis balls from the dressing-table and stowing them
in his tunic. He strutted round showing off his new
bust line. "All girls together," he yelled. "Come and join
the party."

The girl said she never went to parties before breakfast, so they grabbed the bed and started tossing it up
towards the ceiling until she squealed, "All right, but
get out while I dress."

Gibson left the party early, but not for bed; he went
over to the hangar to give Humphries and Chiefy
Powell a hand with the casualty telegrams to the next
of kin. Fifty-six beardless men out of 133 were missing,

and only three had got out by parachute at a perilously low height to spend the rest of the war miserably in prison camp. Gibson had expected to lose several over the Moehne, where those sinister installations had been spotted by the recce aircraft, but they had lost only one there. (It was not till after the war that they discovered that those dark shapes on top of the Moehne had been —trees . . . ornamental pine trees. In the middle of the war the Germans would not send extra guns but had gone to the trouble of decorating it.)

Around lunchtime the party survivors transferred to Whitworth's house and Whitworth's best port. Wallis came tiredly downstairs in a dressing-gown, distressed about the losses, and after a while he left to fly back to Weybridge with Summers. Martin gave him a sleeping-pill as he was leaving so that he would sleep that night. He slept all right. The weary scientist swallowed the pill sitting up in bed at home and went out like a light.

About two o'clock even the durable Martin and Whittaker were ready for bed, but they were all up again at five o'clock and drove over in buses to a party at Woodhall Spa. On the way back David Shannon and Anne were sitting close together, and Shannon leaned closer so the others couldn't hear and asked her to marry him.

"Oh, David," she said, and there was a pause, "n-n-not with that moustache."

Shannon fingered the growth defensively. It was a dear possession; made him look years older—at least twenty-two. He groaned. "What is it?" he said. "My moustache or you?" There was only silence and he sighed, "All right. I'll whip it off."

In the morning 617 Squadron went on leave, three days for the ground crew, seven days for the aircrew survivors—except Gibson, who stayed on two days to write to the mothers of the dead. He refused to let Heveron type the usual form letter but wrote them all out in his own hand, different ones each time, fifty-six of them.

In London and in their homes the crews found they were famous, though the headlines in Germany were not so flattering. A recce Mosquito arrived back from over Germany with the first pictures of the damage, and they were breathtaking. The Moehne and Eder lakes were empty and 330 million tons of water were spreading like a cancer through the western Ruhr valleys, the bones of towns and villages showing lifeless in the wilderness.

The Ruhr, which had been enduring its ordeal by fire, was having it now by water. For 50 miles from the Moehne and 50 miles from the Eder coal mines were flooded and factories collapsed. At Fritzlar one of Hitler's largest military aerodromes was under water, the aircraft, the landing ground, hangars, barracks and bomb dump. Roads, railways and bridges had disappeared. The Unterneustadt industrial suburb of Kassel, forty miles from the Eder, was under water, and the flood ran miles on down the Fulda Valley. Canal banks were washed away, power stations had disappeared, the Ruhr foundries were without water for making steel. A dozen waterworks were destroyed as far away as Gelsenkirchen, Dortmund, Hamm and Bochum. The communications system feeding raw materials to the Ruhr and taking away the finished weapons was disrupted. Some factories were not swept away but still could not work because there was no electricity. Or no water.

In the small town of Neheim alone 2,000 men, including 1,250 soldiers, were diverted to repair damage. Another 2,000 men were trying to repair the dams. And in the months ahead, in the Battle of the Ruhr, there was not enough water to put the fires out.

The official German report said it was "a dark picture of destruction." By the next autumn they might know how much industrial production would be ultimately affected, but estimated it was going to mean the equivalent of the loss of production of 100,000 men for several months.

A hundred and twenty-five factories were either destroyed or badly damaged, nearly 3,000 hectares of arable land were ruined, twenty-five bridges had vanished, and twenty-one more were badly damaged. The livestock losses were 6,500 cattle and pigs.

There was a moral price to pay too; there always is. 1,294 people were drowned in the floods, and most were civilians. Most were not Germans—there were 749 slaves and prisoners among the dead. There had been a Russian P.o.W. camp in the valley below the Eder.

After the raid the Germans diverted hundreds of soldiers with flak guns to guard all the other dams in Germany. While they were working like beavers to repair the Moehne they also built two tall pylons 2,000 yards back from the dam wall and strung between them a heavy cable across the lake. From this other cables dangled to the water, and lashed to them were contact grenades to catch low-flying aircraft. They strung two heavy anti-torpedo nets near the dam wall, and another one 1,000 yards away. On the dry side of the dam they strung a steel mesh curtain on posts sunk into the sloping wall.

Oberburgermeister Dillgardt was vindicated, but it was too late. The stable door was shut, but the horse had gone.

Gibson spent his leave quietly with his wife, Eve, who had had a shock when she had opened the papers and found Guy's name and photographs splashed over the front pages. All the time he had been at 617 he had told her he was having a rest at a flying training-school.

Micky Martin was summoned to Australian Air Force Headquarters, where a dark, pretty girl called Wendy tried her damnedest to get him to talk about the raid for a story for Australia, but all the incorrigible Martin would say was, "Come and have lunch with me," and kept it up until she did.

Back at Scampton, Gibson found a letter for him addressed from a country vicarage. It enclosed, for his information, a copy of a letter which the writer had sent to *The Times*:

"Sir,

In international bird-watching circles, the bombing of the Moehne Dam has caused grave concern. For three years previous to the outbreak of war a pair of ring-necked whooper swans nested regularly on the lake. They are almost the rarest of Europe's great birds. The only other pair known to have raised a brood during recent years were a pair of the Arctic sub-species which were photographed by the aunt of the late Professor Olssen, of Reykjavik, on their nest on the shore of Lake Thongvallavatn, Iceland, in 1927.

Has anything been heard of the fate of the Moehne pair, probably the last in Europe? And, in view of the rarity of these beautiful birds, why was the bombing of their home permitted? Furthermore, assuming that this operation was necessary, could it not have been deferred until the cygnets (if any) were full grown?

Yours faithfully, etc., etc."

The Times must have smelt a rat and did not publish it, which was just as well because Gibson found later it had been written by two intelligence officers at Scampton.

Micky Martin got a letter too. The Australians wrote saying they were collecting souvenirs for a war museum, and could he send them a souvenir of the dams raid. Martin, irreverent where headquarters were concerned, wrote back:

"Sir,

I am very interested in your museum and am sending you, enclosed, the Moehne Dam.

Yours faithfully."

And under his signature he got Toby Foxlee to scrawl in red ink: *"Opened by censors and contents confiscated by the Metropolitan Water Board."*

Then the decorations came through—thirty-three of them. Gibson was awarded the Victoria Cross. Mar-

tin, McCarthy, Maltby, Shannon and Knight got
D.S.O.s. Bob Hay, Hutchison, Leggo and Danny
Walker got bars to their D.F.C.s. There were ten
D.F.C.s, among them Trevor-Roper, Buckley, Deering,
Spafford and Taerum. Brown and Townsend got the
Conspicuous Gallantry Medal, and there were twelve
D.F.M.s, among them being Tammy Simpson, Sump-
ter, Oancia and Pulford.

When he heard the news Gibson rang for Flight Sergeant Powell.

"Chiefy," he said quietly, "if I ever change, tell me."

On May 27 the King and Queen visited the newly
famous squadron, and the crews pressed their uniforms
and stood in front of their aircraft to be presented,
though one noted pilot overlooked one point and was
standing there smartly to attention with an orange
sticking out of his pocket. That day was Shannon's
twenty-first birthday, and Gibson had primed the King
beforehand, so that when Shannon was presented the
King shook him warmly by the hand and said jokingly,
"You seem to be a very well preserved twenty-one,
Shannon. You must have a party to-night."

Gibson had had a competition for a design for a
squadron badge, and after the parade he showed the
King the roughs and asked if he would choose one. The
King called the Queen, and unanimously they picked
a drawing showing a dam breached in the middle
with water flowing out and bolts of lightning above.
Underneath, the motto was *"Après nous le déluge"*;
most apt, particularly as it had a royal background—
Marie Antoinette had used it.

That night, when the Royal party had left, Shannon
had his party. Towards the end an apparition came
leaping into the mess. Charles Whitworth had robed
himself in hunting kit, red coat and white breeches, and
pranced around tootling on a hunting horn, hurdling
the furniture till there was a bellow from the doorway:
"What the devil's going on here!" In the frame of the
door stood an obviously senior officer, rows of braid
up his sleeve, gold oak leaves on his cap and ribbons

plastered across his chest. A hush fell, and then slightly glazed eyes focused and a chorus of catcalls burst the silence.

"Shannon!"

Shannon had slipped away and put Whitworth's tunic and hat on. He stalked in, stopped in front of Whitworth and boomed, "Who is this wretched fellow in fancy dress?"

Whitworth blew him a raspberry on his hunting horn.

"Whip him off to the guard-room!" Shannon shouted. "Clap him in irons!"

He turned to his wireless operator, the lanky Concave Goodale, and roared, "Stand to attention when you look at me!"

"You're not standing so well yourself," Goodale said rudely.

Buckley padded forward, eyeing his skipper indulgently, and said, "Let's have his pants."

Bodies closed in menacingly, but Gibson said, "No. Give him grace. It's his twenty-first birthday."

Someone, patently insober, said, "Shannon, I think you're drunk," and Shannon said with hauteur:

"Sir, if so, it is by Royal Command."

9

THE BLACKEST HOUR

Weeks passed placidly. Gibson wrote and asked the Chester Herald to approve the chosen badge. The squadron got new aircraft and did a lot of training flying, both high and low level, finding it boring, and to give them something to think about Gibson laid on compulsory P.T. for all aircrew. On the second morning three men did not turn up for it, so Gibson made them run round the perimeter track, four and a half miles, and to make sure they ran the whole way he sent the dismayed Chiefy Powell with them. Powell came in a reluctant fourth. A few days later a couple more decided to chance it and stay in bed: Gibson made them do an extra half hour P.T. in gas masks and there were no more absentees.

All those decorated were to attend an investiture at Buckingham Palace on June 22, and on the 21st they went up to London in two special carriages. The staider ones and those with wives were mostly in one carriage, and the bloods gathered in the other, pockets bulging with bottles, and settled down to pontoon and poker.

An hour later Humphries was chatting in the respectable carriage to a few of the wives and W.A.A.F. officers when a wireless operator appeared in the doorway, immaculately dressed except that he had no pants. Long shirt tails kept him technically decent.

"Losht my pantsh," he mumbled. "Very awkward. Can't see King without pantsh."

Humphries jumped up and screened him from the giggling W.A.A.F.s, pushed him into a toilet and walked along to the compartment where Trevor-Roper and

Maltby were noisily playing cards. He tried the casual approach:

"I say, have any of you chaps by any chance seen Brian's pants?"

Screams of mirth.

"Why, Adj., has he lost them?"

"You know he has," Humphries said severely. "It's not really so funny. He just walked into a compartment where there were a couple of ladies."

Louder screams of mirth. They were crying with laughter.

"Quite well made, isn't he?" gasped Jack Fort and the compartment rocked with laughter again.

Trevor-Roper was eyeing Humphries' pants sinisterly, but Humphries held his ground. "You wouldn't think it was funny if it had been your girl friends."

"Ah well," Maltby said, "I suppose not." He pulled a pair of crumpled pants from under the seat and tossed them over.

"Have a Scotch before you go, Adj.," Trevor-Roper said. He whipped the cap off a bottle and poured till the top of the vacuum flask was nearly full. He was grinning; it was clearly a case of sinking the neat spirit or losing his own pants, and Humphries chose the spirit, downing it in one gulp, so that for a fearful instant, through the tears, he thought the top of his head was coming off.

"I'm proud of you, Adj.," Trevor-Roper said. "Have another." But Humphries had retreated with the pants.

They got safely to London, a tribute to Humphries' tireless and tactful shepherding, but that evening he fell into bad company again, finding himself in a suite at the Savoy with the mountain of man from Brooklyn, Joe McCarthy, and Toby Foxlee. He does not remember where he went that night but at some hour in the morning he found himself back at the Savoy. Trevor-Roper walked in and said, "Let's have a drink. The party hasn't started yet."

In the morning, when he tried to open his eyes, Humphries thought the ceiling had fallen on him, but the investiture was at 10.15 a.m. and he just *had* to get up. They were nearly all in the same boat but they all made it, pale and heavy-eyed.

617 Squadron was decorated *en masse* first, taking precedence over the other V.C.s and high orders, a historical precedent that may never be repeated. And when the band struck up the Anthem it was not the King who emerged but the Queen; the first time a queen had taken an investiture since the days of Victoria.

Gibson went up first to get his V.C., and one by one the others. The Queen took Joe McCarthy's great paw and stood chatting with him for a long time, asking him questions about America while the big blond tough from Brooklyn turned pink and stammered out answers.

That night A.V. Roe's gave them a celebration dinner. The only mistake all night tickled everyone; the printers had labelled the menu "The Damn Busters."

More weeks of training, high and low level, and the crews, who were supposed to be the pick of Bomber Command, became "browned off." Men of other squadrons who were doing several ops. a week took to ragging them as the "One op. squadron," and one of the 617 bomb aimers, Jimmy Watson, a droll little Yorkshireman, composed a lament on the subject. Sung to the tune of "Come and join us," the first verse ran:

"The Moehne and the Eder dams were standing in the Ruhr,
But six one seven Squadron went and knocked them to the floor.
Now since that operation six one seven's been a flop
And we've got the reputation of the squadron with one op."

Cochrane told Gibson he had done enough operations and would not let him fly again. Squadron Leader George Holden, D.S.O., D.F.C., arrived to take over, but Gibson stayed on for a few days. Holden was slight and youthful with fair wavy hair but a brusque manner. Before the war he had worn a bowler and carried a

rolled umbrella, but was a very tough young man. He
had felt very sick once but kept flying on ops. for over
a week till he nearly collapsed after landing one night
and went to the doctor, who examined him and said,
a little startled, "Well, I think you've had pleurisy, but
you seem to be nearly all right now."

617 went to war again on July 15, against power-
stations in Northern Italy, at San Polo D'Enza, near
Bologna, and Aquata Scirvia, near Genoa. Mussolini
was toppling, the battle of Sicily was raging, and supplies for the Germans were streaming down Italy on the
electrified railways. They hoped to cripple the railways
by striking at the power. It was a long way, the aircraft
would arrive with tanks two-thirds empty and there was
no hope of flying back to England. Yells of joy when
they were told they would fly on to Blida, an airfield
in North Africa, near Algiers. The only glum one was
Gibson, categorically forbidden to go. Holden was to
lead six aircraft to Aquata Scrivia, and Maltby to lead
the other six to San Polo D'Enza. Gibson sadly waved
them off from the end of the runway.

It was a "cissy" trip; no opposition on the way, but
they found the targets cloaked in haze and bombed
largely by guesswork. Several aircraft were hit and
Allsebrook lost an engine, but they all landed safely at
Blida. At the de-briefing McCarthy threw down his
parachute disgustedly and said, "You know, if we'd
only carried flares to-night we could've seen what we
were doing." No one took much notice just then, but it
was that remark, remembered later, that was partly
responsible for the history they made.

North Africa was a novelty for about two days.
The airfield was a plain of baked earth, and the crews,
sweating in wooden barracks, lay about sipping red
wine and sunbathing. The weather closed in and they
were stranded for ten days, getting browned off by
boredom instead.

On the flight home they called at Leghorn to deliver some bombs over the docks, but again there was
haze and they were not pleased with the bombing.

Martin flew back over the Alps at 19,000 feet, to the

dismay of Tammy Simpson in the rear turret, who had thought they were returning low over France and had worn only his light tropical kit. Back at Scampton they thawed him out with rum.

The squadron greeted them most warmly as they clambered out of the aircraft with bottles of benedictine and wine, and dragging crates of oranges, figs and dates. Martin jumped out wearing a fez.

Gibson was not there to meet them. He had gone. Harris and Cochrane had put a definite stop to his flying by asking Winston Churchill to take him with him to America for a "show the flag" tour, and Gibson had had no option. He'd been so upset he had not been able to face the farewells.

On July 29 the squadron dropped leaflets on Milan to persuade the wavering Italians that the war was profitless. It was singularly unstimulating, and McCarthy summed up the feeling by grumbling, "It's no better than selling goddam newspapers." The only bright feature was that they went on to Blida again and re-stocked with benedictine and oranges.

One aircraft had been commissioned to bring back a keg of wine for a senior group captain. They brought it back all right, but it vanished from the aircraft after landing and there was a great deal of carefree laughter in the ground-crew barracks that night. Also an explosion from the group captain. Chiefy Powell was told to catch the culprits, but after a decent interval of about three days he reported it was a complete mystery, feeling somewhat disgruntled because he was the only man who had been noble enough to refuse a beaker.

In August they were back to boredom. No ops., but training all and every day.

It was about this time that disturbing reports were coming out of Germany about a mysterious new weapon. Apparently Hitler's notorious "secret weapon." Agents could not say what it was but sensed it was something special. A couple of escaped prisoners of war reached England with information that hinted at rockets and indicated an area north-east of Lü-

beck. In the Pas de Calais area thousands of workmen
were swarming about monstrous new concrete works.
A recce aircraft brought back a photograph of a
strange new factory at Peenemünde, north-east of
Lübeck. Lying on the ground were pencil-shaped objects that baffled the interpretive men, but little by
little they began to connect the rocket reports with
the pencil-shaped objects and the concrete structures, which would obviously be impervious to any
R.A.F. bombs. The 12,000-pounder thin-case bomb
was nearly ready, but it was purely a blast bomb,
to explode on the ground and knock over buildings.
It would not dent masses of concrete half embedded
in the earth.

The spies were right. Sixty miles from London,
just behind Calais, Hitler was building his secret-
weapon blockhouses, fantastic structures which would
bombard London and the invasion ports non-stop in
spite of anything we could do. They were all of reinforced concrete, walls 16 feet thick and roofs 20 feet
thick! No known bomb would affect them. The Todt
Organisation promised Hitler that.

At Watten, Wizernes and Siracourt the blockhouses
were to be assembly, storage and launching sites for
rockets and flying bombs. Twelve thousand slaves
were working on them, and deep under the concrete
they were carving tunnels and chambers in the chalk
and rock where Germans could live and fire their
rockets without interruption.

But greatest nightmare of all was the grotesque
underworld being burrowed under a 20-foot thick
slab of ferro-concrete near Mimoyecques. Here Hitler
was preparing his V.3. Little has ever been told
about V.3, probably because we never found out
much about it. V.3. was the most secret and sinister
of all—long-range guns with barrels 500 feet long!

The muzzles would never appear above the earth;
the entire barrels would be sunk in shafts that dived
at 50 degrees 500 feet into the ground. Hitler was
putting fifteen of these guns in at Mimoyecques,
five guns, side by side, in each of three shafts. They
were smooth-bore barrels, and a huge slow-burning

*charge would fire a 10-inch shell with a long, steady
acceleration, so there would be no destructive heat
and pressure in the barrel. In that way the barrels
would not quickly wear out as Big Bertha did in
World War I. These were more monstrous in every
way than Big Bertha; they fired a bigger shell, could
go on firing for a long time and, more important than
that, they had a rapid rate of fire. Thick armour-
plate doors in the concrete would slide back when
they were ready, and then the nest of nightmare guns
would pour out six shells a minute on London, 600
tons of explosives a day. They would keep that up
accurately day after day, so that in a fortnight London would receive as much high explosive as Berlin
received during the whole war. But that fortnight
would be only the start of it.*

The War Cabinet did not know this, but they *did*
know enough to be extremely worried. There were anxious (and very secret) conferences (which coincided
with the fact that Cochrane was strongly pressing for
renewed interest in Wallis's shock-wave bomb—he
wanted to use it on the Rothensee shiplift). Soon the
Chief Executive of the Ministry of Aircraft Production,
Air Chief Marshal Sir Wilfred Freeman, sent for Barnes
Wallis, who was now held in esteem and some awe.
Freeman said:

"Wallis, do you remember that crazy idea of yours
back in 1940 about a bomb?"

"I seem to have had a lot of crazy ideas then,"
Wallis said wryly.

"I mean about a *big* bomb, a ten-tonner and a six-
tonner. You wrote a paper about it. To penetrate deep
into the earth and cause an explosion."

"Ah, yes," said Wallis, his eyes lighting up.

"How soon can you let me have one?"

It was so sudden that Wallis was staggered. He
thought a while.

"About four or five months," and he added quickly,
"that is, if I get facilities. There's a lot of work to it,
you know."

"Right. Will you go and see Craven right away,

please? I'll ring him and tell him you're coming over."

Sir Charles Craven, head of Vickers, was also a Controller of the Ministry of Aircraft Production. Wallis was shown into his office near Whitehall ten minutes later, and before he could say a word Craven was booming at him:

"What the hell d'you want the services of twenty thousand men in Sheffield for?" Apparently Freeman had already been on the phone.

Wallis explained and got a promise of full support. He had little time to relax in the next few weeks. First he held a "Dutch auction" with Roy Chadwick, the Avro designer.

"Roy," he said, "can your Lanc.s carry seventeen thousand pounds for two hundred and fifty miles?"

"Oh, yes," Chadwick said, "Easily."

"Could they carry nineteen thousand?"

"Oh . . . er . . . I think so."

"Well now, Roy," Wallis said persuasively, "how about going to the full ten tons?"

"Oh, good Lord, I don't know about that."

"Now come on . . . if you tried more powerful engines and strengthened the undercarts."

"Well . . . Oh, I suppose it *could* be done."

"Thanks," said Wallis and went off to Sheffield to iron out more of the problems that seemed endless. The bomb had to be made from a *very* special steel; there were only two foundries in the country capable of casting the casings, and both were fully occupied on other vital work.

New methods of casting had to be evolved, new forms of heat treatment for hardening so the bombs could plough into hard ground faster than sound and not break up. The fuses had to stand up to the same shock. There were not enough firms capable of machining the finished bombs. It was a question of finding firms throughout England who might be able to machine one each a month. There had to be special machines designed and built to fill them with explosive, and new methods of testing. The Lancasters would have to be extensively modified to carry them; special trucks and dollies designed and built to handle them, and special winches to get them into the aircraft.

On August 30, 617 Squadron moved to Coningsby, another bomber airfield in Lincolnshire. Scampton had been a grass field, but Coningsby had long bitumen runways, more suitable for aircraft carrying very heavy loads. Flying was still confined to training, high and low level, aimlessly it seemed, and suddenly they were switched to low level. Cochrane told Holden that they had to be as good as they had been for the dams raid, and there were some new crews to train.

Cochrane and Satterly had long conferences with Holden and Group Captain Sam Patch, the station commander at Coningsby. There was a new verve about the squadron, a feeling of expectancy. At nights the aircraft hurtled low over the flat country and heavy lorries drove in to the bomb dump, their loads hidden under heavy tarpaulins. But it was not to be quite like the dams raid: that was obvious because they were still using the orthodox Lancasters. A flight of Mosquito night fighters arrived at Coningsby, and stayed. Apparently they were going to have fighter escort.

On September 14, Holden drew up a battle order for that night; a short one, eight crews, the pilots being Holden, Maltby, Knight, Shannon, Wilson, Allsebrook, Rice and Divall. Target was the Dortmund–Ems Canal, the freight link between the Ruhr and Central and Eastern Germany, including the North Sea. At that time 33 million tons a year passed along it, of which only a small fraction could be diverted to the railways. Near Ladbergen the fields fell away below the level of the canal and earth banks guided the water across the lowlands. One bomb breaching the bank would flood the countryside and there would be no canal. At least, no water in it; and that would starve the Ruhr of coal— and do many other things. Pre-fabricated U-boats were made in the Ruhr, for instance, and they could only be taken to the sea along the canal.

It was to be another very low-level raid, partly for bombing accuracy and partly because they thought the flak low down was less of a risk than fighters high up, concentrating on eight lonely aircraft. Cochrane saw that it was one of the most carefully planned raids of the war. As in the dams raid, the route curled delicately between the known flak. A specially designed beacon would be dropped near the canal as a pin-point and night fighters would engage the flak which guarded the most vulnerable points on the canal, although not the point chosen for the attack, which was some two miles from the nearest guns. A weather recce plane would check the visibility in the canal area before the Lancasters arrived. Most important of all, they were going to drop the new 12,000-lb. light-case bombs for the first time. (Not to be confused with Wallis's developing earthquake bomb.)

They took off at dusk with no illusions; memories of the dams losses were too fresh and they had a human yearning for the placid if less stimulating days of the Italian trips.

They were an hour out, low over the North Sea, when the weather Mosquito found the target hidden under fog and radioed back. Group recalled the Lancasters and as the big aircraft turned for home weighed down by nearly 6 tons of bomb David Maltby seemed to hit someone's slipstream; a wing flicked down, the nose dipped and before Maltby could correct it the wingtip had caught the water and the Lancaster cartwheeled, dug her nose in and vanished in spray. Shannon swung out of formation and circled the spot, sending out radio fixes and staying till an air-sea rescue flying boat touched down beneath. They waited up at Coningsby till the flying-boat radioed that it had found nothing but oil slicks.

Maltby's wife lived near the airfield, and in the morning Holden went over to break the news, dreading it because it had been an ideally happy marriage. Maltby was only twenty-one. The girl met him at the door and guessed his news from his face.

"It was quick," said Holden, who did not know it was his own last day on earth. "He wouldn't have known a thing."

Too stunned to cry, the girl said, "I think we both expected it. He'd been waking up in the night lately shouting something about the bomb not coming off."

Holden came back looking tired and got out another battle order. If the weather was right the raid was on again. Martin came back from leave that morning and demanded to take Maltby's place. Tammy Simpson, who had been flying with Martin for two years now, noted philosophically and a little querulously in his diary: "Mick's a bloody fool volunteering. This is going to be dangerous." Shannon was hoping the weather would be right this time. Moustacheless, he was to marry Anne in a week and was supposed to have left for London that morning to arrange the wedding. Anne had already wangled a posting for herself to Dunholme Lodge, an airfield near Coningsby.

At dusk in the control tower McCarthy watched the heavy aircraft lift off the runway and head east. Also watching was a languid W.A.A.F. who said as the aircraft merged with the darkness, "My God, I only hope they get there to-night! The trouble the A.O.C.'s gone to over this . . ."

McCarthy turned on her and snarled: "The hell with you and all the A.O.C.s. What about the seven lives in every kite!" The building vibrated as the door slammed behind him.

Over the North Sea the Lancasters kept loose formation in two boxes of four. It felt like the dams raid all over again; they were down to 50 feet to fox the radar and on strict radio silence. The faster Mosquitoes would be taking off now to pass them somewhere on the way in and set about the flak as the bombers arrived. Over the canal itself the weather Mosquito radioed back that it was perfectly clear.

The bombers crossed the Dutch coast and there was no sign of flak. Holden seemed to be flying a perfect course, which was just as well because the moon was up and it was full, throwing soft light over the fields as they moved towards Germany and Ladbergen.

Ahead of them a small town loomed up and high chimneys and a church steeple seemed to be rushing at them. Martin waited for Holden to swing to one side, but Holden elected to bore straight across and climbed to clear the steeple till he was about 300 feet. The more low-flying-wise Martin dropped right down to roof-top height and, on the other side of Holden, Knight and Wilson did the same, till even from the ground they were nearly invisible against the horizon. Holden was limned against the moonlight.

There was one light gun in Nordhoorn and its crew had been alerted. Holden was half-way across when a procession of glowing red balls streamed up, and in a shaven fraction of a second Toby Foxlee was firing back, so that only about five shells pumped up before Foxlee's tracer was squirting down and the gun abruptly stopped.

One of the five shells punched into Holden's inner starboard wing tank. There was a long streamer of flame trailing back beyond the tailplane; the aircraft showed clearly in the glow and they could see it was going down. The port wing was dropping and then the nose; she was falling faster, slewing to the left, right under Wilson and Knight with a 12,000-pounder on board! Martin yelled sharply over the R/T: "Break outwards!"

Wilson was just turning away when Holden's aircraft hit on the edge of the town almost under him; the 12,000-pounder went off and the town and the sky were like day.

Martin called the other two anxiously. Knight came right back and said he was all right, but it was twenty seconds before Wilson answered, a little shakily, saying they were jarred by the explosion but he thought nothing serious was broken. A little later they were back in formation, Martin leading. They swept into Germany, grimmer now. Gibson's crew had been in Holden's aircraft. Spafford, Taerum, Pulford, Hutchison; they were all gone.

One by one they picked up pin-points and the canal was only five minutes away when a blanket seemed to come down in front and they found themselves in mist. It was unbelievable. The area had been clear an moonlit half an hour before, no trace of trouble, and now the ground was a smudge, and they edged up to over a hundred feet to be clear of obstacles. The fog had moved in from the east without warning, almost without precedent. Some of the experts said later that Allsebrook, the deputy controller, should have called it off then, told everyone to go home and forget it till next time, but that is debatable. As it was they pushed on.

There were locks along the canal and every one was armed with flak. The trouble was that the Lancasters could not see the canal until they were right on it, and then it was too late to bomb. They would have to bomb from 150 feet—because they could not see the canal if they went any higher—and hope the flak would miss, which at that height was unlikely.

All of them tried flying across the canal to pick it up, hoping they could swing sharply on to it, but found it was nearly impossible. Split up now, they searched the area but kept blundering into the flak, and then they turned away and tried again, refusing to bomb till they were certain they were in position. The Mosquitoes had arrived and, with their greater speed and smaller size, were charging back and forth trying to silence the gunners, but could not pick them up in the fog.

Allsebrooke is believed to have bombed eventually but where his bomb went is not known. They never found the wreckage of his aircraft either. Wilson was heard briefly over the R/T saying something about going in to attack. The bomb was still aboard when the aircraft hit the ground about 200 yards beyond the canal and made a crater 200 feet across. Divall was heard briefly over the R/T, but that was the last anyone ever heard from him.

The gentle little Les Knight shouted over the intercom that he could see water, and then flak was coming at them and they were weaving. Johnson, the bomb aimer, yelled that he could see trees looming ahead and *above* them, and as Knight pulled up hard the bomber shuddered as she hit the tree-tops, and then they were clear with branches stuffed in the radiators, both port engines stopped and the tailplane damaged.

With the two starboard engines roaring at full power the Lancaster, with the bomb still aboard, was just able to hold her height. No chance of bombing in that condition, and Knight called up Martin: "Two port engines gone. May I have permission to jettison bomb, sir?" It was the "sir" that got Martin. Quiet little Knight was following the copybook procedure, asking respectful permission to do the only thing that might get him home.

Martin said, "For God's sake, Les, yes," and as the bomb was not fused Knight told Johnson to let it go. Relieved of the weight they started to climb very slowly.

After the gunners had thrown out all the guns and fittings they could, Knight got her up to about 1,400 feet and headed towards England, the aircraft waffling soggily at 110 m.p.h. The controls were getting worse all the time until, though he had full opposite rudder and aileron on, Knight could not stop her turning to port and it was obvious he could never fly her home. He ordered his crew to bale out and held the plane steady while they did. When the last man had gone he must have tried to do the same himself, and must have known all the time what would happen when he slipped out of his seat. There was perhaps a slight chance of getting clear in time, but as soon as he took pressure off stick and rudder the aircraft flicked on her back and plunged to the ground. Knight did not get to the hatch in time.

Geoff Rice tried for an hour to find the canal, was badly holed by flak and finally had to swing his winged aircraft out of the area, jettison the bomb and head for home. Shannon was seventy minutes before he got a quick sight of the high banks of the canal, wheeled the Lancaster along the water and Sumpter called, "Bomb gone!" There was an eleven-second delay on the fuse, so they only dimly saw the explosion. The bomb hit the tow-path. If it had been a few feet to one side, in the water, it would have breached the canal wall.

Martin spent an hour and a half plunging at 150 feet in the fog around the canal trying to give Bob Hay a good enough sight on the few spots where the high earth bank was vulnerable. Now and then he caught a brief glimpse of the water, but it was either at a spot where the banks were low and solid or the flak was too murderous to give them a chance. It squirted at them when they were right on top of it and they had to wheel away into the fog. The aircraft jolted twice as shells punched into it, and once a sudden burst of tracer ripped through under the cockpit so that Martin jumped with shock, one foot slipped off the rudder bar and the big Lancaster swung so crazily he thought it was all over.

The gunners had been firing whenever they got a chance and Tammy Simpson reported his ammunition was getting low. Martin told him to forget the flak and save what he had left in case they got a chance to fight their way home.

Once or twice he was able to come up the canal diagonally so that it was easier to turn along it, but each time the glimpse of water came too late or the flak was coming point blank at them and they had to pull away.

On the thirteenth run Hay got a glimpse of water in the swirling fog and called, "There it is!" Martin turned away in a slow and regular 360 degrees circle, opening his bomb doors and calculating the exact moment he should come over the water again so the straighten-up would be gentle. It was a beautifully timed turn; they were low over the sliver of water with no flak, just long enough for Hay to call, "Left, left, a shade right . . . bomb gone!" and then Whittaker slammed the throttles hard on and Martin pulled her steeply round in a "split-arse" turn as the flak opened up.

A little later they hurtled back across the canal and saw the water boiling where the bomb had exploded, a few feet from the bank, just a few feet too far, because the bank was still there.

They were still over Germany and dawn was breaking as they came out of the fog. On full throttle, "P

Popsie" was shaking at 267 m.p.h., the fastest she had ever travelled at low level. As they slid round the end of Sylt two last guns sent shells after them and then they were over the sea.

They landed two hours overdue and found Cochrane still waiting. He had heard of the losses from Shannon, who was first back, and his face was leaner and grimmer than ever. Martin was the third back, out of eight. Cochrane knew there would not be any more. He said:

"How was it?"

"I'm terribly sorry, sir," Martin said. "It didn't breach. The mist beat us, and the flak." He told what had happened. Cochrane listened keenly and at the end he was staggered when Martin said, "I'm very disappointed, sir, but if the weather's clear to-morrow—I mean, that is, to-night now—I think we can get it, if you'll let us have another crack."

"How many crews have you got left?"

Martin thought for a while and said, "Well, there are three of us in my flight, and three more in Shannon's flight. That ought to be enough, sir."

"Six!" Cochrane said. "Out of your original twenty-one!"

"It ought to be enough, sir. I'm just sorry about last night."

Cochrane said gently, "I don't think you have to apologise for anything, Martin. I'll let you know about to-night later. Meantime you'd better go and get some sleep." He took Sam Patch by the arm and led him over to the corner and Patch for the first time sensed that Cochrane had let slip the mask of his reserve. There was no mistaking it, and almost no defining it, an intensity about his eyes, his whole face and his voice as he said:

"Patch, I'd like to make Martin a wing commander on the spot and put him in command of the squadron. You know the boy better than I do. Would you recommend him?"

Patch thought for a moment before he made the answer for which he has been kicking himself ever since:

"It's two jumps up the ladder, sir; I'm not sure he's ready for it. He's had no experience in administration."

"Well, I'll at least get him made a squadron leader and give him temporary command." Cochrane caught Martin as he finished stowing his kit away and said in his sudden-death way, "You're a squadron leader now, Martin, and for the time being you're in command of the squadron."

Martin looked after the retreating back and said, "Christ!" A moment before he hadn't even been a flight commander. Patch said, "Well, you've got responsibilities now, Mick. Come and have a walk and talk till you relax." Martin was too exhilarated to sleep. They paced slowly across the airfield, right to the blast walls of the bomb dump, lonely in its isolation on the far side of the field.

"I didn't think anything could have gone wrong," Patch was saying. "I thought we had the perfect plan this time."

"Oh, we should've pranged the thing," Martin said disgustedly. "That bloody mist. You couldn't see a thing."

There was a long silence; the air was fresh, the grass soft and springy under their feet, and Martin, after eight hours in the air, was far from sleep with the light-headed exhilaration you get after you're so tired you can hardly stand and then get your second wind. He had been awake over twenty-four hours. He said suddenly: "Well, there it is, sir. Two real ops. and six crews left. Maybe this is the end. They'll make us an ordinary line squadron . . . or disband us altogether."

"Probably *will* be the end if you try that canal again to-night," Patch said dryly. "You were silly to volunteer again. You're not immortal."

"No, sir."

"D'you think you'd get away with it again to-night?"

"Couldn't be any worse."

"I suppose it occurs to you the flak will be expecting you."

Martin said soberly, "I suppose so."

"Forget it a while, Mick," Patch said. "I don't think the A.O.C.'ll let you try again for a while anyway. He doesn't like losing crews, and you lost five out of eight last night . . . six including Maltby the night before. You'll lose the rest if you go again to-night. We've got to think out a cleverer way of doing it."

There was another silence and Patch broke it by saying tentatively:

"What d'you think about 617 taking a rest for a while? You've taken an awful beating and you've got to fill up with new crews and train them. What d'you think?"

Martin said, "No. Let's do another one right away and get the taste out of our mouths. Otherwise we're going to get scared of going back."

"The A.O.C.'ll decide that anyway," Patch said. "Maybe you've had your day on special duty."

They called at the office on the way back to see about the casualty reports, but Chiefy Powell and Heveron were already attending to them. Patch took Martin over to the mess for breakfast and sat and talked to him. Patch had not been to sleep for nearly thirty hours himself but he never changed his routine when a raid was on. He never failed to visit every aircraft before it took off; always waited up till the last crew had landed and then went over to the mess with them for bacon and eggs and yarned as long as they wanted him to. He never went to bed himself till he'd seen the last of the boys off to bed. He was a round-faced, heavy-set, youngish man, direct and honest. If you did a good job, Patch would go to tremendous trouble to let you know. If you did a bad job he would tell you how and why, so you would do better next time. If you failed to mend your ways he would crack down hard, and then in the mess that night he would be normal and friendly to the punished one.

As Martin was finishing breakfast McCarthy and the laconic Munro came in, clicked their heels and peeled off sizzling salutes. "Good morning, sir," they chorused, and Martin had the grace to blush. They congratulated him and, in grimmer mood, paid their respects to the dead. Martin gave his first orders. "Will you get cracking on making what aircraft we've got left ready for to-night? I'm thinking we'll be on again. Let me know when the target comes through." He added, almost as an after-thought, "May be the same target to-night."

"All right," said McCarthy. "Push off to bed and grab some shuteye."

Shannon had only got to bed himself about half an hour before. He had written a little note to Anne, apologising for not being able to go up to London. Anne got it over at Dunholme Lodge that afternoon. Quite a short note: "Sorry, darling. Couldn't make it. Been up two nights. Lost six out of nine. Please forgive. I'm rather tired." For the first time she saw the writing was shaky.

She had been up all night herself in the ops. room at Dunholme Lodge. About dawn they got a report that five out of the eight were shot down and she was crying when someone ran over and said, "David's all right. He's back." But the tears only fell faster.

Martin got nearly five hours' sleep. McCarthy regretfully woke him at two o'clock, shaking his shoulder and saying, "Target's through, Mick," until the tired boy shook the sleep out of his head and said, "Where?"

"Somewhere in the South of France. Bridge or something."

Martin pulled some clothes on and saw Patch over in the planning room. Patch said, "You're not going back to the canal yet. You're going with 619 Squadron to have a go at the Antheor Viaduct. It's on the Riviera, near the Eytie border, and carries the only good railway into Italy from France. If you prang it you'll stop half the Hun reinforcements to Sicily."

Martin said, "I'm sorry it isn't the canal," and he so obviously meant it that Patch just looked at him.

They found the viaduct without trouble 15 miles west of Cannes, seeing in the moonlight the 90-foot stone arches curving across the beach at the foot of a ravine. The idea was to dive to 300 feet and stab 1,200-

lb. bombs into the stone with delayed fuses. It was
like a coco-nut shy; bang on and the coco-nut is yours,
miss by an inch and lose your money. They missed by
inches. The bombs went through the arches and exploded on the ground all around; the viaduct was
pitted by splinters but that was all. The only real result
was that it woke the Germans up to the vulnerability
of the railway, and soon after that the flak batteries
moved in.

Shannon scrounged a few days' leave, went up to
London and married Anne. They spent part of their
honeymoon in a hotel, and when they walked into the
bar one night Anne heard someone say, "Good God,
that boy looks too young to be in the Air Force."
Shannon turned round and the man saw he was wearing a D.S.O. and D.F.C., and his eyes stuck out like
organ stops.

The Chester Herald answered Gibson's letter about
the squadron badge, questioning the motto. It was
true Marie Antoinette had said, *"Après nous le déluge,"* but she had used it in an irresponsible connec-
tion. Martin chewed it over with Patch, and Patch said,
"Well, change it to *'Après moi le déluge.'* That ought to
fix it." Martin wrote back accordingly.

A day or so later Cochrane sent for him. "I think
we might be able to use this dams bomb of Wallis's
against the *Tirpitz,"* the A.O.C. said. The *Tirpitz* was
still sheltering in Alten Fiord. "You can't fly up the
fiord to get her; that'd be death, but she's moored only
about half a mile from the shore where the land rises
steeply. You might do it by surprise, hurdle the hill,
dive and bomb before they wake up." There was a hill
near Bangor, he said, about the same height and gra-
dient. Martin was to go and practise over it to see if he
could level out soon enough on the water at the right
height and speed.

Martin flew "P Popsie" over to North Wales and
spent an afternoon diving over the coast, climbing and
trying again. It called for most delicate judgment, but

towards the end he found he could do it with 40 degrees of flap down. It meant diving 60 m.p.h. faster than permitted with 40 degrees of flap and that meant the flap was likely to collapse on one side. If that happened at low level the aircraft would spin straight in. He reported to Cochrane that he was willing to chance that. He knew what the *Tirpitz* defences would be like at low level but thought the raid would be possible.

"We wouldn't need too many aircraft, air. Myself, McCarthy and Shannon would go. I don't imagine there will be much chance of a second run, but we know the form of attack well and we could practise over the Bangor hills so we get it right the first time." He suggested they do the raid by moonlight or at dusk or dawn, so there would be some gloom for cover but enough light to see the ship. Matter-of-factly he added: "I think you should be prepared to lose the three aircraft, sir, but we'll have a go and probably get her."

Cochrane, who had not met anyone quite like Martin before, looked at him for some time and finally said, "Well, I'll let you know about it. Meantime start building up the squadron again with new crews. I'll have some picked ones sent to you."

(Actually it was not the *Tirpitz* that Cochrane was after at this time. "Tirpitz" was the "cover plan" to camouflage the real plan. He was, in fact, scheming to smash the big dam at Modane, in Italy, and the hills round Bangor resembled the hills round Modane Dam. Martin discovered that seven years later.)

Martin was interviewing new pilots and crews for the next week, and it was not easy. 617's fame—or notoriety—had spread and it was known as a suicide squadron. Some quite brave men were posted to it but told Martin openly they did not want to stay. Martin did not argue. They were quite willing to fly with their own squadrons, where perhaps one crew in ten finished a tour; in 617 it seemed that no crew had a chance. He did not press anyone who was not willing—they would be no good to him—but sent them back to their old squadrons, and after a week had found only four crews willing to join him: O'Shaughnessy, Willsher, Weedon and Bull. He was doubtful about accepting Willsher because Willsher looked younger even than Shannon, only nineteen, a thin, fair boy a year out of school.

Willsher had trouble finding a crew until a red-faced, broken-nosed, tough-looking Londoner called Gerry Witherick insisted on being his rear gunner. Witherick was unkillable. He had flown nearly a hundred missions and was a hard case with a soft heart and a riotous wit.

A letter came for Martin from the Chester Herald regretting that *"Après* moi *les déluge"* was questionable too. An aged Greek had used it to show selfishness.

"Why couldn't the damn Greek stick to his own language?" Martin growled to Sam Patch. "What d'we do now?"

"Write back politely and explain that the badge had already been chosen by the King," Patch said. "Just say how sorry you are that the King's prerogative should be overlooked."

10

SNIPER SQUADRON

The fate of 617 was decided at high level. "We'll make 'em a special duties squadron," said Sir Arthur Harris. "They needn't do ordinary ops., but whenever the Army or Navy want a dam or a ship or something clouted we'll put 617 on to it. They'll keep like that—keep the Army and Navy happy too. And we'll put all the old lags in 617. That's just the thing for them. Make 'em the old lags' squadron."

"The old lags" was Harris's affectionate and respectful name for the really hard-bitten aircrews who only wanted to do operations. Every now and then there would be a crew who, after finishing their tour, would stubbornly boggle at taking their six months' rest training new aircrews. They insisted on staying on operations and were dearest of all to Harris, probably because they had the same volcanic temperament as himself.

Harris said 617 could stay in 5 Group with Cochrane, and Cochrane had it in his mind to make them a "sniper" squadron for super-accurate bombing with Wallis's 10-tonner. Ordinary bombing, he knew, would waste most of the 10-tonners, and there would be none to waste. He was well aware (it is no great secret now) that bombing had sometimes been almost primitively inaccurate.

They had started the war bombing by moonlight, but as German night fighters multiplied they had had to use dark nights because of losses, and now they were even having to stick to "dirty" dark nights when heavy cloud gave added cover (and obscured targets).

British people who had endured the Blitz read with understandable satisfaction of R.A.F. bombers over Cologne or Essen or Hamburg, or of the Hamm sidings being pounded. They did not know (they would have been shaken to know, and the propaganda people did not dare to tell them) that many of these raids did little damage. Some did none at all, and many people still do not know that. Harris, people like Cochrane, "Pathfinder" Bennett and the "back-room boys" were trying to find how to hit targets in blind weather, and it was about this time that the main force was starting to produce really good results.

Up to this time a little more than one out of three raids were really effective. The Germans built dummy targets outside cities, spread camouflage nets over telltale lakes and rivers in the towns, decoyed the bombers in every way they could, and even lit fires in fields so the bombers would think they were hitting their target. Often the crews bombed open fields instead. A pilot once came back from Mannheim and said he was the only aircraft that had found the city. They barked at him for getting lost himself until he produced his aiming point photograph, which showed he was right. The other bombers had dropped their loads on fields or some other town. By 1943 there had been over a hundred attacks on Essen, anything from eighteen to a thousand aircraft dropping a huge weight of bombs against Krupps, but most bombs fell elsewhere and significant damage was quite limited.

That was why the Pathfinder Force had been formed, and now that they were in action bombing was becoming more effective. P.F.F. found and marked the target areas with coloured flares, and the main force bombed these markers. It stopped them bombing open fields, but it was still "carpet bombing," hateful, and yet, it seemed, necessary.

And losses still mounted. Now they were about 4 per cent; one bomber in twenty-five failed to return. Or average it another way—a squadron of twenty aircraft would lose every one in twenty-five raids. A tour of operations was thirty raids; then, if you were still alive,

you had six month's rest and went back for another
tour. In lives and labour and for the minor damage
done, bombing was not economical enough for Harris.

At Farnborough, in 1941, a man named Richards
had invented a piece of intricate mechanism he called
the Stabilising Automatic Bomb Sight. It incorporated
a gyro; in perfect conditions it could aim a bomb un-
cannily, but Harris thought it was too complicated for
the hellish conditions of actual bombing. For one thing,
a bomber using it had to run perfectly straight and level
up to the target for ten miles, a perfect mark for flak,
searchlights and fighters. Harris said it would mean
death for too many of his boys, who had little enough
chance as it was, and Bomber Command could not
take much heavier losses.

Another school of thought said the S.A.B.S. *could*
be used economically by a small force. Cochrane was
one of them. He argued that from high level the
S.A.B.S. could hit a well marked target so accurately
that they would not have to send the squadrons back
again to the same place again and again. In the long run
they would lose less. He wanted to train 617 till they
could use the S.A.B.S. in battle and deliver Wallis's 10-
tonners, when they arrived, in the right spots.

There were many conferences and then Harris
agreed.

Patch called Martin to his office. "The *Tirpitz* is off
for the time being," he said and Martin sighed gently
with relief. "The A.O.C. has something new for you.
From now on your squadron role is changed to ultra-
accurate high-level bombing and you're going to be
practising till your eyes drop out. You've got to get
down to an *average* of *under* a hundred yards from
twenty thousand feet." Martin's eyes almost dropped
out on the spot. "The reasons," Patch went on, "are
that there's a new bomb coming up . . . a big one.
You'll only be able to carry one and they're so expen-
sive every one will have to be spot on." He said they
were getting a new bomb sight at once.

A day later a tall, thin man with lively eyes walked

into Martin's office carrying a bundle wrapped in oil-
skin and announced that he was Squadron Leader
Richardson come to help 617 convert to the S.A.B.S.

"This is it," he said, carefully unwrapping the
bundle. "It's the loveliest thing in the world." The
S.A.B.S. looked like an ordinary bomb sight except that
a bulky gyro was encased in it. Richardson handled it
lovingly, and in the next few days the squadron found
out why. He was not a bomb-aiming enthusiast, he was
a fanatic who started talking bomb-aiming at breakfast and was still on the subject at bedtime. If he talked
in his sleep no one doubted what the subject would be.
He lectured the crews, flew with them, experimented
with them and after a time no one had any chance of
not knowing everything about the S.A.B.S. Bob Hay,
haunted now by his own profession, christened him
"Talking Bomb." Much of the credit for what happened
belongs to "Talking Bomb," who had been a pilot in
World War I and managed in due course to fly on fifteen raids with 617 to watch his beloved bomb sight in
action.

617 did no ops. for weeks, but night and day the aircraft were 20,000 feet over the bombing range at Wainfleet aiming practice bombs at the white dots on the
sands with the S.A.B.S. It needed far more than a hawk-
eyed bomb aimer; it called for teamwork. The gunners
took drifts to help the navigator work out precise wind
direction and speed, and navigator and bomb aimer
calculated obscure instrument corrections. An error of a
few feet at 20,000 feet would throw a bomb hopelessly
off. Altimeters work off barometric pressure, but that is
always changing, so they used a complicated system of
getting ground-level pressures over target and correcting altimeters by pressure lapse rates (with temperature
complications). A small speed error will throw a bomb
off, and air-speed indicators read falsely according to
height and the attitude of the aircraft. They had to com-
pute and correct this, and when it was all set on the
S.A.B.S. the pilot had to hold his exact course and
height for miles while the engineer juggled the throttles

to keep the speed precise. That, over-simplified, expresses about a tenth of the complications. When the bomb aimer had the crosswires on the target he clicked a switch and the S.A.B.S. kept itself tracking on the aiming point by its gyros, transmitting corrections to the pilot by flicking an indicator in the cockpit. The bomb aimer did not have to press the bomb button; when it was ready the S.A.B.S. did that, and even told the pilot by switching off a red light in the cockpit.

First results were only fair, average error being about 180 yards, but the crews soon started to get the hang of it. "Talking Bomb" flew with them all, the only way of checking. A good bomb aimer might get poor results because of pilot inaccuracy, so "Talking Bomb" switched pilots and bomb aimers and coached the weak ones. There was plenty of scope for error. At 20,000 feet the bombs left the aircraft two miles short of the target and dropped for forty-five seconds before they hit, throwing up the little puffs that were plotted from the sandbagged quadrant stations. Results were phoned to Coningsby and the crews got them as soon as they landed so they could see what had gone wrong.

"Talking Bomb" himself was very accurate with the S.A.B.S., and before long a couple of crews could emulate him. Martin's was one. Within three weeks Hay set an example with an average of 64 yards. Some of the others, however, were still well over a hundred yards, and Cochrane drove over to look into it, got "Talking Bomb" to give him an hour's instruction on the S.A.B.S. and took off as bomb aimer in "P Popsie" to try it. On the ground one or two people indulged in a little anticipatory lip-smacking.

Martin flew sedately and when Cochrane had called his last "Bombs gone!" brought him straight back. "Talking Bomb" met them with the results, and an expression of great respect. Cochrane had achieved the extraordinary average of 38 yards. For a moment the A.O.C.'s face loosened into a faint grin but he froze it off and said crisply, "Well, if I can do it you people ought to be able to."

Someone muttered in the background, "If we all could we'd all be A.O.C.s," and that time Cochrane had to laugh.

After he went Hay said darkly to the other bomb aimers, "Well, you're going to have to pull your fingers out now." He turned to Martin: "Hell, Mick, why didn't you kick the rudder as he was going to bomb?"

A letter came to Martin from the Chester Herald, gracefully yielding in the matter of the squadron badge. He had not realised it had been chosen by the King and by no means would he interfere with His Majesty's prerogative. The badge was therefore approved, with the motto *"Après* moi *le déluge."* He enclosed an imposing piece of prose with the official description:

> *"On a roundel, a wall in fesse, fracted by three flashes of lightning in pile and issuant from the breach, water proper."*

There was a session in the mess that night to celebrate it. Concave Goodale had a bad smoker's cough and had been sitting in a chair coughing to clear his throat for a couple of hours when someone said, "Poor old Concave. He's nearly dead. He's got a foot in the grave." Ivan Whittaker said, "Oh, he *is* dead. Let's bury him." He and Martin slipped away and got a sheet from someone's bed, but Concave saw them come in with it and retreated into the lavatory. There was another door on the other side of it, and Whittaker slipped round and caught Concave coming out, throwing the sheet over his head. They carried him back kicking, wrapped him like a cocoon in the sheet and laid him on a trestle table in the kitchen. Someone brought in the padre, a cheerful grey-haired man with a broad Irish brogue who gazed, startled, on the shrouded victim and said, "What's all this about?"

"Goodale's coughed himself to death," Whittaker said lugubriously. "We're going to bury him." Concave raised his head with a sickly grin. Eight volunteer pallbearers lifted the table to their shoulders and set off in a wavering slow march, followed by an entourage banging on tin plates, singing "Abide with him" and moaning the "Volga Boatman." In the anteroom they set the table on its trestles again and Concave lay in state in front of the fireplace, the others standing around in a solemn circle. The padre grinned but declined to read the burial service, so someone grabbed a paper-backed novel and chanted an improvised service.

As he intoned "Dust to dust and ashes to ashes" the elderly local defence officer sprinkled ash from the fireplace on Concave and bawled, "Slack away." He nudged one of the trestles, the table-end lurched and Concave rolled off and landed in a half-sitting position on his bottom vertebrae. He let out a groan, his head dropped back with a bump and his eyes rolled up so the whites were visible. He lay still and everyone saluted him. They unwrapped him and said, "O.K., Concave, you're in hell now," but Goodale did not move and the laughter became uncertain and died. Someone said, "He's really out." They carried him away and laid him on his bed; the doctor arrived and found a lump on Concave's spine as big as an egg.

The elderly defence officer ran contritely in with one of his dearest possessions, a bottle of very old brandy, pulled the cork, put the bottle to Concave's lips and up-ended it. Concave spluttered and coughed, brandy running down his chin; his eyes opened, he licked his lips and a soft smile dawned. He closed his eyes again, opened his mouth and the defence officer poured in more brandy.

"He'll be all right," said the doctor. They stayed a while encouraging him to absorb more medicine and then softly retreated, all happy (particularly Concave) except the defence officer, who could not find his bottle of brandy.

There are some who solemnly lament that wartime flying men were known on occasion to drink more than was seemly. That not-always-tactful man Arthur Harris

called the worst examples of disapproval "unctuous
rectitude." Perhaps the rigidly virtuous might acquire a
more flexible understanding if they followed the young
pilot to the airfield and watched his face in its hood
when the chocks were pulled away. Better still, follow
him into the air, strapped to a seat and deafened by
noise, held precariously aloft by wings relying on in-
constant engines and petrol tanks, highly vulnerable to
the assaults of flak and fighters, fog and ice-cloud.
Follow him up there not once but sixty times till violent
death is a threefold statistical certainty.

They played hard because they had little time to
play, and more often than not it was high rather than
potent spirits which affected them.

Higher circles were satisfied now that in Peenemünde
lay the heart of Germany's secret weapon, rockets or
whatever they were, and Harris sent 600 heavy bombers to dissect the spot. Pathfinders lobbed their markers
in the middle, and for the first time the main force used
the "master bomber" technique that Gibson had
started over the Moehne Dam; a "master of ceremo-
nies" circled low directing the bombers by radiophone
on to the choicest markers, and Peenemünde rocket
centre was almost wiped off the map, putting the ad-
vent of rockets over England back by six months. Having failed to protect it, Hans Jeschonnek, Hitler's night-
fighter chief, committed suicide. The Germans learnt
anew the virtues of dispersal.

617's bombing kept slowly improving. Three more
crews arrived; Bill Suggitt, a Canadian squadron leader, to take over A Flight, Clayton and Ted Youseman,
an Englishman, who never stopped talking flying. There
were the usual incidents—two aircraft hit trees low
flying and were written off (though no one was killed),
Martin had an engine catch fire in the air but doused it
with the extinguishers. Shannon's aileron cables
snapped over the North Sea, but he made an emergency landing, using trimmers to keep his wingtips

level and making a wide, flat turn on rudder alone. He claimed it was better than his usual landing, which, Sumpter said rudely, was nothing to boast about.

Spurred on by Cochrane, Sam Patch and Martin tried to find a way of minimising the danger of the ten-mile run-up to the target using the S.A.B.S. "Talking Bomb" was a fertile source of ideas.

"This is what you ought to do," he said. "You all fly round the target in a great big circle like Red Indians, see? and then someone gives the word and you all turn inwards and come in like the spokes of a wheel. The Hun won't know who to shoot at."

"That's O.K., 'Talking Bomb,' " Martin said, "but what happens when they all get into the middle?"

"Oh, put 'em at different heights."

"What about the bombs falling on the lower aircraft?"

"There must be a way over that," "Talking Bomb" muttered.

It was a somewhat similar idea that they adopted, and it depended on immaculate timing and navigation. The aircraft, at different heights, would circle a spot in sight of the target but outside the defences, and when the markers were down the leader would assess their accuracy, give the order to bomb and they would all come in, converging slightly. If there were twenty guns below, for instance, and only one aircraft coming in, the twenty guns would all be firing at it, but with twenty planes coming in at the same time, too widely scattered for a box barrage, there would be only one gun against each aircraft—twenty times less chance of being hit.

New troubles kept cropping up with the S.A.B.S. For instance, the thermometers (necessary in getting outside temperatures for computing precise height from the altimeters) were showing errors up to 5 degrees, enough to throw a bomb over a hundred feet the wrong way. Farnborough put in new-type thermometers, but two more corrections were still necessary. Airflow against the bulb caused friction and heat, and this had to be corrected by a table based on the indicated air speed at the time. Then cockpit heating affected part of the thermometer which was inside the aircraft and that, too, had to be calculated and allowed for, but by early November the squadron had an average bombing error of only 90 yards.

Good enough, Cochrane thought, and at dusk on November 12, Martin led the squadron off to try out the S.A.B.S. in battle. The target was the Antheor Viaduct again, an easy one so that they could give the S.A.B.S. fair trial. In the bomb bays hung 12,000-lb. light-case "blast" bombs.

They found the viaduct in half-moonlight, but this time it was different . . . four searchlights and half a dozen guns round it. Running up, the viaduct was hard to pick up in the glare of the searchlights; the next little bay looked exactly the same and several crews bombed the wrong bay. Some of them got the right bay in their graticules, but could not distinguish the viaduct. Rice, O'Shaughnessy and one other got near misses, 60 yards away, but the blast was not enough to damage the viaduct.

They flew disgustedly on to Blida again, and it was then that Martin recalled what McCarthy had said about flares after San Polo. Everyone agreed that if they had had flares to mark the viaduct they could have hit it. Two days later they flew back to England, but Youseman never arrived. No one ever found out what happened to him and his crew, but a German fighter probably got them over the sea.

Martin reported to Cochrane the need for target marking, and Cochrane sent him and Patch to Pathfinder Headquarters to talk it over with the experts. Pathfinders promised to mark their next target, and Martin put the crews back on training to perfect their S.A.B.S. technique.

Martin's time as temporary commander was up. Cochrane would not replace him with any ordinary squadron commander (none of whom, in any case, was eager to take on the suicide squadron), but he had found the man he wanted. Leonard Cheshire, at twenty-five, was the youngest group captain in the R.A.F., and was not only willing to return to operations but actually asked Cochrane to drop him back to wing commander so he could take over the squadron. He did not look the part at all. Gibson had looked the part; Gibson and glamour were indivisible, but Cheshire looked more like a theological student thinly disguised as a senior officer; yet he had done two tours and won a D.S.O. and bar and D.F.C. He was tall, thin and dark, a strange blend of brilliance (sometimes erratic), self-consciousness, confidence and soft-spoken charm. Highly sensitive and introspective, he yet lacked, quite illogically, the foreboding imagination that makes some sensitive men sweat with fear before a raid. Once he had walked from Oxford to Paris without a penny in his pockets to win half a pint of beer. He liked a suite at the Ritz on leave and to bask in a Mayfair cocktail bar. At twenty he had an Honours degree in Law at Oxford (where his father was Vinerian Professor of Law —England's highest such appointment), and at twenty-four, in a few weeks' joyous leave in New York, he had met and married Constance Binney, who had been America's top film star, successor to Mary Pickford, in 1922. She was a bride of forty-one.

He had a gentle consideration for other people and a Puckish sense of humour, but in the air he was cool, efficient and calculating. In a way he had a mind like Barnes Wallis, liable to get ideas that horrified people but turned out to be right. He had been flying a certain type of heavy bomber at a time when losses of that type were inexplicably heavy. They had acquired too much extra equipment, so that fully loaded, at operational height, they were slow, flew soggily and were inclined to yaw and drop into a final spiral with the rudders locked over. Then they added kidney cowls to blanket the exhaust flames from night fighters, and that, for Cheshire, was the last straw. He considered it made the aircraft more dangerous than the enemy and asked permission to take the cowls off his squadron's aircraft.

Everyone flatly disagreed except his A.O.C., Air Vice-Marshal Carr, who let Cheshire do so, with the result that his losses fell. It was the first step to taking off a lot more: front turret, mid-upper-turret and armour-plate; freed of the excessive drag and weight the plane flew more comfortably, the engines were not over-worked and losses fell further.

For two days after Cheshire joined 617 little Doris Leeman, his W.A.A.F. driver, sat in the shooting brake outside his office with nothing to do. She watched Cheshire walk away several times, and at last she could stand it no longer and went in to Chiefy Powell. "Doesn't he *know* I'm waiting for him?" she asked, with the anger of a woman kept waiting inexcusably. "You'd better tell him," Powell said, so she knocked at his office door and told him, and was staggered when he confessed he didn't know he had a car at his disposal. It was fairly typical of the man: never taking for granted what lesser men demanded.

The destruction at Peenemünde had put Germany's rocket programme back six months, and they stopped work on the monster rocket blockhouses to go ahead with the more dispersed flying-bomb sites. Recce air-craft were bringing back to England photographs show-ing mysterious new activity in the same areas, the erec-tion of many low, curved buildings in clearings in woods, and next to them short sets of rails that seemed to start and end in nothingness. Intelligence men chris-tened them "ski sites" because the long buildings were the same shape as skis, and bit by bit they connected them more definitely with secret-weapon reports.

It was clear that these and other satellite launching sites could be put up very quickly and were more or less mobile. They were springing up all over the place and ordinary blast bombs could smash them, but after Peenemünde, Hitler seemed to be relying for pro-tection on dispersal—numbers, camouflage and mobil-ity—instead of three or four centralised targets.

In Whitehall, Churchill, the Air Council, Harris, Sir

Stafford Cripps (now Minister for Aircraft Production) and Sir Wilfred Freeman discussed the situation uncomfortably, and one day Freeman sent for Wallis.

"We're stopping work on the ten-ton bomb," he said. "The big targets we had for them aren't so important now, and Sir Stafford doesn't think the ten-tonner justifies all that work."

Wallis could not dispute the logic of it. The biggest bombers would have a very short range with a ten-tonner—little more than across the Channel, and in that area there seemed no other targets important enough. There were plenty in Germany, of course, but the Lancasters could not carry the ten-tonner as far as that.

Wallis pleaded with Freeman to let him go ahead with the 12,000-lb. scaled-down version of the ten-tonner, to penetrate deeply in the same way and cause an earthquake shock. The Lancasters could drop them deep inside Germany on the kind of targets he had originally had in mind. Freeman thought for a long time, and in the end he said yes—a bold decision to make on his own. He knew that neither the Air Council nor the Ministry of Supply liked the idea of either the 10-tonner or the scaled-down version, because they were designed to be dropped at 40,000 feet for proper penetration. The Lancaster could not drop them from higher than 20,000, and the Council and Ministry considered they would not thus penetrate deeply enough for the proper earthquake effect.

Freeman made the decision so much on his own initiative that no Requirement Order was issued for the bombs, which meant that the Air Force did not have to accept them—or pay for them. He gave the scaled-down bomb the code name of "Tallboy," and Wallis hoped to have one ready for trial by March.

Cochrane had his eye on the mobile launching sites as targets for 617 but left them in peace while Cheshire kept his crews perfecting the S.A.B.S. technique, and for some weeks the squadron did no operations until, on December 10, Cheshire got a call from Tempsford for the loan of four crews. Tempsford was the hush-hush airfield where planes took off to land agents in occupied countries and drop arms to Resistance fighters. Cheshire chose McCarthy, Clayton, Bull and Weedon, and they flew their aircraft to Tempsford.

McCarthy landed back at Coningsby two days later, walked into Humphries' office and dumped two kitbags on the floor. "Bull and Weedon's kit," he said. "They've had it."

"Oh God! When?"

"Last night. We did a special low-level thing, dropping arms and ammunition. They must have hit trouble." He added disgustedly, "I didn't even find the damn target area."

He went back to Tempsford that afternoon, and he and Clayton tried again that night—successfully.

Cheshire, meantime, had had one of his most spectacular ideas. His brother had recently been shot down and captured and Cheshire had been thinking a lot about prisoners of war. He sent for Martin, and Martin found him in the planning room huddled over maps spread out on the table. Cheshire greeted him with bright eyes and a pleased grin. "Mick," he said, "we're going to drop Christmas parcels to the prisoners of war on Christmas Day."

"Oh," Martin said. "Sounds interesting, sir. Whereabouts?"

"Stalag Luft III. Here." Cheshire stabbed his pencil at a spot on the map, and Martin leaned over and saw the point was resting on a small town called Sagan, between Berlin and Breslau, up near the Polish border. They had never flown so far as that over Germany and Martin said cautiously, "It's a long way."

"We've got the range all right."

"How're we going to find a little thing like that at night?"

"Won't have to, old boy. Going by day. Christmas morning."

"By day!"

"Yes."

"By *DAY!*"

"Don't worry. We can do it. Nip in over the Baltic low level and surprise 'em. We'll get away with it."

"How many aircraft?"

"Three ought to be enough."

"Who?" Martin felt that his ears were laid back and the whites of his eyes showing.

"Me, you and either Shannon or Munro."

"Uh!" Martin looked at the map silently. "What sort of food were you thinking of taking, sir?"

"Oh, things like chickens and raisins and chocolate. It ought to give them a hell of a lift."

Martin said, trying to keep the edge out of his voice, "D'you think we could drop some parcels addressed to ourselves? We'll still be there on Boxing Day, you know, either on the ground or under it."

"Oh, I don't think it'll be that bad, Mick. We'll paint the aircraft white, put red crosses over them and take the guns out."

"Oh! No guns!"

"We can do the trip in by night," Cheshire said, "arrive about dawn so we'll have no trouble pin-pointing it, drop the stuff about a hundred feet to make sure it gets into the compounds and nip out across the Baltic. That's the shortest way out, and I'll get Pickard to meet us with his Mossies and take us home."

Martin said: "If there's any cloud we could try and make our retreat in them, if there's any retreat."

"O.K.," Cheshire said cheerfully. "That sounds good enough."

He called the others to the briefing room and told them: they listened in startled silence, but had acquired such faith in him that he soon had them planning a fund to buy chickens and hams and volunteering to give up their sweet and cigarette rations. They went round surrounding farms, bargaining for chickens, cheeses and bacon; and Cheshire, Martin and Shannon practised low-level formation. Cheshire had warned everyone to keep quiet about it because if Cochrane got to hear there would be no chickens for the prisoners, but probably bread and water for Cheshire.

11

DIRECT HIT

Harris had been sending bombers by day to smash at the mysterious "ski sites" in the Pas de Calais, but too many German fighters swarmed up to protect them. It left him with a pretty problem . . . the targets were so small and well hidden that the squadrons would not be able to pin-point and bomb them accurately by night; what was good enough for a big industrial area was not precise enough now. Cochrane asked permission for 617 to try their precision bombing with P.F.F. (Pathfinder Force) to mark the pin-point with incendiaries, and Harris agreed.

Night after night 617 was briefed, but the target was smothered under low stratus cloud until, on December 16, Cheshire led nine Lancasters off. A Pathfinder "oboe" Mosquito flew with them to mark the target. "Oboe" was a new way of radar pin-pointing; two beams went out from England and crossed exactly over the target to let the pilot know when he was there. This night the "oboe" plane dropped a casket of incendiaries, and they cascaded into the wood that hid the "ski site." At 10,000 feet 617 saw them winking among the trees like tiny glow-worms, swung in together according to the drill, nicely scattered so that the flak was ineffective, and all the 12,000-pounder "blast" bombs went down within a couple of minutes. Around the incendiaries the wood erupted in flame.

Back at Coningsby they developed the aiming-point photos (taken by photo-flash) and a groan went up. The markers had been 350 yards from the target; the bombs were all round the markers with an average error of only 94 yards, but that meant that the bombing was so good that the ski site was untouched. It was the most accurate high-level night bombing of the war, but that made it all the more bitter.

It confirmed a suspicion both Cheshire and Cochrane had had . . . Pathfinders were fine for area marking but not precise enough for pin-point targets. Martin suggested they drop parachute flares over the target, lighting up the area so that a couple of aircraft could dive to low level and drop incendiary markers "spot on" the target. Cheshire agreed, but Cochrane, with the memory of the Dortmund–Ems painfully fresh in his mind, would not hear of more low-level work.

Cheshire and Martin went off quietly and tried low-level markings on the ranges in the hope that they could get Cochrane to change his mind. They dropped practice bombs from about 200 feet using the low-level bomb sight and were only mildly satisfied with the results. They found they could land a bomb accurately but the trajectory was so flat that the bomb tended to bounce and skid 200 yards beyond the target. And at nighttime they found in the Lancasters that they were shooting past the range target before they saw it.

On December 20 they tried P.F.F. "oboe" marking again on an armament factory near Liége but found the town hopelessly cloaked under low cloud. On the way back (with their bombs) Martin saw a Lancaster going down in flames with one of the gunners still firing at the fighter. Back at Coningsby they waited up, more out of conscience than hope, but Geoff Rice, one of the five survivors of the original squadron, did not return.

They tried again with the "oboe" Mosquito on a ski site, but again cloud defeated them.

Cheshire called on an intelligence officer in London for a final check on his P.o.W. "chicken run." The intelligence man listened to the plan with horror and said, "My God, you can't do that! If you drop things in the compounds the Germans'll think you're dropping them arms, and as the prisoners rush out to pick them up they'll be mown down."

Cheshire said, "I didn't think of that," went back and told Martin and Shannon sadly that they would have to call it off, but it didn't sadden the other two at all.

The weather closed in until the night of December 30, when they went with an "oboe" plane to another ski site. Three bombs were direct hits on the "oboe" markers, but the markers were again a couple of hundred yards off the target and the ski site escaped.

Cheshire pleaded with Cochrane for permission to mark at low level. His idea was that P.F.F. should drop flares by "oboe" to illuminate the area, and he and Martin should fly low enough to put a marker right on the spot.

Cochrane replied with a flat no, and added, "Try and find another way. Try marking with the S.A.B.S. from about five thousand feet. If you can light the area enough with flares to get a sight, you ought to be able to do it accurately."

Cheshire suggested in that case that 617 might as well carry their own flares and dispense with the Pathfinders. Cochrane agreed and on January 4 they flew to the Pas de Calais without the "oboe" plane. From 12,000 feet the squadron dropped floating flares, but cloud foiled Cheshire and Martin at 5,000 feet, so they both dived to 400 feet (pre-arranged and strictly off the record) and skimmed over the dim clearing from different directions. The markers landed in the clearing but both sets bounced and skidded 100 yards into the woods, so that the clearing was straddled by them.

The squadron managed to put most of their bombs between the markers, badly damaging the ski site; Cheshire thought it was fairly successful but was not exactly delighted . . . skidding markers were too uncertain to rely on. In the next few days he, Martin and "Talking Bomb" kept experimenting to find a permissable way of marking.

Between 3,000 and 6,000 feet on a clear aiming

point by day they found they could put down a marker
within 40 yards of a target—near enough for Cochrane
—but could not do it on a hazy target, and there was
little chance of getting a clear enough aiming point at
night. Moonlight and flares would help, but any important target was going to be camouflaged.

That was the week the squadron moved from Coningsby to Woodhall Spa, about ten miles away. Woodhall was a one-squadron station and that was the reason for the move. As a "special duties" squadron on
new and rather hush-hush projects, Cochrane wanted
them to go on working in somewhat exclusive isolation.

Snowstorms had mantled the field and the runways
were under a 6-inch carpet. Everyone on the squadron, officers and aircrew too, turned out to shovel the
snow off the runways so the planes could get off
the ground. They worked from dawn till midnight for
two days, long lines of men shovelling at the white
acres while W.A.A.F.'s brought them coffee and
sandwiches and rewarded them with a rum ration
when they finished work at night.

About this time a Military Brain conceived that, if a
large dam just north of Rome could be breached, the
flood would tangle German communications in Italy
and help the imminent break-out from the Anzio
beach-head. 617 was the logical squadron for the job,
and Cochrane—a little reluctantly—put them on to
intensive dams-type training . . . low flying. It would
have to be Wallis's dams bomb again, dropped from
60 feet, but the Italian dam lay in a lake surrounded by
high hills, a worse proposition even than the Eder. It
meant sliding over a hill and losing 1,800 feet in
3,000 yards to be at 60 feet over the water in time to
bomb, a frighteningly steep dive in a heavy aircraft at
night. It was going to need a lot of skill. They measured 3,000 yards out over the airfield, marked the
extremities, and Martin stood off from one mark with
a theodolite to measure height while each pilot came
over the far mark at 1,900 feet and tried to cross the
next mark at 60 feet. Pilots who could not do it after a

couple of trial runs got the benefit of Martin's salty vocabulary and were spurred on to achieve success next time.

One other complication was that they would have to take off for it from North Africa because the all-up weight would be too great from England; and if the Germans got an inkling that the Dam Busters' Squadron was flying to Africa for a raid they would very likely put two and two together, put balloons and guns by the dam and save their dam as well as kill most of the crews.

Cochrane and Cheshire hit on the solution. Cochrane sent in lorry loads of enough arctic equipment and clothing to outfit the whole squadron, and Cheshire stored it under guard in a locked hangar, then dropped a hint that they were going to North Africa. From that moment the whole squadron was convinced they were going to Russia. The more they were told it was to be Africa the surer they were that it was Russia.

The pilots practised low flying constantly over Lincolnshire and Norfolk. On January 20, O'Shaughnessy was practising diving over the sea by the Wash and levelling out at 60 feet, but he was concentrating so hard on his altimeter that he did not notice the land looming up. The Lancaster smacked her belly on a hill rising off the beach, bounced, charged into another rise in the ground and rolled into a flaming ball, cremating the crew except for Arthur Ward, the wireless operator, who was thrown clear with a broken leg. That was the day the Authorities decided that if the dam were breached it might kill many civilians and perhaps disrupt the Allied advance more than the Germans, and so they called it off. Such is war.

In between low flying Cheshire and Martin had kept experimenting to find a way of marking, and one day, flying back from the range, Martin saw a patch of seaweed in the water that took his fancy. Always ready to spice his flying with a little variety he peeled off in one of his usual spectacular turns, dived steeply and dropped a bomb. It was a direct hit.

When he landed he jumped out of "P Popsie" quivering with excitement. "That's it, sir," he said jauntily to Cheshire. "We've got it. I didn't use the bomb sight when I dropped that thing over the seaweed and it was a piece of cake. If we can dive-bomb markers point-blank over a target we can put 'em right on the button without the bomb sight and they won't skid off. What's more, we could see the target much better from above than coming up to it down low."

Cheshire went out and tried it that afternoon and it worked like a charm, almost without practice.

Next night they went back to the Pas de Calais. Munro dropped flares and Martin, turning a blandly blind eye to orders, tried his new method, peeling off, sticking his nose steeply down and aiming his whole aircraft at the ski site. He found that dive-bombing low at night in a four-engined plane was a slightly hair-raising business but dropped his markers in the dive and pulled out at about 400 feet. They were a new type of marker, red and green flares known as "spot fires," and as he pulled up and levelled off Martin saw the two lights like red and green eyes winking in the middle of the clearing. It was a clear night; from 12,000 feet they were plainly visible, and the rest of the squadron plastered the rocket site out of existence.

A couple of nights later they went to another flying-bomb site; Martin dived low again, laid his spot fires accurately and a few minutes later the target was littered about a few smoking craters.

Cheshire went to Cochrane and told him of the new method (that is, told him of the seaweed and the trials over the range, not of Martin's actual dives over the targets). Knowing that Cochrane approved of low-level marking on every count except the risk, Cheshire assured him that the diving attack, straight down, up and away, with only a few fleeting seconds near the ground, was reasonably safe. He added earnestly: "Sir, if we're going to mark accurately we *must* be low enough to see exactly what we're doing, and I'm sure that Martin is right when he says that right down low we're actually safer. I can't find any way of marking accurately from medium level. Will you let us try this new way on some lightly defended target?"

Cochrane considered for a moment, looked up and said, "All right, we'll give it a trial."

The target he chose was the Gnome-Rhone aero-engine factory at Limoges, 200 miles south-west of Paris. The Germans had taken it over but there was hardly any flak for miles.

There was an immediate complication. War Cabinet vetoed the target because the Germans had 300 French girls working in the factory on night shift and there were French homes nearby. Churchill would not have French people killed if he could possibly avoid it, particularly as this was not a vital target.

Cheshire replied that as far as the homes were concerned he would guarantee they would put all bombs on the target itself. To protect the girls in the factory he offered to make several dummy runs over the factory to give everyone plenty of time to get clear. Cochrane backed him up and, after a silence from Whitehall, permission came through for the raid, on the understanding that if one Frenchman was killed there would be no more. Cochrane told Cheshire: "Our future stands or falls on this one. If anyone slips you won't get another chance. Not in France or Belgium anyway, and I won't let you make guinea-pigs of yourselves over Germany." Cheshire, at briefing, told the crews the same thing. Cochrane and he planned it with fanatical care.

Twelve aircraft took off into bright moonlight and reached Limoges just before midnight. The town was evidently not expecting bombs because the blackout was bad. Lights showed all over the place and in the factory itself all the workshop lights were on and it was obvious that the Germans had them working hard. Pat Kelly, Cheshire's gay, chunky little navigator, looked down on the lighted streets, making wistful comments about the bistros and French girls he imagined he could see.

Cheshire dived low and hurtled over the factory at a

hundred feet, and as he climbed and turned he saw all the lights vanish. He dived back over it again, and Astbury, his bomb aimer, could see people running below and throwing themselves flat. A third time he dived in warning, and on his fourth run held her down to 50 feet till he was practically scraping the workshop roofs. Astbury called "Bombs gone!" and a cluster of brilliantly glowing incendiaries cascaded into the exact centre of the workshops. In the Lancaster the camera-man filmed it.

Martin dived in the same way and two red spot fires joined the incendiaries. Cheshire called, "Markers dead centre. Bomb as ordered."

At "Zero plus 1" (one minute past midnight) Shannon dropped the first 12,000-pounder from 10,000 feet. It exploded in the middle of the incendiaries and blew them to smithereens but started a big fire that was just as good. In the next eight minutes nine more bombs fell right on the factory, and one fell just outside in the river. The last man, Nicky Ross, had a "hang-up"; his bomb did not release, so he went away and came in on another run. At "Zero plus 18" his 12,000-pounder lobbed in the crater that Shannon's bomb had made.

Cheshire cruised overhead for a while, but there was nothing to see but flames and smoke and soon he turned for home. Apart from two machine guns there was no opposition and none of the Lancasters was holed, not even Cheshire's.

In the morning a recce aircraft brought back pictures which showed that of the factory's forty-eight bays half were scars on the ground and the rest were only shells. A target had never been more completely expunged, and Cheshire knew that, on undefended targets at least, he had proved his point. Cochrane was delighted.

(A message reached England from Limoges not long after. The girls of the Gnome-Rhone factory wished to thank the R.A.F. for their considerate warning and would be pleased to welcome the people concerned after the war.)

Bob Hay also deserved credit for the bombing at Limoges. He and "Talking Bomb" had the bomb aimers so well trained in the S.A.B.S. that from 15,000 feet *at night* they could guarantee two direct hits on any target, 15 per cent of bombs within 25 yards of the centre and 75 per cent within 80 yards, a remarkable feat when it is considered that the crack Pathfinders were never called upon to mark with more than 150 yards accuracy.

12

GALLANT FAILURE

In Italy the Allies were preparing to break out from Anzio and the Germans were preparing to stop them. Trains carrying 15,000 tons of supplies a day were passing over the Antheor Viaduct, and for the third time 617 was ordered to smash it.

Cochrane thought a 12,000-lb. "blockbuster" within 10 yards of the viaduct might knock a span down but this time he warned Cheshire that he must not try "deck-level" marking unless it were absolutely necessary. There were twelve heavy guns and several lighter guns around the viaduct, plus searchlights.

With heavy bombs the range was dangerously far from Woodhall Spa, so they refuelled at Ford in the south, Cheshire flying McCarthy's "Q Queenie" as his own aeroplane was being overhauled and McCarthy was on leave.

They found the bay at midnight but it was so dark they could not see the viaduct from above 3,000 feet, and as soon as Cheshire and Martin slipped down to that height the flak opened up terrifyingly, nearly twenty guns predicting and concentrating on the two of them. Cheshire made a run to drop his markers, but the searchlights caught him long before he was in position and shells were bursting all round him, so that he had to turn away. Martin tried a run but the same thing happened. Cheshire came in again and Martin flew parallel, higher and about a mile out, to draw the flak. It took some of the flak off Cheshire, but not enough; his aircraft shuddered in the blast of near misses and jagged lumps of flak ripped holes in his wings and fuselage. He slid out to sea and swung in again, but as he straightened up for the run Martin's voice sounded in his earphones: "Hold off a minute, Leader. I think I'm in position for a low run. I can see everything."

He had dived over the hills inland, was hugging the ridges so that the flak could not see him against the dark mass, and turning down the long ravine that cut down to the viaduct across the bay. When they had looked at the maps at briefing it did not seem possible that an aircraft could get down that way but Martin, who could land a Lancaster out of a steep turn, had his nose dipping into the ravine and could see the viaduct dead ahead, limned against the phosphorescence of the surf on the beach.

Cheshire called back, "O.K., Mick, go ahead."

"Try and draw the flak as long as you can," Martin said. He was deep into the ravine; the viaduct was about a mile in front and some 1,500 feet lower; he throttled his engines back to keep the sound from the guns and at 230 m.p.h. opened his bomb doors and knew he was making the best bombing run he ever had. The guns down by the viaduct were all firing, but their target was Cheshire weaving in towards them from the other side at 4,000 feet.

In the nose of "P Popsie" Bob Hay said over the intercom, "Target markers selected and fused."

"Right," said Martin. "I'm going to level out in the last second."

"O.K." The bomb sight was no use in a dive. Hay relied on Martin for the signal.

The ravine ridges were towering on each side and the viaduct was rushing at them, growing hugely. One gun on the eastern end suddenly swung and out of its muzzle-flashes a chain of shells was swirling at them. Hay called, "Now?" and Martin yelled, "No! No!" He eased the nose up, a second dragged into eternity, he shouted, "Now!" And as he shouted a shell smashed through the nose and exploded in the ammunition trays under the front turret. The aircraft rocked in the crashing din and jagged steel and exploding bullets shot back into the fuselage, hitting flesh and ploughing through hydraulic and pneumatic pipes, control rods and fuse boxes.

Hay must have pressed the button as the bomb-release contacts parted, and then they shot a bare couple of feet over the viaduct and dipped towards the water as half a dozen more guns swivelled and spat at them. Foxlee was still alive; for the first time in months he was in the mid-upper turret instead of the nose, and now he was cursing and shooting back, and so was Simpson in the rear. Martin pulled the nose off the water and Whittaker rammed the throttles forward but there was almost no response from the engines.

"P Popsie" was bathed in glare but Simpson and Foxlee put three of the searchlights out with long bursts. They were practically in the water now, and in the glow of the last light Simpson saw the spray hissing up from the prop-wash and thought for a moment it was smoke from a burning engine. Then they were out of range and Martin lifted "P Popsie" a few feet off the water, praying with thankfulness as he found she still had flying speed.

Whittaker leaned over and yelled in his ear, "Port inner and starb'd outer throttles gone and pitch controls for the other two gone." That meant two engines would stay throttled back as they had been for the run down the ravine, and the other two, in fully fine pitch, were straining themselves at maximum revs. on extreme power to keep the aircraft flying.

Martin became conscious of Cheshire's voice: "Are you all right, 'P Popsie'? Are you all right? Can you hear me?" Nearly a mile above he had seen the Lancaster rocket over the viaduct, caught by the searchlights and with all the guns pounding her.

Martin called back: "Still airborne, Leader. Hit badly, I think. Two engines gone and crew hurt." He had felt the sting in his own leg as the shell went off in the nose and knew he had been hit. Whittaker was doubled up now, holding his legs.

Cheshire's voice came back: "Can you make it back home, Mick?"

"Not a hope, sir. We'll try and make for the nearest friendly land."

"All right, boy. Good luck!"

Martin was calling the roll round his crew. The tough little Foxlee was all right. Bob Hay did not answer. Whittaker gave him a twisted grin, swearing and hunched, holding his legs. The rest were all right. He called Hay twice more but there was only silence, so he said, "Toby, see if Bob's all right. His intercom must be busted." Foxlee swung out of his turret and wormed down towards the nose. He lifted his head towards Martin. "He's lying on the floor. Not moving."

Over the viaduct Cheshire was trying to drop his markers but again was coned by searchlights and hit by flak, so he had to stand the Lancaster on a wingtip and pull her round to the safe darkness at sea. It meant several miles for another run. He came in again about 3,000 but again he was battered and had to pull away. He climbed to 5,000 but the flak caught him once more, and now there was another worry on his mind. Out to sea the squadron had been circling for half an hour waiting for the markers and he knew they were getting short of petrol. Met. had radioed that England was under fog and only two fields were suitable for landing. They would need plenty of petrol to search and land through the fog . . . or risk losing the whole squadron.

On his sixth run he dived to upset the predicted flak and was able to drop flares that lit the viaduct. He turned back for another run and this time the searchlights did not find him. The guns predicted on him but he threaded through them and soon his markers sprang to glowing life as they hit; he saw in the light of the flares that they were on the beach about a hundred yards from the viaduct.

He swung in again with his last two markers but four seconds short of release point two shells hit "Q Queenie" and she almost stood on her head in the blast. It threw Astbury off his bombing aim, but

Cheshire got her back under control and found she would still fly and there was no fire.

The squadron headed in, unable at 10,000 feet to pick up the viaduct from the flares but trying to allow for the error of the markers. The gap was fiendishly hard to judge in the darkness. One 12,000-pounder went off brilliantly 15 yards from the side of the viaduct, but that was 5 yards too far and the viaduct shook but was not damaged beyond chipping from fragments. Six more exploded a few yards further on and pitted the great stone piers a little more. It was good bombing, but not quite good enough. Long after they were supposed to, they turned for home.

Whittaker had taken his tie off and wrapped it round his thigh as a tourniquet. There were a dozen pieces of flak in his legs but the pain was passing into numbness now. He grabbed one of the roof longerons, pulled himself up and found he could stand. Foxlee stuck his head up from the nose and said, "Bob's unconscious. Get a first-aid kit, will you?" Whittaker pulled one of the little canvas bags out of its stowage and eased himself down into the nose. Hay was lying on his side, his head pillowed on the perspex right up in the nose. "Give him some morphia," Foxlee shouted, and Whittaker nodded, unclipped the canvas pack and took out one of the tiny morphia hypodermic tubes. Foxlee unzipped Hay's Irvin jacket sleeve and rolled the battledress sleeve up till Whittaker could see the soft flesh of the forearm, pale in the gloom. He felt the flesh was still warm, jabbed in the needle and squeezed till the tube was empty.

"Let's get him over and see where he's hit," he shouted. Together in the cramped space they edged him over on to his back and Whittaker crawled up and gently turned the head over. He saw the great hole in the side of the head and felt the stickiness in the same moment. He said, "Oh, my God!" and felt he was going to be sick, looked up at Foxlee, but Foxlee was looking down. He had lifted his hand off Hay's chest and the blood showed darkly on his fingers. "He's got it in the chest," he said, and Whittaker said, "Yes, the poor devil's had it."

He crawled back up into the cockpit to his seat beside Martin, leaned over and said, "Bob's dead." Martin looked at him a moment, then looked ahead again and gave a little nod.

Whittaker noticed Kenny Stott, the new navigator, standing by Martin's seat. "Where're we going?" Whittaker said, and Martin gave him a wry little grin. "Somewhere friendly, I hope," he said. "Just been talking it over with Kenny. Got any ideas?"

"Whatever's nearest. How 'bout Gib.? Or Sicily? Or North Africa?"

Stott said, "What about Sardinia? Or Corsica? Aren't they closer?"

"Is Corsica ours?" Martin asked, and Whittaker cut in, not sensing then the unconscious humour of it: "Yeah. I saw we got Corsica in the *News of the World* last Sunday."

"O.K. Fair enough. Kenny, give me a course for North Corsica."

Stott went back to his charts and Whittaker said he would try and assess the damage. Martin found "Popsie" had just enough power to claim a little more height, very slowly, so he edged the nose up a little, and soggily, not far from stalling speed, the Lancaster started climbing laboriously. In the darkness she was full of noise, the high-pitched screaming of the two good engines battering at the ears in waves because they would not synchronise properly.

He felt his right foot in the flying boot was wet and remembered he had been hit in the calf. He had enough sense not to strip his leg to investigate because the trouser leg and high flying boot would help staunch the blood. The trouble was, if he lost too much blood, he would pass out and they would all die because no one else could fly "Popsie," particularly the way she was. Against the ragged thrust of the engines the trim would not hold her either straight or level and he was working all the time to keep her flying. With one hand he pulled his tie loose and wrapped it round the calf over the spot where the shrapnel had hit him, knotting it tightly so that it would press the trouser leg against the wound with the effect of half bandage, half tourniquet.

Whittaker came back. "Not too good," he said. "The floor's all smothered in grease. It's from the hydraulics, so you can count them out. Air pressure's gone too."

"I know," Martin said. "I can't get the bomb doors up."

"The CO_2 bottle seems all right," Whittaker said, "so you'll probably be able to get your undercart and flaps down but you won't have any brakes to pull up with."

"Oh, Christ!"

"I've kept the best bit to the last," Whittaker said morbidly. "The bomb-release fuses have gone for a Burton and we've still got the bombs on board."

"I thought so. That's why she's flying like a bloody brick."

Stott came up with a course for North Corsica, and Martin swung on to the new heading. They were about 2,000 feet now.

"We'll have to get rid of the bombs," Stott said. "The fusing circuit's bashed in too, so they must still be fused. We can't unfuse 'em. If you can get high enough I might be able to prod the grips through the floor with a ruler and trip them."

Martin was trying to coax more height out of the stricken plane. He had a 4,000-pounder and several 1,000-pounders in the bomb bays, and the minimum safety height for dropping a 4,000-pounder was 4,000 feet.

Curtis was tapping out a "Mayday" (S.O.S.) and excitedly reported, after a while, he had made contact with Ajaccio in Northern Corsica. An advanced R.A.F. fighter unit had just moved in there and the airfield and flarepath were serviceable.

Foxlee came up from the nose and said in a puzzled voice, "Bob's still warm. His body's quite warm. I think he might be alive." Whittaker went down to investigate and came back up again, a little excited. "He *is* warm," he said. "He *must* be alive still." Martin told

Curtis to warn Ajaccio to have a doctor to meet them.
Curtis made contact again and came back to the cockpit. "They say they haven't got a doctor with any
facilities to look after a bad head wound. They say if
the kite'll hold together we ought to make for Cagliari.
That's in South Sardinia. There's an American bomber
base at Elmas Field there, and they've got everything,
but it's another hundred and fifty miles."

Martin said feelingly, "Christ, what a party! Give
me a new course, Kenny." The aircraft was still full of
numbing noise; a gale was howling through the shell-
hole in the nose and the two good engines still screamed
in high pitch. Whittaker was watching his gauges nervously, waiting for the engines to crack under the
strain.

They were about 2,700 feet when the stars blotted
out and they were in heavy rain, followed soon after by
hail. Water was sweeping in through the nose, and
then darkness swallowed them as they ran into heavy
cloud. It was ice cloud. Martin saw supercooled water
droplets filming over the leading edge of the wings,
forming the dangerous glazed ice that altered the aero-
dynamic shape and robbed the wings of lift. He had no
spare speed to give him lift, and then the propeller of
one of the two good engines slipped right back into
coarse pitch and could not be budged out of it. The
revs. dropped down to about 1,800; the engine was
still giving power but the propeller could not use it all.
Martin felt the controls getting soggy; he held on to
her, correcting the waffling with great coarse movements, trying to coax her to stay up because Stott was
shoving a ruler down through the floor into the bomb
bay against the bomb grips. He got a 1,000-pounder
away and then the aircraft stalled, Martin couldn't
hold her; the nose fell, she squashed down and the
starboard wingtip dropped and they were diving and
turning, on the verge of a spin. He had hard left rudder
on and the rudder caught her, the spin checked and
she was diving, picking up speed. He eased her out
but they were down to 1,800 feet. That was clear of the
cloud, and soon the thin ice cracked and flicked off the

wings. He started climbing again. They still needed 4,000 feet to drop the 4,000-pounder.

It took a long time. At 2,500 feet they were in the ice-cloud again, but Stott prodded two more 1,000-pounders free before the ice started to make "Popsie" soggy again, and this time Martin eased her down out of the cloud before she stalled. He started climbing again and found they were running clear of the worst of the cloud. It was still there, but higher and thinner, and only the barest film of ice seemed to be shining on the wings. "Popsie" slowly gained height, passed the 3,000 mark, but then progress was terribly slow and when at last they reached 3,200 she could not drag herself any higher. She was still at the climbing angle but moving no higher, like an old man trying to climb a fence and not being able to pull himself up.

"She's only squashing along," Martin said. "Can't make the safety height, Kenny. What're our chances if we drop the big one here?"

"Better than trying to land with the bloody thing," Stott said. "Let's give it a go."

He went back to the winch slits in the floor and probed. Martin felt the aircraft jump weakly in the same moment that Stott yelled, "She's gone!" Martin tried to turn away but knew he could not get far enough for safety. The 4,000-pounder took fourteen seconds to fall and it felt like fourteen minutes. The sea below and a little to one side opened up like a crimson rose and almost in the same moment the shock wave hit the aircraft. She jumped like a startled horse and a wing flicked, but Martin caught her smartly with rudder and they were all right.

Curtis came up a couple of minutes later. "Elmas Field says the best way in is over the mountains in the middle of Sardinia."

"How high are they?" Martin asked. Stott said they were 8,000 feet and Martin showed his teeth sardonically.

They got a landfall on Sardinia about 3:30 a.m. and turned to follow the coast all the way round the south tip, and on e.t.a. Martin let down through light cloud

and they came out about 1,000 feet and saw the flarepath.

"Thank God for that," he breathed, and a minute
later changed his mind. Elmas was on a narrow spit of
land. It had one runway only, a dangerously short one
for an emergency landing. Martin steered low over it to
see what the overshoot areas were like because they
were probably going to need them, and felt a chill as
he saw that some genius of an airfield designer had had
the fabulous idea of building the runway *across* the
spit of land, so that the runway started very abruptly
at the beach and stopped just as abruptly and dismay-
ingly quickly at the cliff, where the sea started again.
No overshoot.

He still had two 1,000-lb. bombs that Stott could
not reach and they were almost certainly fused, so a
belly landing was out of the question. With the emergency CO_2 bottle the undercarriage might go down,
or it might not; the tyres might be all right or they
might have been punctured, and if they were the
aircraft stood a good chance of ground-looping so that
the undercart would collapse on to the fused bombs. If
his first approach was not perfect the aircraft, without
brakes, would certainly run over the far cliff. There was
not enough power to go round for a second approach.

Whittaker yanked down the handle of the CO_2 bottle, and the undercart swung down and seemed to
lock. In the gloom they could not see the tyres. There
was just enough pressure left to get some flap down.
Martin headed in on a long, low approach, dragging in
from miles back, while the crew snugged down at emergency stations. Coming up to the runway he was dangerously low, deliberately, and in the last moment
he cut all engines and pulled up the nose to clear the
dunes. The speed fell and at about 85 m.p.h. she
squashed on the runway about 30 yards from the end,
not even bouncing. The undercart held, and as she
rumbled on Martin started fish-tailing his rudders.
The far cliff was running towards them and he pushed
on full port rudder. "Popsie" swung and jolted over

the grass verge, slowing more appreciably. She started to slew, tyres skidding just short of a ground-loop, and came to a halt 50 yards from the cliff-top.

Foxlee said, "Well, you old bastard, I'll never bitch about your landings any more."

An ambulance and fire truck had been chasing them along the runway, and a young doctor swung up into the fuselage and they directed him up to the nose. He was out a minute later and said, "I'm sorry, but your buddy's gone. He was dead as soon as it happened."

He went over to Whittaker, lying on the grass, and cut his trouser legs away, exposing the legs messy with blood and torn flesh, and where there was no blood they had a distinct blue tinge. He worked for quarter of an hour on them, dabbing, cleaning and bandaging, while Martin gingerly pulled up his own trouser leg to inspect the damage to himself. The doctor finished bandaging Whittaker and as they loaded him into the ambulance told him, "That's a close call, boy. You nearly lost a leg." He turned to Martin. "Now let's have a look at you," but Martin said as off-handedly as he could, "Don't bother about me, Doc. I'm quite all right."

When he had uncovered his leg he had found one tiny spot of blood on a tiny puncture where a tiny piece of flak, at its last gasp, had just managed to break the skin. It had stung at the time, and imagination had done the rest. The wetness he had felt round his foot was not blood gushing into his flying boot but sweat!

About the same time the rest of the squadron was landing at Ford in thick weather. Tommy Lloyd, Woodhall intelligence officer, had flown to Ford and debriefed them, and then the weather worsened and it looked as though they were stranded for a while. Suggitt thought he could make it to Woodhall Spa all right and offered a seat in his aircraft to Lloyd, a gallant and revered World War I veteran. The immaculate Lloyd accepted but insisted on having a shave before take-off. A little later, spruce and monocled, he climbed into "J Jug" with Suggitt, and five minutes later the aircraft flew into a hill and everyone was killed instantly except Bill Suggitt, who lingered a couple of days before he died.

The rest flew back later, and Cheshire's "erks" found 150 holes in "Q Queenie." The port wing had to be scrapped. McCarthy, back from leave, was outraged to find his beloved "Queenie" so battered and a comic but slightly acid note edged his Brooklyn accent when he said loudly and meaningly in the mess (Cheshire was standing near): "It's a remarkable coincidence that the wingco has been flying his own aircraft for three months without getting a spot on it, and then sends me on leave and takes mine and does this to it."

They buried Bob Hay in Sardinia. Whittaker stayed in hospital while the rest made rough repairs, flew "Popsie" on to Blida, where R.A.F. "erks" did a thorough overhaul, and then filled her up with benedictine, wine, fruit and eggs and flew back to Woodhall Spa, where Cheshire met them with the news that Cochrane had vetoed any more operations for them. "It's no use arguing, Mick," Cheshire said. "He means it. He says you'll only kill yourself if he lets you go on." Martin *did* argue, but Cochrane posted him to 100 Group Headquarters, where he immediately wangled himself on to a Mosquito night-fighter squadron doing "intruder" work over Germany.

[I have a letter which Cheshire wrote to a friend some four years after this, talking about the old days. He said: "The backbone of the squadron were Martin, Munro, McCarthy and Shannon, and of these by far the greatest was Martin. He was not a man to worry about administration then (though I think he is now), but as an operational pilot I consider him greater than Gibson, and indeed the greatest that the Air Force ever produced. I have seen him do things that I, for one, would never have looked at."]

It is not a bad tribute from a man who has himself often been labelled one of the world's greatest bomber pilots. I have these words of Cheshire's in my notes: "I learned all I knew of this low-flying game from Mick. He showed me what you could do by coming in straight and hard and low, and I never saw him make a mistake."

Cheshire himself, in fact, was perhaps the most outstanding of the 617 pilots, though if one suggested this he would decry it with a gentle and faintly derisive smile. Always he had a talent for self-effacement, a soft-spoken modesty, and many qualities not usual in hearty men of action and courage. His courage could match any man's, and in addition he was always a strange blend of leader, intellectual, man of action and man of ideas and ideals (sometimes eccentric and seldom conformist). Inevitably he has an awareness of this and balances it by a deprecating introspection. He has never quite rid himself of the idea that he lost his nerve at Antheor, that he should have tried to go in low like Martin, and does himself no justice, because he and his crew would almost surely have died, probably before being able to lay their markers, and that would have destroyed any chance of success for the raid.

As it was, the raid was within 5 yards of success, but that is a sore point with 617. Antheor seemed to have a hoodoo on them.

13

THE MOSQUITO PLAN

Cheshire reported to Cochrane that the Antheor raid had convinced him of three things:

(a) Accurate marking was essential for accurate bombing of small specific targets.
(b) Accurate marking could only be done reliably at low level.
(c) Low-level marking was *very* dangerous on defended targets with a big aircraft like the Lancaster.

Cochrane was not yet convinced that low-level marking was practicable, but he told Cheshire he would lay on more lightly defended targets so the experiment could go on. He wanted the system perfected by the time Wallis's "tallboy" was ready; the first one was nearly ready for testing, and after that they would be some time building up stocks. Meantime the squadron needed some re-forming. With Martin and Suggitt gone there were no flight commanders.

It was Cochrane's idea to split 617 into three flights for easier organisation and training; a happy idea, because it gave Cheshire a chance to promote Shannon, McCarthy and Munro, now the only three of the original squadron left, and all battle-tested, reliable and ideal in temperament and training for 617's unique role. Shannon was an old-young man now, venom-tongued on occasion, highly strung on the ground (though not the slightest neurotic), but calm and detached as an iceberg in the air. McCarthy, strong as an ox and even-tempered, stood no trifling—his way with a young fool who forgot himself was swift and vigorous. Munro, the slow-speaking, taciturn New Zealander, so earnest and dour that he was known as "Happy," did most of the tedious routine work in the squadron and never even suspected that the W.A.A.F.s on the station adored him as a strong, silent man. The Australian, the American and the New Zealander, each in some way typifying their national characters, led by the subtle and audacious Englishman, a strong combination of leaders in a squadron that ever was an oligarchy, but a respected and revered one.

McCarthy, incidentally, now that he was a squadron leader, let himself take on a little of the colour of his surroundings. With a touch of Brooklyn wit, he bought himself a pipe, a walking-stick and a dog, and took the dog for long walks in the countryside, claiming that, as he had to be pretty much of a gentleman officially, he was goddamned if he wasn't going to have a crack at looking the part too.

The squadron had several new pilots now, including another American, Nicky Knilans, a droll youngster from Madison, Wisconsin, with precisely the quality of nervelessness that Cheshire wanted in 617. Knilans had already done about twenty trips with 619 Squadron and been in strife on nearly every one of them. Several times on the way to the target he had had engines shot out, and more shells had ripped chunks out of his aircraft, but he had always pressed on and bombed and had a D.S.O. to commemorate that laudable habit. Once his rear gunner had been cut in two by a night fighter, and it was such a terrible mess that, when they landed back at base, the ambulance driver who met them had had hysterics and largely left it to the nerveless Knilans to get the remains out of the turret.

Knilans had joined the Canadian Air Force before America came into the war and had just recently been transferred. Now a "lootenant" in the U.S. Air Force, he wanted to stay and finish his tour in the R.A.F., and

had a row with his crew when he had them posted
with him (without telling them) to 617. They claimed
it was a suicide squadron, but, as Knilans pointed out,
few people on 619 had ever finished a tour either, so it
didn't make much difference. The crew was even more
unhappy when Knilans suddenly seemed to develop into an exceedingly ham-fisted pilot. He was given a new
aircraft, "R Roger," when he joined 617 and could not
make his usual three-point landings any more; even the
take-offs were frightening, as "R Roger" seemed most
reluctant to leave the ground, and when she did leave
climbed like a tired brick. "Give the game away,
Nicky," one of his gunners said. "You're getting flak-
happy. You can't even fly any more."

"Doggone, it's not me," said the badgered American. "It's this bloody-minded aircraft. You don't
have to fly it, you have to understand the son of a
bitch."

In the next few weeks 617 was busy training new
crews and settling down with the new flight commanders. Cheshire and "Talking Bomb" kept flying around
at 5,000 feet trying medium-level marking, but could
find no way of lining-up an indistinct target. Cochrane
told them to keep trying.

The first couple of prototype "tallboys" were finished,
and at Ashley Walk range, in the New Forest, the complicated process of testing them started. They were sinister objects, 21 feet long, shining blue-black steel, slim
and perfectly streamlined, weighing 12,030 lb. A Lancaster dropped one on test from 20,000 feet, and it
sliced through the air like a bullet till it was falling faster
than a bomb had ever fallen before. Long before it hit it
passed the speed of sound, and as the compressed waves
of the sonic barrier piled up round it the bomb vibrated
in flight so that it almost toppled and was deflected
slightly from its even course, just enough to interfere
with the fanatical accuracy that Wallis wanted.

He overcame it with a brilliant idea, offsetting the
tail fins so that, as the next bomb dropped and gathered

speed, the offset fins began to revolve it. Faster and faster it whirled till by the time it reached the speed of sound it was spinning like a highspeed top, and the gyroscopic action held it perfectly steady as it plunged through the sonic barrier. At Shoeburyness the blind Air Commodore Huskinson put other prototypes through heat and cold and rough-usage tests, dragging them over rough ground on bomb dollies and throwing them against concrete walls. They filled one with RDX, stood it on its nose and exploded it. Instruments scattered for hundreds of yards registered the effects, and in a concrete shelter a very high-speed camera took a slow-motion film of it. It was obviously impossible to point the camera at the bomb; they shielded the camera behind a shelter pointing at a mirror so placed that it reflected the explosion into the lens, and got some extraordinary photographs showing the bomb slowly swelling under the tremendous pressure within, like a balloon blown to bursting point, till it was nearly twice its normal size, and then the casing burst with deeply satisfying results.

At Ashley Walk they dropped a "tallboy" with dummy filling from 20,000 feet and it sank 90 feet into the earth, almost enough for the maximum camouflet that Wallis had planned from 40,000 feet, and certainly enough to make a respectable earthquake.

Came the day of dropping the first "live" one, and they buried a movie camera in the earth to film it. There was some discussion as to where the camera should go, and perhaps it was logical (if a little cynical) that they decided to bury it right in the centre of the white circle that was the target, on the assumption that it was the safest spot.

The result was a lesson for anyone who doubted Wallis's genius. Peering over the edge of the sandbagged dug-out half a mile away, they saw the slim shape streak down and hit the centre of the target, right on the camera! The dug-out trembled, and where the camera had been was a smoking stinking crater 80 ft. deep and 100 feet across.

Cochrane called Cheshire to Group H.Q., told him the earthquake bomb had passed its tests with honours and they were now building up stocks for "a big operation" in the spring and summer. 617 was still the only squadron good enough to drop it with the S.A.B.S. but they still had not perfected their marking technique.

On March 2 Cheshire led fifteen 617 Lancasters to an aircraft factory at Albert, in France. Over it the Germans had spread enormous camouflage nets painted with dummy roads and buildings. Cheshire identified the factory from surrounding landmarks, dived low through flak, but his bomb sight was out of order. Munro dived and planted incendiaries and two red spot fires, and a few minutes later the blockbusters crashed down. One toppled and fell outside but the rest, with 617's uncanny accuracy, were direct hits. No more aircraft were made at Albert for the Germans.

Next night to La Ricamerie needle-bearing works at St. Etienne, near Lyons, smallest and hardest target yet. It lay in a narrow valley with 4,000-ft. hills on each side, and the actual target, in the middle of a built-up area, was only 40 yards by 70 yards. Cochrane warned Cheshire again that on no account was a single Frenchman to be hurt.

Met. forecast good weather but the squadron found the target blanketed under unbroken cloud and brought their bombs back. The attempt, however, was notable for two incidents that illustrate the remarkable spirit of the squadron.

Les Munro lost an engine on take-off but got into the air safely and, instead of turning back, which would have been normal, flew on with three engines, arriving only a minute late.

The second concerned a Warrant Officer Rushton, a gunner in Duffy's crew, a hard-boiled bunch of Canadians. Duffy was ill that night and could not fly, so Rushton begged Cheshire to take him along with him. No particular reason, except that he did not want to be left out of an operation. That sort of thing happened often on 617. A navigator broke his collar-bone in a football game one day and sneaked out of sick quarters next night to fly with his crew.

Duffy's crew had made themselves notorious the night they had arrived on the squadron. When they went upstairs to bed they could not find the toilets but, being resourceful men from the backwoods, had relieved themselves out of the window. In the morning they were brought before the group captain, who eyed them coldly and said: "If you fellows do your job properly you can get away with almost anything on this squadron, but one thing you *can't* do is piddle on the group captain."

He had been walking below at the wrong moment. The rest of the squadron thought it wonderful that a crowd of new boys should do that to a senior officer from a great height.

The weather cleared and they tried La Ricamerie again, finding the valley dark under broken cloud. Cheshire dived low between the hills and made six risky runs up and down trying to mark but found he could only see the factory at the last moment. On the sixth run he judged his distance, shoved his nose down and let go his incendiaries; they lobbed on the main factory building but had such a low trajectory that they bounced a hundred yards beyond. Munro dived and undershot. Shannon came in; his markers hit a workshop roof and bounced. Arthur Kell, a lanky Australian who had been a champion amateur boxer and taken over Micky Martin's "P Popsie," came in at roof-top height, and his incendiaries stayed in the middle of the factory.

Cheshire told the bombers above to aim at the last marker, and soon the darkness was lit by flashing explosions and flames. Morning revealed that only the wall round the factory remained; the rest had disappeared and there was no damage outside.

More nights of waiting for the weather; it had been snowing for days and they turned out every day to try and shovel the drifts off the runways and crack the ice off the wings, but as soon as they had finished the snow was coming down again. One night they got off in freezing cold to plaster an aero-engine factory at Woippy, near Metz, but flew through ten-tenths cloud the whole way and found the cloud just as thick over the target. No hope of bombing.

On the way home Duffy's plane was "jumped" by two JU88s and a F.W.190. The first burst sent a bullet through the hand of McLean, the rear gunner, but McLean, after a few salty comments, found his hand was still working and more than evened the score by shooting down both 88s, and possibly the F.W.190 as well.

It was so cold in the rear turrets that the oxygen mask studs on Gerry Witherick's helmet had stuck to his face. He did not know it till he dragged his helmet off and a couple of square inches of skin came away with the studs. The M.O. consoled him with a rum ration.

Next night to the Michelin rubber factory at Clermont Ferrand, partly sabotaged but still making the Germans 24,000 tyres a month. This was an amazing raid. The factory consisted of four large buildings—three workshops, and the fourth was the workers' canteen, just beside them. War Cabinet was still worried about the risk of killing French people, and from a high level the startling instruction came down that they were to smash the three workshops but on no account damage the canteen. It would be such a fine gesture and such good propaganda! (It would also be, a high officer remarked, "a bloody miracle.") To make it more difficult it was a black, moonless night.

Cochrane drew up a most detailed plan and also sent six Lancasters from 106 Squadron with a special new radar navigation aid to drop flares. McLean, his hand swathed in bandages, wanted to fly as usual with Duffy but Cheshire flatly forbade him.

The flares brightly revealed the factory, and Cheshire made three low runs over it at a hundred feet to warn the workers, and on the third run his markers fell short. He called on Munro, Shannon and McCarthy to mark, and they all dive-bombed their spot fires on the workshop buildings.

Seven minutes later the bombing was over and the factory was smothered in flame and smoke. Cheshire radioed back, "Michelin's complexion seems a trifle red."

In the morning a Mosquito took a picture of the smoking ruins. Six of the 617 aircraft had been carrying 12,000-lb. "blockbusters" and every one was a direct hit on the workshops, which could work no more. Just beside them the workers' canteen was untouched. Cochrane sent the picture off to War Cabinet.

Cheshire had been pondering some new marking ideas. Remembering Martin's experiences at Antheor and his own and Munro's troubles marking the needle-bearing factory up and down the dark valley, it seemed to him that Lancasters were too big and clumsy for marking; too big a target for the flak and too clumsy for manoeuvring low over rough ground on pin-point targets. He went to Cochrane and suggested that he try marking in a Mosquito, and Cochrane liked the idea. The twin-engined Mosquito was much faster as well as smaller and "nippier." Provided Mosquitoes could be used, Cochrane for the first time began to feel more comfortable about the idea of sending crews out to mark at low level.

A new idea was already growing in Cochrane's mind: to have 617 mark for the whole of his 5 Group, about twelve squadrons, instead of the Pathfinders. He did not consider the Pathfinders accurate enough for his purposes and a polite "cold war" had, in fact, been developing between 5 Group and the Pathfinders, aggravated a little by 617, who were already tending to consider themselves "Pathfinders to the Pathfinders." Cochrane had already sounded out Harris on his new idea and Harris had reacted favourably. Cochrane reasoned that if they could show that low marking in Mosquitoes was reasonably safe, Harris would probably give 5 Group its chance. He said to Cheshire:

"Well, I'll see if I can get you a couple of Mosquitoes, and then I'd like you to try them first on easy targets. If it seems all right, you could have a go at a tough one."

A bond was developing between the two men. Cochrane did not have an easy personality and few of the hundreds who were daunted by him ever realised that underneath the crisp and almost ruthless front he was shy, with rigid control over his emotions. His precise brain dwelt on operational efficiency. He watched his men from close quarters and visited them constantly. He never, for instance, missed attending a squadron dance, so that he could know them and gauge their temper (and so that they could gauge him). Yet the reserve that covered his shyness made him wary of the embarrassments of easy-going familiarity that might lessen his unswerving concentration. Cheshire was brilliant in a more erratic way, and Cochrane's relentless logic was a brake on this occasional waywardness. They were an ideal combination. Cheshire was a natural tactician in personal relationships, gentle and unobtrusive but with a quiet confidence and the charm that comes from treating everyone, high or low, as a real person and not as a Thing.

It was not easy for Cochrane to get hold of Mosquitoes for 617. They were in short supply and great demand; Pathfinders and other squadrons had priorities for them, and the idea of a heavy-bomber squadron using some experimentally evoked sturdy protests in some high places. While Cochrane was working on this, 617 went ahead perfecting their technique with Lancasters on several small French targets. On March 18 they visited the explosives factory at Bergerac, on the banks of the Dordogne, under rigid orders that there was to be *no* low flying. Cochrane would not risk his choice crews before the Mosquitoes arrived.

For once, in the light of flares, Cheshire's bomb aimer, Astbury, got a good sight at 5,000 feet and put his markers on the factory. Munro did the same. Shannon and McCarthy branded the explosives dump nearby, and Bunny Clayton put a 12,000-pounder in the middle of the dump. For fifteen seconds it looked as though the sun was coming up underneath; the ground was one great orange flash that Cheshire described as "fantastic." It lit the sky for miles so clearly that Cheshire looked up and saw the remaining ten aircraft of his squadron heading in to bomb, and five minutes later the factory as well as the dump was a sea of flame. Cheshire radioed back, "The powder works would seem to have outlived their usefulness." No bomb fell outside the works.

The Germans had another explosives works in France near a town called Angoulême, in a bend of the Charente. Cheshire led fourteen aircraft there the following night, put his spot fires in the centre and ten minutes later was able to radio back, "In accordance with tradition." The factory had ceased to exist. Again no damage outside.

A pleased Cochrane rang Cheshire next day. "Pack your over-night bag," he said. "You're coming down with me to see Air Chief Marshal Harris about a couple of Mosquitoes."

That night they dined with Harris in his house near High Wycombe, Cheshire for all his urbanity feeling uneasy in the company of the two most terrifying commanders in the R.A.F. He needn't have worried; the fire-cracker and the meticulous planner chatted nostalgically about their days in Iraq when they were both young flight lieutenants not fanatically addicted to administration.

Over the port Harris suddenly said, "Cheshire, what makes you think you can mark from nought feet in a Mosquito and get away with it?"

"There's no question that we can mark accurately, sir. The only thing is having a reasonable chance in the face of heavy opposition. Air Vice-Marshal Cochrane thinks a Lancaster is too big and slow. Against heavy opposition I'm inclined to think now he is right, but I believe he agrees with me that the chances in a Mosquito are good. I believe in a Mosquito we can

have a go at any target under the sun and mark with
under twenty yards accuracy."

"I've always wanted to bomb Munich properly, and
I've never succeeded," Harris said. "It's got four hundred guns. D'you think you could mark that on the
deck and get away with it?"

"Yes, sir. I do."

Cochrane cut in, saying that they should practise
first with the Mosquito on less lethal targets so they
would know precisely what was possible.

"All right," Harris said, "I'll see if I can get you two
Mosquitoes . . . just on loan for a month. If by that time
you can mark Munich accurately for me, you can
keep them."

Just behind Calais the Germans had started work
again on the bomb-proof rocket and long-range gun
bases. Thousands of slaves were crawling over the massive blockhouses and it was obvious that the secret-
weapon project was nearing completion again. Whitehall knew now that the weapon was to fall on London
and the invasion ports, but kept it very secret. (They
still knew nothing of the long-range guns, the 500-ft.
barrels of which were then being brought up through
Belgium.) If the secret weapon started up before the
invasion and the R.A.F. could not destroy the blockhouses, London would be destroyed and it was likely
that the invasion would also be wrecked.

Churchill was insisting on twice-daily Intelligence reports. Some reports put the weight of the secret-weapon warhead as high as 10 tons of explosive and suggested they might fall at a rate of thousands a week.
Churchill ordered the preparation of plans for the evacuation of London and told Sir Arthur Harris that the
blockhouses were to be destroyed without fail before
they were ready for action.

Wallis's "tallboy" was the only weapon Harris knew
of that might smash them, but the "tallboys" would not
be ready for some time. They would have to be dropped
from at least 18,000 feet to get enough speed for pene-

tration, and only one squadron could drop them accurately enough. But the sites would be so well camouflaged in the bomb-pocked earth that a bomb aimer would have trouble getting them in his bomb sight from 18,000 feet even by day. Though the sites were fairly plastered with flak, they would have to be marked clearly and with unprecedented accuracy because there would be no "tallboys" to waste. It was a pretty problem, and Harris called the Pathfinder chief, Bennett, and Cochrane and Cheshire to a conference at his headquarters.

Bennett said frankly that the Pathfinders were not equipped to mark with such accuracy, and Cochrane suggested that 617 might be able to do the marking as well as the bombing.

Cheshire said: "I doubt if it could be marked accurately at medium level. You'd have to run-up straight and level, and at that height the searchlights would blind you so you couldn't see the target, and the flak would pretty surely get you anyway. I should think, sir, we could mark it at very low level in a diving attack."

Cochrane said warningly, "Not in a Lancaster."

"No, sir. In a Mosquito, as we discussed before. She's so fast we could be in and out before the defences could nail us."

Bennett said, "I don't think you'd find the Mosquito fast enough to dodge the defences . . . you'll have enormous casualties."

Cheshire held stubbornly to his own viewpoint and added, "In any case, sir, I can't see that there is any other way."

The conference was virtually stalemated. Harris said grimly, "Well, the job's got to be done. If P.F.F. aren't equipped for it, how about your boys, Cochrane?"

Cochrane accepted the challenge. "We'll get down to it, sir," he promised.

A day later Cochrane phoned Cheshire: "I've got two Mosquitoes for you. They're over at Colby Grange. Go and learn to fly them and be quick about it. Let me know as soon as you're ready to use them."

Cheshire was delighted with the Mosquitoes, and within two days felt at home in them. The only possible fault he could find was that, carrying a load of heavy markers, their range might be a little short for some of the more distant targets. Munich, for instance, would be barely within range, so he asked Group to get him some long-range drop tanks as soon as possible.

A gratifying indication that their bombing success was spreading to the outside world came when the two American Air Force generals, Spaatz and Doolittle, flew over to Woodhall to inspect them and inquire about the marking technique. Cheshire explained it with pride, and Spaatz wanted to know if there was any particular problem they had not solved yet.

"Well," said Cheshire, straight-faced, "there is still one problem actually, and that's to find some way of de-calibrating the bomb sights, because the damn bomb aimers are lobbing all their bombs in the same hole."

"Oh, is that so?" Spaatz said with a fierce grin. "Well, how's about you and us having a bombing contest, and we'll show you how to land a bomb in a pickle barrel?"

Cheshire accepted the challenge eagerly, but it never came off because there were sterner things to do, which was a pity because it would have settled a lot of arguments. 617 was confident of the result, and probably with justification. With the S.A.B.S., the direction of Cochrane and the skill of Cheshire and Martin, they were showing that bombing—and night bombing at that—could be confined almost completely to military targets and that there need be no slaughter of the innocents. 617 were entitled to feel proud of themselves. Morale had climbed far above the grimness of the "suicide" days, and in the past months they had flown 149 sorties and dropped 473 tons of bombs without, as far as they knew, hurting any civilians.

Significant peaks are seldom seen through the smoke

of battle; it is only when time moves the beholder to a
clearer perspective that the peaks stand out. No one on
617 at this time realised that they were already a workshop of tradition. Still only a fledgling squadron,
they had a spirit probably unequalled by any other unit.
Achievement lay behind them already; that was one
reason, but only a part of it. More subtle factors in-
voked the rest.

First, the aircrews were volunteers. They were where
they wanted to be; not square pegs in round holes. They
could leave whenever they wanted to, and none of
them ever wanted to. They had pride in their special
competence and purpose and were honoured for it.

Secondly, there was Cochrane, dedicated to his job.
His lively little personal assistant, Carol Durrant, deftly
warded off all distractions from him and left him free
to concentrate on his precise work. Having carefully
chosen his squadron commander, he briefed and guided
him and then shrewdly left him to choose his own team
and run it.

Cheshire had the perception to recognise the peculiar character of a bomber squadron. The Air Force is
the only fighting service where one section of the same
unit does the most dangerous job of the war and the
other the safest. With an expectation of death far higher
than the Navy or Army, the aircrews had to face action
day after day, week after week, virtually alone, with
only their consciences as monitors. The ground crews,
on the other hand, were liable to frustrations which
could only be soothed if they could be assured of
their value, and Cheshire delicately gave them those
assurances.

When he landed in the early morning after a raid
his driver usually found him under the wing sharing
cocoa and sandwiches with his ground crew. As anxiously as they asked him how he had got on he would
be asking them if they had managed to get any sleep
while he was away, or thanking them for the performance of the aircraft, all with a friendly touch and a
few jokes thrown in.

With flying or ground crew he was a leader and never a driver, never bullying, overbearing or petty, though his tongue could be quietly devastating if you merited it. His aircrews almost worshipped him, and the ground crews' feelings were probably deeper because he treated them with warm consideration, and they were not used to it.

Incompetence was never tolerated on the squadron but high spirits were, and the result was what Cochrane had aimed at: a unit of functional quality. He had long thought that one good performer was worth ten bad ones, and with 617 he proved it. The intriguing thing was that, so long as they were completely efficient, the rather punctilious Cochrane never unduly interfered with their somewhat spirited attitude towards life, and so in the intrinsic lunacy of war they found a purposeful comradeship.

Signs of their growing prestige were not lacking. March brought them nine more decorations; popular ones. Among them were a bar for Martin's D.S.O., a second bar for Cheshire's D.S.O., a bar for Whittaker's D.F.C., and the D.F.C. to add to Foxlee's D.F.M.

Cheshire flew down to Weybridge to see Wallis about tactics for dropping the "tallboys."

"I haven't really designed this thing for concrete," Wallis said, "so I think, my dear boy, it might not be a good thing to drop them right on the roofs of those wretched concrete affairs; they might bounce out again like corks. However, you needn't worry; just drop them down at the side in the earth and they'll bore down and blow them up from underneath." He stuck pins in a diagram to show the vulnerable points and added disapprovingly, "The Germans are very silly not to put twenty feet of concrete *under* these things, not on top."

Cheshire suggested as tactfully as he could that, though he had enormous faith in his squadron, it was one thing to stick pins in a diagram and another to drop a bomb in that spot from 20,000 feet.

"Oh well," Wallis said huffily, "if I'd known you propose to scatter the bombs around the countryside like grass seed I'd never have bothered to design them."

14

THE UNAPPEASING OF MUNICH

On April 4 Cheshire reported to Cochrane that he was ready with the Mosquito. Cochrane rang Harris and asked permission for his whole group to operate by themselves, led by 617 to mark the target, which was to be a large aircraft factory just outside Toulouse. Harris agreed, and next night they took off.

Cheshire found his Mosquito handled delightfully. A flare force lit up the factory and Cheshire dived fast and low over it, but, not satisfied with his positioning, pulled up sharply without dropping his markers. Heavy flak opened up on him as he corkscrewed away. He would almost certainly have been hit in a Lancaster, but the shells did not even scratch the Mosquito's paint. He dived again, once more was not satisfied and pulled up in a hail of shells. The third time his markers fell in the centre of the buildings, and again he climbed steeply away, unscathed. At 10,000 feet the squadrons moved in. Munro put an 8,000-pounder right on the markers and the rest of the bombs slathered the spot.

In the morning a recce aircraft found the factory flattened and only an occasional crater in the fields beyond.

Four days later 617 continued the experiment, going alone, led by Cheshire in the Mosquito, to attack the biggest German air park and signals depot in France, at St. Cyr, some two miles west of Versailles. Cheshire put his nose nearly straight down from 5,000 feet, let his markers go from 700, and they lobbed on the western corner of the target. He ordered the bombers in and soon rolling coils of smoke hid the target.

Cheshire landed as dawn was breaking and found Cochrane in the de-briefing room; he had been waiting up all night to see how the raid went and took Cheshire aside.

"That's the end of the experiment, Cheshire. I'm satisfied you can do it low in Mosquitoes now, and we're going to start thinking of the big targets. I'm getting you four new Mosquitoes. Train three or four picked pilots to use them and be quick about it."

The four Mosquitoes arrived that afternoon, and in the next six days McCarthy, Shannon, Kearns and Fawke spent their waking hours flying them. They were to fly Mosquitoes exclusively from now on and their crews were split up. Shannon kept the tough Sumpter as his navigator. Danny Walker stayed as squadron navigation officer, Goodale went off for a well-deserved rest, and Buckley joined another crew. The lanky and good-natured Concave had won a D.F.C. and bar as a wireless operator, which is not far short of a miracle, because decorations for good work by a crew usually went first to the pilot, then to the navigator and bomb aimer. Or to a gunner who shot enemy aircraft down, or an engineer who had a chance to keep battered engines going in the air. A wireless operator had little chance.

Decorations were a vexed question because there was no way of equitable distribution. Cheshire had strong views on the subject; as usual, unorthodox views but extraordinarily perceptive. Generally he divided courageous aircrews into two categories: (a) men with acute imagination who realised they would probably die and who forced themselves to go on, and (b) men who, though intelligent, could shut their minds off from imagination and carry on without acute forebodings of the future. Cheshire puts himself in the second group and, typically, regards the first group as the braver men.

"That's the highest form of courage," he said once.

"They have a hell of a time but keep going. Usually they're not the spectacular types and they don't win the flash awards, but they're the bravest.

"Actually, as far as I could, I tried to get men of the second type, like me. Not thinkers. We didn't have the hard inward struggle and weren't in danger of being deflected by imagination."

The peculiar thing is that Cheshire *is* a thinker, a highly imaginative one, but with that queer capacity for ignoring the probabilities of personal catastrophe. I don't believe it is escapism either, because he is too coldly perceptive and introspective for that. He examines himself so closely that he would realise in a second if he were trying to delude himself. There is something deeper in it, some sort of fatalism. Most aircrew men had a mental defence mechanism that led them to believe, "This can't happen to me," even when they knew it *could* and probably would. Cheshire must have had some of that. Somewhat baffled, I have tried to classify him as a practical mystic, whatever that means.

He told me once: "Decorations are not particularly a test of courage but a test of success. There aren't many awards for failure; a few, but not many, no matter what bravery was shown."

It is not a bad comment from a man with his decorations. There is a clash in Cheshire between self-conscious ego and honesty, and the honesty is the stronger.

On April 18 Cheshire reported to Cochrane that the Mosquito crews were all ready, and that night 617 marked for 6 Group against Juvisy marshalling yards, eleven miles south of Paris.

Munro's flares lit the area beautifully; Cheshire, Fawke, Shannon and Kearns dived to 400 feet and lobbed their spot fires into the middle of the web of rails, though one bounced outside. It all went like clockwork. 617 bombed the spot fires accurately, as usual, and then the rest of 5 Group, 200 Lancasters, surged in and excelled themselves. They were used only to area bombing and not precision bombing, but this time, with the bright aiming points of the markers, they put nearly all their bombs in the target area. Some fell outside on the marker that bounced but morning reconnaissance showed the ragged end of rails in acres of erupted earth where a thousand craters overlapped each other. (It was eighteen months after the war before the yard was again in action.)

From the spot fire that bounced, Cheshire learned the importance of releasing the markers before the Mosquitoes started to flatten out of the dive, and that was another step towards perfection of the technique.

Next night they led 5 Group to the other important Paris marshalling yards, La Chapelle, a very ticklish target because these yards lay just outside the Gare du Nord and were fringed by high tenement buildings. Light and heavy flak hosed up at them, but the Mosquitoes plunged through it and laid all their spot fires except one in the centre of the rails; the one that missed fell on the tenements. The bombing that followed was as accurate as ever, but inevitably some of the bombs fell on the inaccurate marker and the whole tenement buildings were flattened. (For a year Cochrane worried about the French people who he thought must have died in them, until he discovered that the tenements had been occupied by a regiment of the Luftwaffe.)

Once again 617 lost no aircraft and the Mosquitoes did not have a single hole among them. To Cheshire and Cochrane—and to Harris too—it was further confirmation of their ideas.

Cochrane flew to Woodhall that morning after the raid, saw Cheshire privately in Cheshire's office and, as usual, wasted no words:

"Now you can have a crack at Germany. To-morrow you're going to Brunswick. . . . One Group as well as Five Group, so you'll be leading about four hundred aircraft. Pathfinders will drop flares and you'll mark with red spots."

There was one alternative, he said. If cloud hid the target, special radar Pathfinders would mark "blind" with green spots instead.

The first P.F.F. flares went down over Brunswick, but Cheshire could see no target (rail yards) by their light. More flares went down seven miles north, and over that spot Kearns and Fawke saw the target and dropped their red spots "on the button." Cheshire gave the order to bomb, and the first bombs were just exploding when the reserve radar Pathfinders ran into cloud nearby and dropped their green spots on fields three miles away. Most of the main force, according to orders, turned for them.

Cheshire called till he was blue in the face, but the radio was jammed and only a few aircraft picked up his message. Nearly all the bombs fell on the wrong markers out in the fields.

After they landed back at Woodhall, Cochrane flew over in his Proctor and Cheshire started apologising for the mix-up. Cochrane cut in:

"All right, Cheshire. Don't you worry about that. You did your part perfectly. We've learned a bit more from it and we'll see the trouble doesn't happen again. How do you feel about Munich?"

"As soon as you like, sir. We're ready."

"I've been on to Air Chief Marshal Harris. If the weather is all right you're going to-morrow night, leading the whole group again. You'll go for the rail yards."

Together they planned it, and this time it looked as though it could not miss. Bomber Command was to raid Karlsruhe half an hour before to draw the fighters. 617 was to lead 5 Group towards Switzerland as a feint; six Lancasters were to swerve south towards Milan dropping bundles of "window" (thin strips of metal foil) to delude German radar into thinking 5 Group was heading for Italy. Just before the Group reached Munich, radar Pathfinders were to drop flares, and Cheshire and the Mosquitoes were to mark, the rest of 617 were to drop more markers from medium level with the S.A.B.S. in case the early markers were blown out, and then the 200 Lancasters were to bomb.

One point worried Cheshire. "Munich is about as far as a Mosquito can get without overload tanks," he said. "I've asked for them but they haven't come yet. We're not going to have enough margin for bad winds or upset timing without them."

"Give Group a sharp nudge about them," Cochrane said. "I'm going down to the C.-in-C. with the plan."

Cheshire phoned Group, and they said they would do all they could. He phoned them again next morning and was dismayed when they told him the tanks were in acutely short supply and other Mosquito units had priorities. It seemed that one or two people still tended to regard 617's Mosquitoes as an unorthodox and slightly reprehensible novelty.

Cheshire got hold of Pat Kelly, his navigator, and they worked out a new plan for the Mosquitoes: to fly first to Manston, in Kent, a hundred miles nearer the target, pour in all the petrol they could and fly straight to Munich across all the defences. Kelly plotted the distance, worked out their range from Manston and looked up grimly.

"If everything goes dead to time—which I've seldom seen—and if the winds are all in our favour—which I've never seen—we might just get back, but probably won't."

Cheshire went to a high officer at base and explained respectfully that, even taking off from Manston, he doubted if the four marking Mosquitoes would get back. It was usual to have a couple of hours' petrol in reserve—at least—to allow for contingencies. With the very best conditions they might arrive back with a few minutes' petrol. Personally he had never had to fly on a raid in such conditions. Nor did he know anyone who did. What should he do?

The answer was not inspiring.

"If you can't do this marking in Mosquitoes," the high officer said, "you'll have to do it in a Lancaster. Whatever you do the raid has to go on."

Cheshire said, "Yes, sir."

He went back and collected the four Mosquito crews. They got a preliminary Met. report: heavy cloud—possible ice cloud—over the western half of

Germany; perhaps clear over Munich. At 14,000 feet the winds might be reasonably favourable. The four navigators bent over their calculations and looked up grimly.

Kelly said, "If everything goes perfectly we might get back to Manston." They all knew that a raid rarely went perfectly.

One of them exploded: "Hell, sir, we don't mind sticking our necks out over the defences. That's just part of the job, but we can't see any point in such a bloody unnecessary risk. What sort of fools are we supposed to be?"

Cheshire said, "I'm sorry, but we've got to go." There was a brief silence and one of them said, "All right."

The four Mosquitoes flew down to Manston and were refuelled and parked at take-off point so they would waste no fuel taxi-ing. Sitting silently over dinner with the others, Cheshire got a phone call from Cochrane.

"I'm deeply sorry about the overload tanks," Cochrane said. "Can you make it?"

"We'll have a go, sir. I think it will be all right."

"I just want to let you know," Cochrane said, "I've had a word with the C.-in-C. When you get back he's giving the whole squadron a week's leave."

Cheshire went and told the others, and Kelly said acidly, "Fat lot of good that's going to do *us*." Cheshire had never seen them like that. They seemed almost on the verge of mutiny, not because they were too scared (they were scared all right, but so is nearly every airman before a raid), but this time it *was* unnecessary.

Around dusk Cheshire said, "Well, let's get it over." They walked out silently; it was clear over England, the sun dipping under the horizon and the sky above flaming orange. Cheshire said, "What a glorious sunset!" From the others a sullen silence, and then Shannon, without even lifting his eyes towards the west, said, "Damn the sunset. I'm only interested in the sun*rise*."

They took off without warming up, climbed straight

on course to 14,000 feet and over the North Sea ran into heavy cloud.

They were coming up to the Rhine. Or hoped they were. Cloud lay on the earth like a deep, drifting ocean, rolling up unbroken to 17,000 feet, and in the hooded glow of the cockpits each pilot found comfort in the dim shape of his navigator beside him, feeling they were outcasts sealed in a small world. Beyond the numbing thunder of engines lay nothing but blackness and they only sensed that somewhere in a few square miles of sky they were together, unseen. Cheshire broke radio silence to ask Shannon how he was finding the weather and felt his scalp prickle as a voice out of the past spoke in his earphones, "Is that you, sir?" He recognised it instantly, through the static and the careful anonymity . . . Micky Martin.

He called back, "Is that you, Mick?"

"Yessir."

"Where on earth *are* you?"

"Oh, I'm around "

"What the hell are you doing?"

"Sticking my neck out for you types."

(Martin was a hundred miles away in another Mosquito, a night fighter, his job being to "beat up" German night-fighter fields, encouraging the fighters to stay on the ground while the bombers plastered Karlsruhe and Munich; another part of Cochrane's planning.)

One wastes no time in radio chatter over enemy soil. Plotting stations need few seconds for a "fix." Cheshire said, "Good luck to you, Mick," and Martin answered laconically, "Good luck to you too. Be seeing you."

The other Mosquitoes heard it and flew on a little more cheerfully. It seemed an omen somehow, but whether for good or bad they were not quite sure.

Apparently it was for good! The clouds thinned, winds stayed kind and exactly on zero hour they came out over Munich. No mistaking it; the flare force had arrived and massed guns were vomiting upwards. At

14,000 feet the flashes of bursts split the night and lines of red balls were marching up from the lighter guns. There must have been a hundred searchlights; pale fingers probing the dark, lighting now and then on aircraft which glinted like ants and turned to burrow into the crevices of the night. Mostly they vanished, but one was caught in a second beam, and a third. They saw it coned and held as it dived and turned and climbed, a trapped little ant. The flak hunted it; in the glare they saw the brighter flashes all round and then the ribbon of flame as the Lancaster dived again; this time the nose never lifted.

A flare abruptly glowed in the darkness, then another, a third—five . . . one by one they lit till thirty hung flaming in the sky over the naked city, so that Cheshire recognised from the photographs the kidney-shaped park, the long lake, drilled streets of pygmy houses and the lined acres of the rail yards. He shouted over the R/T, "Marker Leader going in" and peeled off from 10,000 feet, holding the nose down till the little Mosquito was moving into the flak faster than she had ever travelled. Sliding past 5,000 feet he lined her up on the rail yards, focused his mind on them, still aware in a curiously detached way of shells, balloon cables and searchlight dazzle, hoped he would miss them and coldly shut his mind to them. The little plane was shivering with the headlong surge and the busy fury of the engines; Cheshire barely heard the screaming noise: she was twisting in the rising speed against the trim and he was coaxing her to arrow dead straight in the dive, forcing himself to wait for the dragging seconds till he suddenly jabbed the bomb button and eased back on the stick. He felt her lifting out instantly, the mounting "g" ramming him hard down into his seat, a phantom load dragging at his lips, his cheeks, his eyeballs and his blood, heavier and heavier, till his vision was greying out as the Mosquito flattened low over the roof-tops, curved up and climbed nimbly away. He let her lift into the darkness over the flares before he rolled her out on one wing, looked

over the side and saw his markers, two red eyes glowing in the rail yards.

Shannon dived in the same way and put his markers
within a hundred yards of Cheshire's. Kearns did likewise. Cheshire called the 617 Lancasters, told them to
back up, and minutes later their clusters of incendiaries
splashed into brightness on the rail yards.

It was the spearhead that Bomber Command had
never had over Munich; even the giant flashes from the
8,000-pounders and the coils of smoke soon rolling
over the rail yards did not hide the pin-points of the
markers, and the bomb aimers made the most of it.

The destruction was not all on one side. Cheshire
several times saw the trails of flame, like shooting stars,
streaking for the ground and the explosions when they
hit. It was the flak that caused most of them. Nearly all
the fighters had been sent to Karlsruhe or down to
Milan, and few had enough petrol to fly back to
Munich.

Petrol shortage or not, Cheshire flew full throttle
round and round the inner city at 1,000 feet, checking
the accuracy and ready to call up with new instructions if the bombing looked like moving off the target
area. The gunners below could hear him and the
searchlights and flak chased him, but the Mosquito
was too fleet. Once a beam held him for a second and
destroyed his night vision, but he was too fast to hold
low down and passed into darkness again. Light flak
exploded around him; he heard the crack of the shells
and the aircraft shook from near misses. A dozen
lumps of shrapnel gashed it and hit the engines but
hurt no vital spot.

Satisfied he could do no more he turned for home;
the other Mosquitoes were already on their way. It
was not a happy trip back; no flak or fighters to speak
of, but Kelly doing intricate petrol calculations, thumb-
ing the fuel gauge, plotting his track and e.t.a., and
trying to look philosophical. It seemed the longest
trip they had ever made, and then they came in over
Manston with ten minutes' petrol on the gauges. Some

gauges on low tanks are as reliable as a woman's intuition. They might have petrol for ten minutes, or fifteen minutes, or ten seconds, and were going to need at least five minutes for approach, circuit and landing.

Throttled right back in coarse pitch, Cheshire flicked his navigation lights on and dipped his nose towards the long runway, where the flarepath shone like a stolid but comforting guard of honour. Kelly said: "What's wrong with their runway? Look at those funny lights down there." Cheshire looked . . . puzzled. There *were* lights blinking in and out of the flarepath. "Funny," he said. It hit him suddenly and he shouted to Kelly, "Turn those bloody navigation lights off. It's a Jerry fighter."

The target, they found out later, was Gerry Fawke, just settling down on the runway. The fighter had stalked him round the circuit and gone for the kill when Fawke had his flaps, undercart and speed right down and was helpless, unable to turn sharply—unless he wanted to stall and spin in. Luck, it seemed, stayed with 617 that night. The German fighter, with a "sitter" in front of his guns, missed completely. Fawke rolled to a stop and the flarepath flicked off. Cheshire made a careful approach, took a quick sight at the last moment with his landing lights and set his aircraft down safely. In the briefing room he found the other Mosquito crews. None had got down with more than fifteen minutes' petrol to spare (a terrifyingly small margin).

Shannon said, "Wake me at sunrise. I want to see it."

Back at Woodhall later in the morning, they found the 617 Lancasters all back except Cooper. No one ever found out where Cooper went down. Cochrane flew over, showing what was, for him, extravagant delight, a wide but faintly embarrassed smile, as he congratulated and thanked them. He said to Cheshire, "You might like to look at this." It was an aerial photograph of Munich, brought back by recce Mosquito an hour earlier. Round a couple of scars on the outskirts were circles of ink, and Cochrane tapped the spots with his finger. "That's how it was up to yesterday afternoon after all the other raids." He put his finger on the cratered rail yards. "Last night," Cochrane said. "It seems to justify us."

The photograph staggered even Cheshire, who knew what the bombing had been like. There must have been a hundred times more damage in that one raid than the dozen previous ones, especially as the previous damage had been on no significant target. This time they had struck an effective blow.

It proved Cheshire's contention that he could mark a heavily defended target at low level without undue risk, but the photograph also showed that one solitary marker from the high force had fallen outside the target area and drawn some of the bombs, so that a lot of houses were either gutted shells or mounds of rubble. Unfortunate though that was, it led to further improvement in the marking technique. Cochrane and Cheshire had both thought it too dangerous to rely on one marker only since it might be obscured by smoke or hit by a bomb. Now they realised that dropping too many markers could also be risky, and thereafter they tended to cut the number of markers down to try and eliminate such accidents as the one stray marker at Munich.

Many ordinary people probably died in those crumbled houses, and the post-war domestic moralists, whose virtue increases as the memories of Nazism recede, are likely to point the accusing finger. Most will probably keep pointing it until, Heaven help us, another war starts and their virtue will become tempered by the slightly more powerful instinct of self-survival. A few will continue to point the finger with wistful idealism until one day, perhaps, morals and the practical affairs of man become compatible.

On the strength of Munich, Cochrane drove down to see Harris and asked for four extra Mosquitoes so that another of his squadrons could learn the 617 way of target marking.

Harris, who never did things by halves, said, "Not four Mosquitoes, Cocky"; and almost before Cochrane could feel his disappointment Harris went on, "I'm sending you a squadron of Mosquitoes from Pathfinders and two Pathfinder Lancaster squadrons. You can operate as a group by yourselves now. Get 617 to teach the new Mosquitoes low marking, and then they can mark for your group, with the two Lanc. squadrons as flare force. That'll release 617 for some special jobs."

15

EARTHQUAKE BOMB

Cochrane sent for Cheshire and took him walking in the grounds of headquarters away from listening ears.

"You'll be doing no more operations for a month," he said, "and then you'll be doing a very special one. You'll spend the next month training for it. I warn you now it's going to be dull training, but it may be the most important job you've done. You will have to fly more accurately and carefully than you've ever imagined."

He would say no more, but next day a scientist, Dr. Cockburn, arrived at Woodhall from London and also took Cheshire walking. They lay alone on the grass by the airfield, obviously for privacy, and the imaginative Cheshire was highly intrigued by the "cloak and dagger" atmosphere. Cockburn said: "I understand you can be trusted to keep your mouth shut, so I'm going to tell you something a lot of Cabinet Ministers and generals don't know yet. You know by now an invasion is coming off very soon. If the weather is right it will be in about a month, and landings will be made west of Le Havre. We want to fool the Germans we're going in somewhere else."

Cheshire waited.

"On that night," Cockburn went on, "there's going to be a big convoy fourteen miles wide passing across the Channel at seven knots."

"Sounds a pretty big invasion," Cheshire said.

"That isn't the invasion. They'll be heading towards Cap d'Antifer, on the other side of Le Havre."

"A diversion!"

"Yes."

"I must say," Cheshire said, "it sounds a pretty big diversion. Have they got all those ships to spare?"

"No. They won't be ships. They'll be you and your boys."

Cheshire rolled over and looked at him. "Us!" he said blankly and then got the glimmerings of an idea. "Dropping window?"

"That's it," said Cockburn. "It's going to need the most precise flying you've ever done. Can you do this ... can you all fly in a very wide formation, invisible to each other, and do a lot of intricate manoeuvring, keeping within three seconds of all your e.t.a.s and within twenty feet of your height?"

"My God! I don't know. Doesn't sound very possible."

"It'll have to go on for hours and hours," Cockburn said, "so you'll do it in two waves. Eight aircraft for a few hours and then the second eight taking over from them." He went on to explain the technique: lines of aircraft a set distance apart, flying precise courses at precise speeds and height, throwing out window at intervals of a precise number of seconds. The planes would fly thirty-five seconds on course, turn evenly, fly a reverse course for thirty-two seconds, a slow turn again back to the first course and start throwing out more window. They would thus start the original course again at a point slightly ahead of where the previous one started and the first of the new lot of window would drop from the aircraft at the moment that the first bundle dropped on the previous leg hit the water, so there would be no interruption of the steady blips on German radar. It would go on like that for eight hours, timed to give an effect of a large convoy several rows of ships deep moving at seven knots towards the French coast.

"We've got the theory worked out," Cockburn said at the end. "Are you good enough to do it?"

Cheshire said, "I think my crews are good enough for anything, but I don't think they're going to be happy doing a stooge job on invasion night."

"It so happens," Cockburn said, "that there'll be no

flying job more important than this on that night. You might tell them that. The fact that they may not be fired at is beside the point."

The training never let up except for one day when the weather closed in. Otherwise there was no moment, night or day, in the next month when some 617 aircraft were not flying, particularly by night, cruising at a steady 200 m.p.h. on a steady course and height, curving in even turns to reverse courses, turning back on the stop watch, unspectacular, tedious and demanding meticulous care and skill. Understandably the crews, with the uninhibited sap of youth running in them, became restless, and Cheshire, bubbling as ever with ideas, evolved schemes to occupy them. The first was a route march that left them limp and protesting.

Next, from the Commandos, he got the idea of an escape exercise so that, if they were ever shot down and got away with their lives, they would have a few clues about getting back through hostile territory. It was a Sunday afternoon when he lined up all the crews who were not flying, took away their hats and all their money, packed them in covered vans so they could not see outside and drove them to different spots twenty miles from the airfield. He warned them that the Home Guard and police had turned out with orders to nab any airmen without hats, and promised every one who got back safely a bottle of beer. So the game started.

Some cut across the fields to walk, some stole bikes to pedal, some hitched lifts in lorries. The police and Home Guard nailed at least half of them and there were some thrilling chases across country. One man, running from the Home Guard, fell into a canal; another, caught by a policeman, entered a little too warmly into the spirit of the thing and laid the constable out with a sizzling punch. After that the police entered more warmly into the spirit of things too, and locked six of them up for the night.

Nicky Knilans and his team had the best idea; they hitched a lift to the White Horse pub, where they were known to the point of affectionate notoriety, borrowed money from the publican and drank ale till

closing time, whereupon they borrowed their bus fare
home. Police stopped the bus, so they jumped off the
back, took to the woods and straggled home hours
later to demand their prize beer.

With only monotonous training instead of ops. at
night the tension had relaxed and the mess became
almost a home from home. Cheshire's ex-film-star wife,
Constance Binney, was a cheerful influence; she played
the piano beautifully, and after dinner the crews clus-
tered round and sang.

Several dogs haunted the mess, and one Scottie used
to jump out from dark doorways and snap at passing
ankles. It became a favourite trick among the boys to
imitate the Scottie. Nicky Knilans saw McCarthy coming up the stairs one day, so he got down on his knees
in a dark doorway and waited. He heard the footsteps
clumping along the hall and as the legs appeared leapt
out with a growl and grabbed the nearest ankle in his
teeth, looked up with a grin . . . and the grin faded.
McCarthy had turned off into a room and Knilans saw
a strange wing commander looking down at him blankly. The wing commander shook his head and walked
on, all his views on Americans fully confirmed.

They all sensed the invasion was drawing near;
Cheshire had the idea that the Germans might drop
paratroops on British airfields on D-Day, so he per-
suaded Doc Watson's armament section to issue as
many aircrew as they could with either a revolver,
Sten gun, rifle or hand grenade. It was one of his few
sad mistakes. For three days life was a precarious possession at Woodhall. First they set dinner plates up on
the lawn near the mess and loosed off at them with
Sten guns from the second-floor windows. That palled
after a while, so they started lobbing hand grenades in
the general direction of the sergeants' mess. At night
time Buckley became a terrible menace, keeping a vigil
by his bedroom window and loosing off clips from his
Sten gun over the heads of late home-comers so that
they had to crawl to bed over the back lawn on their
bellies.

Sten Gun

Even Witherick, who was known to be too durable for death by any of the known methods of war, commented uncomfortably, "Hell, the only time you're safe on this damn squadron is when you're in the air!" It became obvious that German paratroops were less of a menace than the local aircrew army, so Cheshire collected all the weapons and returned them to the armoury. Peace descended once more on the mess, to the regret of Shannon and McCarthy. Shannon and McCarthy were rarely seen apart; they drank together and dined together and it was logical, therefore, that they should act together to revive the reign of terror, climbing to the roof of squadron headquarters to drop a Véry cartridge down the adjutant's chimney. They knew the innocent Humphries had a fire in the grate.

A Véry cartridge in artful hands is like a semi-lethal firework; exploding in a confined space it resembles a small but concentrated bombing raid, providing a monstrous crash, sheets of coloured flame and clouds of choking smoke. Half the beauty of the thing is that it goes on for about fifteen seconds. They dropped it down the chimney and started laughing as the waves of sound came rocking up from below.

Unfortunately it was not Humphries' chimney, but the commanding officer's. Cheshire scuttled out, pursued by flashes and rolling fumes, ran on to the tarmac and spotted his two flight commanders hiding behind a chimney. With aristocratic dignity he said nothing, but for several nights Shannon and McCarthy found themselves doing duty officer together, an irksome task which kept them out of their beds and abstemiously patrolling the station buildings.

Throwing Véry cartridges into the mess fire had long been a favourite sport, so Cheshire thought it time to issue a stern order that no firearms, cartridges or pyrotechnics of any kind be brought into the mess building.

He was woken that night by a scuttling outside his window, threw it wide open and saw a rat running across the roof. Quick as lightning he grabbed his own .38 revolver from his dressing-table and took a pot-shot that bowled the rat over and echoed through the quiet night like a small cannon. Cheshire was still leaning out of his window, revolver in hand, when the next window shot open and the head of Danny Walker poked out. "Got the dirty rat that time," Cheshire said triumphantly and became conscious of Walker's eyes staring coldly, focusing on the hand that held the gun. He felt his face going red and ducked inside, laying the pistol down, and heard Walker's voice next door, talking loudly to a mythical roommate, "But I tell you, old boy, I distinctly heard the man say that *no* one under *any* circumstances was to have a firearm inside the mess."

On June 1 Avro experts fitted new automatic pilots in the Lancasters for the D-Day operation, and Nicky Knilans at last found out why his much-cursed "R Roger" flew like a lump of lead. They found it needed longer elevator cables than the others, inspected to find out why and discovered that the elevators had been put on upside down at the factory.

Knilans had been flying it for months like that and, as Cheshire said, "Only you and God, Nicky, know how you stayed up."

"Not me, sirrrr," Knilans said in his American drawl ... "Only God. I didn't know."

At any rate he was very relieved, but not so much as his crew. "R Roger" had so often frightened them.

On June 5 everyone was confined to camp, and at dusk, with guards on the doors of the briefing room, Cheshire told the crews that the invasion was about to start. The first wave of eight planes took off about 11 p.m. with twelve men in each aircraft, an extra pilot, extra navigator and three men to drop the bundles of window out.

They made absolutely no mistakes that night, though it would have taken an error of only four seconds in timing to make the convoy suspiciously change position on the German radar. Hour after hour they flew in the blackness over the Channel, turning on stopwatches up and down on reversed courses while the window was tossed out at four-second intervals. Round 3 a.m. the second wave of eight aircraft took over, the trickiest part of all because they had to come in directly behind with split-second timing to carry on. They saw nothing of the invasion.

They were to break away just before dawn, before the light was good enough for the Germans to see from the shore that they had been tricked. By that time they should be within seven miles of the French coast, and that is exactly where they were. Farther north another squadron was doing a similar task with at least as much success.

They had their reward as they turned for home; the German coastal batteries opened up . . . not the flak but the big guns, aiming 12-inch shells by radar prediction at the ghost armada. German E-boats came out from Calais and Boulogne but they would have needed aerial torpedoes to do any damage.

It is history now that the Germans really thought the main invasion was aiming at that area. (In prison camp in the heart of Germany that day, I heard the German radio announcing two huge armadas heading in towards Cap d'Antifer and Calais. It gave us great joy, but we wondered for months what had happened to those convoys.)

Inland from Boulogne and Dieppe the bulk of the

German Army, which should have been hurrying to the
real invasion area on the other side of Le Havre,
waited . . . and waited, poised to swoop on the armadas that were not there. By the time the Germans
woke up to it other squadrons had blasted bridges over
the Seine between them and the invasion and the Allied troops were consolidating their landings with greater freedom from counter-attack than they had dreamed
possible.

Cheshire was driving round the perimeter track with
Munro that evening for no particular reason that he
can remember, and just past the A Flight hardstand-
ings they passed a huge tarpaulin-covered lorry cruising slowly along.

"What's that doing here?" Munro murmured, not
very curiously, and Cheshire, his head still full of D-
Day precautions, said, "Lord knows. Let's find out."

They drove across the lorry's bows; it stopped and
they climbed out of their jeep and went back to the
lorry driver. "What have you got in there?" Cheshire
asked.

"Boilers for the cookhouse, sir," the driver said.

"Aren't you going the wrong way? The cookhouse is
over there." Cheshire waved a hand to the rear.

"Well, I dunno, sir. They told me to deliver them
over there." The driver pointed to the far side of the
field.

"The bomb dump! That's the bomb dump. Who told
you that?" A suspicious edge had crept into Cheshire's
voice.

"That's what they told me, sir."

Cheshire said, "Let's have a look at this, Les.
Something funny here." He heaved himself over the
tailboard of the lorry. Another tarpaulin covered a
shapeless bulk in the back; he tugged a corner clear and,
unbidden, a grunt of surprise came out of him. "My
God," he said, "look at these!"

Lashed to the floor were two shining steel monsters.
They were like sharks, slim, streamlined and with sharp
noses. "Bombs," Cheshire said, almost in awe. "Wallis's 'tallboys'."

They followed the lorry to the bomb dump and were staggered to find the dump nearly full of "tallboys," snugged down under tarpaulins. An armament officer said apologetically, "They've been coming in at night time for the past week, sir. I was told to keep quiet about them."

Cheshire tore back to his office, got Cochrane at Group on the secret scrambled phone and told him he had just been inspecting "the new boilers for the cookhouse in the bomb dump." He heard what sounded like the ghost of muted amusement in Cochrane's voice:

"Just see they're safely in storage, Cheshire. You'll be using them soon."

The call came without warning forty-eight hours later. Intelligence had reported a German Panzer division moving up from Bordeaux by rail to attack the invasion. The trains would have to pass through the Saumur Tunnel, near the Loire, over a hundred miles inland, and in the late afternoon Harris suggested to Cochrane that they might have a chance of blocking the tunnel before the trains reached it. They would have to move fast; it would be nightfall before bombers could reach the spot, and a tunnel on a dark night would be an elusive pin-point of a target. Only one squadron could do it; that was obvious. And probably only one type of bomb!

Cheshire got the order about 5 p.m. to take off as soon as they could, and there was a mad rush to collect everyone (Shannon and Munro, for instance, were playing cricket at Metheringham), trolley the "tallboys" out of the dump and winch them up into the bomb bays. They were airborne soon after dusk, and it was shortly after midnight that Cheshire, in his Mosquito, dropped flares by a bend of the river and saw where the rails vanished into the tunnel that led under the Saumur hill.

He dive-bombed from 3,000 feet, aimed his red spots point blank, and as he pulled up from about a hundred feet saw them lying beautifully in the tunnel mouth. Ninety seconds later the Lancasters were steady on their bombing runs, and a couple of minutes later the first earthquake bombs ever dropped on business were streaking down.

Ten thousand feet above, the crews felt disappointed. The "tallboys" did not make a splash of brilliant light like the blockbusters but showed only momentary red pin-points as they speared into the earth and exploded nearly a hundred feet deep. The little flashes they made were all round the markers but the crews turned for home with a feeling of anticlimax, and it was not till the recce Mosquito landed next morning with photographs that the impact of what they had done hit them. With one exception the fantastic craters were round the tunnel mouth, two of them in a line along the rails as though giant bites a hundred feet across and 70 feet deep had been torn out of the track bed.

But what really staggered everyone was the bomb that had fallen on the hill 60 yards from the tunnel mouth. No one ever found out whose bomb it was, which is a pity, because some bomb aimer would have received an instant decoration (though the credit should really go to Barnes Wallis). The hill rose steeply from the tunnel mouth, and under the spot where this bomb hit lay 70 feet of solid earth and chalk down to the tunnel. The bomb had bored straight through it into the tunnel itself and exploded there. Something like 10,000 tons of earth and chalk were blown sky-high and the mountain collapsed into the tunnel. It was one of the most startling direct hits of all time.

The Panzer division did not get through. It was several days before dribs and drabs of them started to reach the invasion front on other transport, but by then it was too late for the decisive counter-attack they were supposed to have made. The morning after the raid the Germans collected all the excavation gear in the district and slaved for weeks clearing the tunnel, filling in the craters and laying new rails. They just had it nicely finished when the Allies broke out of their bridgehead and took it over. (They found then that only one "tallboy" had fallen outside the target area . . . it had exploded among a group of very old Frenchmen and blown them to smithereens, but no one else was upset, because they had been there a long time, lying several feet deep in a cemetery.)

The morning after the Saumur raid a high officer from Bomber Command burst into Sir Wilfred Freeman's office waving a recce photograph of the smashed tunnel.

"My God," he yelled, "why haven't we been able to use this incredible thing before? How many more of them have we got?"

"None for you, I'm afraid," said a Vickers' executive who happened to be in the room, and the high officer looked at him open-mouthed.

"What d'you mean?"

"Well, we've got some more, but they're all ours. None for you."

"What *are* you talking about?"

"Your boys have never given us a Requirement Order for them, so we had to make them on spec. They all belong to us."

"I see," said the High Bomber Officer. "We'll fix this Requirement Order business right away." He crossed to the desk, picked up the phone and the Requirement Order was delivered that afternoon.

In the nights that followed the invasion, German E-boats sneaking out of Le Havre caused death and destruction among the convoys ferrying men and guns over to Normandy. The darkness that covered the convoys from the Luftwaffe also hid the speeding E-boats that weaved among the landing-craft, loosed their torpedoes and vanished. By day they sheltered in the concrete pens at Le Havre, and around dusk they slid out of the pens and gathered in the harbour, preparing for the night's forays. Cochrane thought that, if the "tallboys" could make an earthquake on land, they might just as easily make a tidal wave in water. Wallis promised him they would, and so as soon as the weather cleared, on June 14, 617 flew over at dusk to Le Havre on the second "tallboy" raid. Some 400 more Lancas-

ters of 1 and 5 Groups followed them, loaded up with
1,000-lb. bombs.

Cheshire, in his Mosquito, whipped round the harbour area at 3,000 feet, saw the dozens of E-boats lined
up, and as he peeled off in a dive-bombing attack the
flak came up in streams. He'd never seen flak like it. In
the dusk it looked like green and red bubbles rising in
shaken soda-water. The air was full of rushing tracer
and he knew that that was not even the half of it . . .
only a quarter. One in four of the light flak shells
were tracer; the rest were rushing with them, but not
visible. Two miles outside the harbour the other Mosquitoes saw him diving into the beaded curtain of red
and green and thought he had no chance. At about
700 feet (as he let his markers go) they saw the nose
start to come up. The little Mosquito flattened low

German E-boat

over the water, holed half a dozen times already, and Cheshire held her straight, heading out to sea, relying on speed alone to beat the guns. A minute later he was back to 3,000 feet and out of range. On the quay, by the lines of E-boats, the red markers were winking clearly.

Shannon, deputy marker, who had seen the flak like a wall of flame, called up: "Hello, Leader, shall I go in and back up?"

Sitting beside and slightly behind him, Sumpter picked a heavy torch out of its stowage, held it over Shannon's head and muttered, "God, David, if he says yes, I'll brain you! We can die more peacefully out here."

A few seconds dragged while Cheshire looked again at his markers and called back, "No, David; they'll do," and ordered the Lancasters circling a few miles away, at 12,000 feet, to head in.

Fifteen "tallboys" dropped almost together into the water by the pens and then the 400 other Lancasters moved in and the harbour vanished under smoke.

When the recce photographs came back in the morning even Wallis was staggered. Not one E-boat was left afloat in Le Havre. Two were still visible, thrown bodily up on to the quay, and the rest were swallowed in the maelstrom of water torn apart by the "tallboys" and then by the smaller bombs. (For a time they thought that some may have slunk out of the harbour that night to a safer port, but weeks after, when the British took Le Havre, they found that none had escaped.) The crashing water had even smashed through the doors of the pens and destroyed any chance of shelter in them. In fact, three of the "tallboys" had been direct hits on the pens, bored through the concrete and wrecked the neat little quays inside.

Next night the squadron went to repeat the dose at Boulogne, also a troublesome E-boat base. Thick cloud hung over the port with heavy flak bursting through it. Cheshire marked alone (his Mosquito newly patched from last night's damage), but the crews above found it nearly impossible to draw a bead on them. About ten were able to drop their "tallboys" without being able to see results, and the remaining ten brought their bombs back. (Cochrane had made a strict order that no "tallboys" were to be wasted. Crews were never to jettison them except in extreme emergency. If they could not see their target reasonably clearly they must bring their "tallboys" back. Landing an aircraft with a 6-ton bomb on board is not as difficult as it sounds.)

We know now that in these two raids on Le Havre and Boulogne 133 small ships (mostly E-boats) were sunk. As Harris said the morning after Boulogne in his message of thanks to Cheshire and his squadron, "If the Navy had done what you have done it would have been a major naval victory."

That was the morning the V1 "buzz-bombs" started to fall on London. The V2 rockets would follow soon. . . . Intelligence was sure of that.

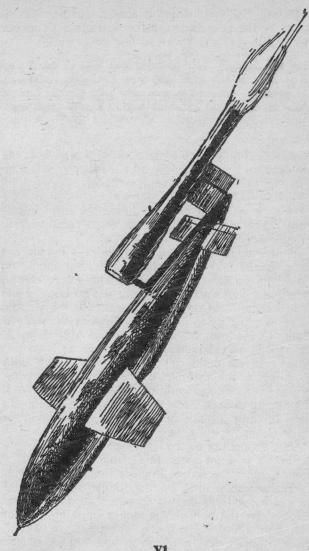

V1

16

SMASHING THE SECRET WEAPON

Cheshire had only tumbled into bed at 5 a.m. after the Boulogne raid, and was dragged out of sleep at 9 a.m. to find his batman tugging at his shoulder.

"Phone, sir."

He took up the phone and heard the Base Intelligence Officer's voice: "Can you please come over to the ops. room right away? It's urgent, sir."

He was there in ten minutes, and the intelligence officer greeted him with a few words that shook the last of the tiredness out of him: "The secret weapon has started, sir. They're landing missiles on London and the invasion ports. Don't know how serious it is yet, but you're to stand by to take off as soon as the weather clears. This is your target." He passed over an aerial photograph, an enlargement that showed an enormous square concrete building. "We don't know how thick the concrete is," the intelligence officer was saying, "but as far as we can gather from agents over there it might be up to twenty feet thick . . . roof as well as the walls. It's near a place called Watten, just behind the Pas de Calais."

Air Commodore Sharp, the base commander, bustled in. "You know about these from the A.O.C.," he said. "I gather the rest of Bomber Command is cracking at the mobile sites, but they think the worst trouble will come from these four blockhouses, and your 'tallboys' are the only things with a hope of touching them. You'll have to go in daylight to see your aiming points properly and mark them with smoke bombs. We'll give you fighter cover."

Cochrane had a word with him over the phone a little later, brief and to the point: "We've got to knock these out somehow, and we'll have to go on until we do. Whitehall is all set for the evacuation of London and we don't know yet whether these things might wreck the invasion. You'll have to work hard."

To lay on a raid, plan it, brief the crew, bomb and fuel the aircraft took at least two hours. This time it was more difficult, because the "tallboys" needed special handling, but they did it inside two hours that morning. The crews were briefed and they all went down to the flights, pulled on their flying kit and waited. Over the Pas de Calais a sheet of ten-tenths stratus stretched for miles at 2,000 feet, making it impossible to bomb. They could not have seen any aiming point from above, and they would have to bomb from at least 15,000 feet for penetration. The idea was to get near misses as much as direct hits. A direct hit might not pierce the concrete roof, but near misses would bore into the earth by the foundations and shake the structure with earthquakes. Wallis thought that a near miss up to 40 yards away would do more damage than a direct hit. The concrete monster at Watten was not the great primary source of power that Wallis had at first visualised for his earthquake bomb, but, fortuitously, it was an even more important target.

The crews stood by all day at the flights. Lorries brought food and coffee from the mess for them, and over the radio they heard the grim reports of the flying bombs falling on London. But the cloud stayed over the Pas de Calais, over Watten and the other concrete rocket sites.

At eleven o'clock they were released but no sooner had they climbed into bed than they were called up again, pulled on their clothes and rushed down to the flights. Before they had their kit on the raid was cancelled once more. Back to bed . . . and at 4 a.m. called out again. A cup of tea and down to the flights and then it was cancelled again. They went back to bed and were called at 7 a.m. Down to the flights once more. Met. thought the cloud might be clearing.

It did not clear but the crews stood by all day, lying
on the grass by the tarmac waiting for the call, but the
call never came. It went on for three days like that
till bed was only a memory. They lived down on the
flights while the low cloud lingered over France and
the buzz-bombs kept falling, ate cold food brought
from the mess and tried to sleep curled up in blankets on the floors.

The eighteen Lancasters bombed-up on the hard-
standings brought another complication. Under the load
of petrol and bombs the undercarriages began to sink.
The bombs would have to come off, at least temporar-
ily. But it would take hours to bomb up again and they
could not afford the time if the weather cleared briefly.
Cheshire had them de-bombed on a rota system so that
at any one time only two or three aircraft were without
bombs. As soon as their undercarts had been relieved
they winched the bombs up into them again and gave
temporary relief to other aircraft.

On the morning of the third day, exhausted, they
were stood down and went off to bed, and in the early
afternoon the clouds over France rolled away. From
Group came the instant call ordering a "time on target"
which gave them a bare ninety minutes to get airborne.

No one at Woodhall will easily forget that hour and
a half of mad rush. In the middle of it Cheshire was in
the ops. room settling the hundred and one final details
inseparable from a raid—time and place of fighter
rendezvous, bomber marshalling point, codes and so
on—when a young pilot officer rushed in and said that
a headquarters group captain wanted to see him immediately outside. "Ask him if he'll please excuse me
just now. I'm terribly busy," Cheshire said. The P/O
rushed outside and was back again in a few seconds.
"He says he's sorry, sir, but it's most important. You
must come."

Cheshire groaned, "What the hell's happened now?"
and dashed out, thinking it was another cancellation.

The group captain was waiting on the grass verge.
He had just arrived and had not heard about the raid.
Cheshire saluted and the group captain looked a little

severely at him. "Do you realise, Cheshire, that your
squadron is last in the Group war savings scheme?" he
said. "I'm very concerned and you've got to do something about it immediately."

Cheshire looked blankly at him.

"Yes, sir, I'll do something right away," saluted and
was running back to the ops. room before the group
captain could stop him. By some sort of miracle the
eighteen Lancasters, headed by two Mosquitoes, were
climbing away from Woodhall on the scheduled minute.

Cheshire flew over Calais at 8,000 feet and searched
the area for several minutes before he was able to pin-
point the camouflaged mass of concrete in the ground
haze. The earth for a mile around was torn up by the
fruitless bombs of other raids, so that nothing stood out
clearly. As he flew over it seventy guns opened up and
black puffs stained the air all round him. He felt reluctantly that there was only one thing to do: 10 miles
away he peeled off, held the nose steeply down and
came in straight and fast on high power, so the engines
were screaming in his ears and the plane shaking like a
live thing. He let his smoke bombs go at 2,000 feet (as
it was daylight the smoke would show more clearly
than red flares), pulled steeply out of the hail of fire,
marvellously untouched, looked back and saw no sign
of smoke. The markers had failed to ignite.

Shannon dived the other Mosquito in the same way,
and as he pulled up smoke puffed on the ground near
the target. In the haze it seemed near enough, and there
were no markers left anyway, so Cheshire called the
Lancasters and saw them wheel in at 18,000 feet, open
bomb doors and track stolidly through the flak. Fascinated, he saw the "tallboys" for the first time falling
in daylight, the sun glinting off them as they streaked
down, picking up speed till they were moving faster
than sound, and then they vanished in a wisp of dust
in the moment of impact. They had eleven-second delayed fuses and the seconds dragged till the ground
burst in the shadow of the concrete and tens of thousands of tons of earth reared up in a climbing mush-

room. Cheshire gaped, and beside him, dumbfounded, Kelly muttered, "God help the Jerries!" The target was hidden.

Recce photos later showed the bombs had circled Shannon's smoke markers, but also showed the markers had been about 70 yards wide. Some of the "tallboys" had fallen some 50 yards from the concrete target and, in the hopes that they had done the job, Cochrane sent 617 next day to Wizernes, where a huge concrete dome, 20 feet thick, lay on the edge of a chalk quarry, protecting rocket stores and launching tunnels that led out of the face of the quarry, pointing towards London.

The squadron reached the spot but found it hidden under cloud and brought their "tallboys" back. Cheshire landed with a new idea forming in his mind. If a Mosquito was better for marking than a Lancaster, then an even smaller and faster aircraft should be better still. He took his idea to Sharp, and the base commander said: "The American fighters have got the range you want. How about a Mustang or a P.38?" Cheshire said he thought that either would be ideal, and Sharp promised to try and get one through Air Ministry. He tried for the next two days but Air Ministry did not seem to be able to help, so Sharp said he would fly over to an American base himself and try "off his own bat." He had worked with the Americans before and appreciated their methods of direct action.

Meantime Cheshire took 617 to Wizernes again but once more the cloud hid it. On the 24th they tried again and this time located the camouflaged dome dimly in the ground haze. Cheshire dived through brisk flak but his smoke bombs "hung up," so Fawke dived and laid his markers on the edge of the dome and the bombs fell spectacularly round the markers. Three of them exploded next to the tunnels in the side of the quarry, one sliced deep under the edge of the dome, and Dicky Willsher, who had just had his twentieth birthday, sent one right into the mouth of one of the tunnels. The face of the quarry seemed to burst open.

The flak got Edward's plane on the run-up. A shell exploded in the port wing and the tanks caught fire. The others saw the Lancaster lose height slowly for a few seconds and then the nose dropped into a steep dive and she went over on her back. Two parachutes came out before she hit and the "tallboy" blew up. It was the first crew the squadron had lost for several weeks. Several men had been wounded in the air and a few aircraft written off, but for some weeks death had taken a holiday, the longest holiday it ever took in the squadron.

Though they were on daylight raids now the squadron did not fly close shoulder-to-shoulder formation as the Americans did. The S.A.B.S. was one reason; having to fly undeviatingly for ten miles on the run-up would make a close formation a sitting target for the flak. On the run-ups they flew what Cheshire called a "gaggle"—lines of five aircraft abreast, each 200 yards apart and each rank 300 yards behind the one ahead. Every plane flew at a different height as well, so that, while they were a most dispersed target for the flak, they could converge on the target and bomb almost together.

That had another advantage. Smoke from the first bombs had often obscured the target from later bomb aimers, but with the gaggle formation the last bombs were on the way down before the first bombs hit.

When he landed back at Woodhall, Cheshire found a Mustang waiting. Sharp's American friends had promptly said, "Sure," and an American pilot had flown one over. The pilot explained the cockpit to Cheshire, bade him a cheerful farewell and left him inspecting his new toy. It was only then he began to realise fully what he had taken on. He had never flown an American aircraft before; in fact, had not flown a single-engined aircraft since his early training days five years before. He had never flown a single-engined fighter at all, nor had he had to do his own navigation for years. The ground crews had their problems too. For a long time they could not even find where to fill the petrol tanks.

Cheshire decided that before he took it for a practice flip he would try and learn a little more about it, but those prudent hopes crashed in the morning when Cochrane ordered the squadron off for the Siracourt rocket site. They found then that the smoke markers would not fit in the racks under the Mustang's wings, and the armourers worked like furies rigging a make-shift wire contraption to hold the markers on. One of the navigators helped Cheshire work out his courses, and he wrote them on a piece of paper and strapped it to his knee. He took off in the Mustang half an hour early to get the feel of it, but did not try any practice landings; there was too much chance of breaking it on his first landing, and if he was going to do that he preferred it to be after the raid had been done.

It is unlikely that a pilot has ever before or since done an operation—particularly such a specialist one—on his first flight in a new type of plane. The change in his case from multi-engined to single-engined fighter makes the feat all the more remarkable. It bristled with difficulties. His timing had to be within thirty seconds over the target to co-ordinate with the bombers, and the Mustang cruised about 90 m.p.h. faster than the Lancasters. He could not very well work out changes of wind as well as map-read and fly. He had to be his own navigator, bomb aimer, gunner and wireless operator as well as learn to fly a new type well enough in an hour to be able to dive-bomb through thick flak.

From the start the Mustang delighted him and inside half an hour he felt he had the "feel" of it. She was lighter than the Mosquito and there was no comparison at all with a Lancaster. From 7,000 feet he spotted the concrete slab that protected the underground Siracourt rocket dump, and when the bombers reached marshalling point he dived to 500 feet, revelling in the way the Mustang picked up speed, and put his smoke bombs within a few feet of the concrete. Someone put a "tallboy" through the middle of the slab, and it pierced 16 feet of ferro-concrete before it exploded. Another hit the western wall and blew it in, and another erupted deep under the rim of the slab.

Night had fallen when they got back from Siracourt, and Cheshire's first Mustang landing had to be a night landing, which makes it about twice as difficult. He remembers little about it (in the same way that a man who bales out never remembers pulling the rip-cord) except that suddenly the little fighter was rolling smoothly on the runway, to his mild surprise and relief.

(If 617's bombing seems monotonously "dead-eye" remember that they dropped them at nearly 200 m.p.h., 18,000 feet up and several miles back from the little squares of concrete that merged with the earth and were usually unseen by the bomb aimer. From that height and distance even the white square on a bombing range looks the size of a pin-head. Cheshire's smoke bombs were as good an aiming point as possible, but usually the ground haze veiled the smoke. No other squadron could have done it.)

Grey cloud still hung over the Pas de Calais; it was forming over the North Sea and blowing over the land, and 617 stood by at dawn every day waiting for it to lift while the buzz-bombs fell on London. To the south the invasion was locked in the bridgehead, and even if they broke out the Seine still barred the way to the rocket sites. In London the nation's leaders (though not the unaware people) waited anxiously in case the mystery sites should start up. They guessed they must be nearly ready.

Several times the crews ran to the aircraft, and once actually took off, but the cancellation came instantly. The raids a squadron did never reflected the ordeal behind them, the nerve-fraying sequence of briefing every morning about 5 a.m., followed by postponement, by stand-by, ready to take off when the order came, never knowing if one would still be alive by nightfall. And then the dusk would come, bringing release till 5 o'clock the next morning. It went on like that day after day, not only at this time but all through the war for every squadron. Often they took off and battled through the flak and fighters only to find the target lost under cloud, so that they had to bring their bombs back, to be ready at dawn next day.

Cheshire had done ninety-eight raids now. At the ruling casualty rate he was living strictly on borrowed time. Statistically he should have been killed for certain four times. Arthur Pollen, the Woodhall intelligence officer, asked him how he felt about it, and Cheshire answered, "You don't feel the strain, Arthur. You keep on going more or less automatically and don't worry." Pollen noticed as he was talking that Cheshire's right eye was twitching, but Cheshire was not aware of it.

At last, on July 4, the weather cleared. Not a moment too soon. London was taking a beating. As the clouds rolled away over France 617 took off to hit back, target this time being the big store of rockets and buzz-bombs hidden in a cave at Creil, near Paris. It ran deep under a hill—at least 25 feet of chalk and clay over it—and the idea was both to collapse it and seal it up. Fawke went ahead in a Mosquito to get weather and wind information in advance. Cheshire flew his now beloved Mustang, and seventeen Lancasters carried the "tallboys."

Cheshire dived to 200 feet and aimed his markers so accurately that Fawke did not have to back up. Several "tallboys" then smashed through the cave roof with great ease; others collapsed the entrance and wrecked the railway that brought the rockets into the cave.

Next afternoon to Mimoyecques, where the Germans were sinking the fantastic gun barrels 500 feet into the ground to fire 600 tons of explosive a day on London. War Cabinet still did not know this; they only knew it was one of Hitler's secret-weapon sites. From above it was nearly invisible, a 30 by 20 yards square of camouflaged concrete shielding the gun tunnels beneath.

An hour before dusk Cheshire, in the Mustang, found the spot in the chalk hills behind Calais, dived and lobbed his markers on it. When the "tallboys" came down he saw one direct hit, and four were "very near misses," which were probably more effective.

A message summoning him to Cochrane met him

Mustang

when he landed and he drove straight over to Group. Cochrane said when he walked in: "I've been looking at the records and I see you've done a hundred trips now. That's enough; it's time you had a rest. I've got hold of Tait to take over." Cheshire opened his mouth to argue and Cochrane said, "It's no use arguing. . . . Sorry, but there it is. A hundred is a good number to stop at." He went on and thanked him, quietly and with no flowery nonsense, and dropped another bombshell: "Shannon, Munro and McCarthy will come off too. They've been going continuously for about two years and it's time they had a rest as well."

There were, as Cheshire expected, protests from Shannon, Munro and McCarthy, but from that moment they were changed men, gayer, but in a less violent way, and only then he realised that the strain had been telling on his three durable flight commanders. Munro, known so long as "Happy" because he never smiled, became like a small boy, running round the mess cracking puns and laughing at anything.

They had earned a rest; all of them had D.S.O.s, D.F.C.s and bars. The squadron gave them a send-off at which one or two (prodded perhaps by alcohol) were near tears, but before the hangovers had subsided Wing Commander Willie Tait had arrived to take over. He put Fawke up to flight commander and brought two veteran pilots, Cockshott and Iveson, as his other lieutenants. Tait was a Welshman, belonging to no recognisable type but with a unique Celtic streak of his own. Smoothly brown-skinned and slim, with straight black hair, he had his own brand of introspection and dry wit. He had a habit sometimes, when he was with you, of saying nothing at all for long stretches of time, standing with his mouth primly pursed, a half can of beer held in extraordinary fashion under his armpit, his arm curled round and the glass caught between his hand and wrist. If he opened his mouth at all it was to stick a large pipe in it and hold it tightly to his mouth with his whole hand clenched over the stem, as though he were trying to hold thoughts inside himself. He was twenty-six, and two D.S.O.s and a D.F.C.

The cloud was back over France, so that for ten days there was no bombing; a lucky reprieve for the rocket sites, but at least it gave the squadron a chance to settle down under the new leaders, and Tait a chance to learn the marking technique in the Mustang.

On July 17 Met. reported the clouds rolling away, and a couple of hours later 617 was on the way to Wizernes. For this, his first marking effort, Tait flew one of the Mosquitoes with Danny Walker as navigator. Thick haze lay over the ground and they circled a long time in the flak before they could faintly pick up the great blockhouse merging with the torn earth. Tait dived from 7,000 to 500 feet before he let his smoke marker go accurately, and Fawke backed up. A few minutes later both Knights and Kearns got direct hits with "tallboys," and several more "tallboys" sent up awe-inspiring eruptions 40 to 50 yards away, more or less where Wallis preferred them.

More days of waiting for the weather, and on the 20th they went back to Wizernes. Tait, flying the Mustang for the first time on business, found wisps of broken cloud drifting over the area and thick haze on the ground. A lot of flak was coming up; he dived through it and lobbed his smoke markers, pulled steeply up to 4,000 feet, looked down and could only just see the smoke drift. Obviously the bombers, miles back at 18,000 feet, would never see it, and so he did an unheard-of thing . . . called up the bombers and said, "Try and aim at me," then dived into the bursting flak directly over the blockhouse and circled it at 1,000 feet, hoping the glinting of his wings would draw the eyes of the bomb aimers on the spot.

The Mustang shook in the shell blasts, and little holes were suddenly appearing in the wings and fuselage as machine-gun bullets and shrapnel punched through. Two bullets went through the petrol tank (which was self-sealing) and just missed the glycol coolant tank (which was not), and even then the bomb aimers did not see him.

They called up on their bombing runs and said they could not identify a thing, and Tait at last swung away out of the flak, an extremely lucky young man to be still airborne and personally unpunctured. The squadron turned and brought their "tallboys" back home.

They waited five more days for the cloud to clear and on the 25th went to Watten, Tait again in the Mustang. Murderous flak came spitting up all around the blockhouse, but this time, for the first time in weeks, there was neither haze nor cloud and in the crystal-clear air the target stood out so clearly that the bomb aimers reported they could see it from miles back, and Tait did not have to mark.

They had half-hour delay fuses on the "tallboys" that day, so they saw no explosions, but as the bombs sliced into the earth puffs of dust shot into the air from the shadow of the blockhouse.

Fawke lingered half an hour near the spot with a

camera in his Mosquito and brought back beautiful photographs of the explosions . . . five direct hits and half a dozen very-*very* near misses. The squadron did not escape scot-free. Three aircraft were badly hit by flak, one gunner died, his throat cut by flak, and one aircraft had to jettison its "tallboy" to stay in the air. Harris sent them special congratulations.

Again they waited for the weather and on July 31 flew to deal with a flying-bomb storage dump in a railway tunnel near Rilly La Montagne. Once more the air was crystal clear, no marking was needed and they caved in each entrance to the tunnel with their uncanny accuracy. They lost one of their most distinguished crews this day. F/Lt. Jock Reid had won a V.C. on a previous tour; a quiet young man, bashful about the red ribbon under his wings. Flak got his Lancaster as they were driving up to the target and only two parachutes came out.

Next day they tried to go back to Siracourt but once more the cloud beat them and they brought their bombs back. Actually it did not matter. The battle of the rocket sites was over. The liberating armies burst out and reached the Pas de Calais area and, as it happened, there was nothing for them to do about the rocket sites except stare in wonder. 617 had destroyed them.

At Watten they found that "tallboys" had smashed the roof and wrecked the building inside so badly that the Germans had abandoned it.

The great rocket assembly and launching site at Wizernes was reduced to rubble. The 10,000-ton dome on top was knocked off its foundations, the launching tunnels below had caved in and so had most of the maze of galleries where men were to have lived and stored and fired their rockets.

At Creil they found that the deep limestone caves which were to have protected their rockets and buzz-bombs had collapsed for hundreds of yards and buried them instead. Much the same at Rilly La Montagne.

A "tallboy" had gone right through the 16-ft. concrete roof at the Siracourt site, exploded beneath it and

wrecked it. Near misses had shaken two of the four
sides of the lower walls to pieces. The Germans had
stopped work on the site to dig deep air-raid trenches
and then abandoned the lot.

Most spectacular was the wreckage at Mimoyecques,
where the fabulous guns of V3 were to have fired on
London. One "tallboy" had ripped a corner off the
20-foot thick concrete roof and completely blocked the
left-hand gun shaft. A near miss had collapsed the
right-hand shaft and shaken the remaining shaft out of
plumb. Five hundred feet down when the bombers
came, 300 workers had been sheltering in what they
must have thought was complete safety. They are still
there, entombed.

Hitler had squandered men and materials to shield
his "impregnable" rocket sites, only to find, too late,
that for all the fabulous concrete on top his *Festung
Europa* had no roof . . . all because a stubborn, white-
haired old scientist in 1939 would not believe that the
world's experts were right about bombing.

When the first cannon-ball smashed a breach in a
castle wall it was not only the stonework that fell; it
also burst the bulwarks of the powerful isolationist
barons and was the beginning of the end of the feudal
system. And when the first "tallboy" fell on Watten it
not only pierced the shield of the secret weapons, but
stripped another layer of protection from Germany.
Hitler could not, or would not, believe it and tried to
build more protection on top. He sent nearly 10,000
workmen to the great U-boat pens at Hamburg, Bremen, Ijmuiden and Bergen to pile more concrete on
top. They already had ferro-concrete roofs 16 feet
thick, but the Germans wanted to increase this up to
30 feet. After the waste of work on the rocket sites it
was an enormous diversion of his war effort.

It was logical that Churchill, Freeman and Harris
should send Wallis over to France to see what his
"tallboys" had done, with an eye to what they might do
in the future. After Churchill, Wallis was probably the
first man to go over there as a civilian. He refused to
wear uniform. "What's the use of uniform to an old

man with white hair like me?" he said. "Good heavens, I couldn't even stand being tortured!" So he went in a dirty old raincoat and grey slacks, and an American major wanted to arrest him in France as a spy.

The Calais area had not yet been properly cleared, but Wallis was so fascinated by the great blockhouses and the damage that he pottered about abstractedly, oblivious of the guns going off all round. When he flew home they took him to Harris's office in the trees near High Wycombe, and Harris silently showed him photographs of the workmen swarming over the U-boat pens at Hamburg, Bremen, and Ijmuiden. They were enormous pens, some of them 300 feet square and 70 feet high. It was obvious that they were being further strengthened. Agents' reports confirmed this.

"Looks as though we're going to have some more substantial targets," Harris said. "After what you've seen of the rocket sites, do you think a 'tallboy' could cope with these?"

"I think one or two 'tallboys' broke up on the concrete," Wallis said. "If we're going to have something still bigger to deal with, I think we should throw something bigger at them." He added artlessly, "Something like a ten-tonner. I've been suggesting a ten-tonner for some time now, and I believe the Lancaster has developed enough to carry it into Germany."

Harris looked at him. He said after a while, "Mr. Wallis, I said once you could sell me a pink elephant. I think perhaps this time you might at last sell your ten-tonner."

That was a *very* satisfying day in Wallis's life.

17

VICTORIA CROSS

617 was a delighted squadron; not because of the coming 10-ton bomb (they were not told about that yet) but because Leonard Cheshire had just been awarded the V.C. It was the second V.C. to the credit of the newest squadron in the R.A.F., and one of the most remarkable V.C.s ever awarded.

The citation specified no one act of superb gallantry but listed some of the things he had done: the time a shell had burst inside the aircraft and he had continued on to the target, his volunteering for a second tour as soon as he had finished his first, his third tour, and then his insistence on dropping rank to do a fourth in a "suicide squadron." There was a piece on his part in the Munich raid, when he cruised through the flak over the roof-tops, and it noted that he had done a hundred raids.

A V.C. is often won in a moment of exalted heroism, but there can be no tougher way of winning it than by four years of persistent bravery. It was Cochrane who put Cheshire up for the medal. High commanders sometimes lose touch with the men under them, but the brusque Cochrane, who was always round the Group, never did that, and his crews sensed it. He won their utter faith not by geniality but by hard work and clear thinking to avoid tactical blunders that would have wasted their lives.

The perceptive Cheshire probably saw that more clearly than anyone. I quoted a letter of Cheshire's earlier paying tribute to Micky Martin. There is another part of the letter that reads: "In tracing the evolution of our low-level bombing technique don't under-estimate the contribution of Cochrane. He is the only senior officer with a really clear, unbiased brain that I have met. He followed our course with great attention to detail, was remarkably quick to grasp the fundamentals and was seldom hoodwinked. If I ever asked for anything and he refused, he always gave me clearly his reasons.

"If we ever needed anything we usually got it immediately. I used to think that if I asked him for an elephant I'd get it by return of post. As a matter of fact I once *did* ask him for an elephant because the tractors kept getting bogged in the mud, but the mud dried up and he said we didn't need the elephant then.

"One day I asked him for two Lancasters fitted with nitrogen tanks (a guard against fire) for the leading high-level crews. He hadn't a hope on earth of getting them officially because they were all booked up months in advance by the Pathfinders, who, though they didn't need them as badly as we did, had the highest priority of all. Cochrane merely called up the makers, asked them to let us have the first two that came off the line without letting anyone know, and we got them three days later.

"It was much the same with everything else, and we should have been lost without someone as strong and critical as Cochrane behind us. He is, of course, a strict disciplinarian, ruthless in dealing with inefficiency, and there is no doubt that he was the key figure behind all that 617 achieved."

617 had lost its priority targets now and Cochrane was busy finding new ones of sufficient importance and diminutiveness to merit the "tallboys'" and 617's specialist attention. Tait had been completely accepted by the squadron. An *élite* corps, they had regarded him a little aloofly (after Cheshire and Martin) until he had gone down to circle Wizernes in his Mustang as a personal aiming point for the bombs as well as the flak; then they went so far as to chide him with fond concern for sticking his neck out so imprudently. Tait, on the other hand, had completely accepted 617, find-

ing in it a rare spirit he had not seen since the first year of the war, before the full impact of it had hit the squadrons. In his fifth year of the war there were few volunteers for rugged ventures. 617 was different. They were all volunteers liable for any dangerous but profitable task.

They bombed a bridge at Etaples with 1,000-pounders (the rocket sites had drawn heavily on "tallboy" supplies), but though they hit the bridge the bombs did little damage to it.

Cut-off German garrisons were fiercely defending the French Atlantic ports of Brest, Lorient and La Pallice, while the Kriegsmarine used the ports as U-boat bases. Cochrane switched 617 on to the massive concrete U-boat pens in those ports, and on June 5 the squadrons bombed the Brest pens in daylight, battling through the heaviest flak they had met for some time to score six direct "tallboy" hits before smoke covered the target.

On the bomb run a salvo of three flak shells slammed into Cheney's Lancaster. The last one exploded in the bomb bay, badly wounded the navigator and wireless operator, and fire broke out in the starboard outer engine. Cheney feathered, pulled the extinguisher and got the aircraft back under control. He asked for a new course, and the navigator, unable to speak, crawled up and pointed out the figures in his log book. Both wounded had lost their oxygen masks, and Cheney pushed the nose down to lose height so they could breathe, and then fire broke out all along the starboard wing. The aircraft was riddled with holes and the end was near. Cheney shouted, "Bale out!" and held the plane steady while all the crew except himself and the wireless operator got out.

The wireless operator could not move and Cheney tried to trim the aircraft in a slow climb while he went back to help him. Several times he had to scramble back to the controls as the Lancaster fell into a dive, but he finally got the wounded man to the escape hatch, saw that he was conscious and able to pull the rip-cord and pushed him clear. The hatch jammed then, and he sweated and tugged at it while the aircraft plunged down till he forced it open and slipped through himself.

He landed in the sea and after a couple of hours a French fishing-boat picked up him and two others, and later they got back to the squadron. No one ever found out what happened to the others.

The day after Brest they went to the U-boat pens at Lorient and scored at least two direct "tallboy" hits and several near misses before smoke blotted them out.

Duffy and his crew of tough Canadians did not go on that trip. Tait had told them the previous night that they had finished their tour and were to go on rest, so Duffy took up his navigator in one of the Mosquitoes for a final local flip. It was the one that Cheshire had flown to mark on the Munich raid and it may have been that he strained the mainspar on that mad dive, because when Duffy was pulling out of a dive over Wainfleet Sands the starboard wing folded and at about 400 m.p.h. they went many feet deep into the mud.

Duffy's D.F.C. and promotion to flight lieutenant came through that afternoon.

The weather stayed fine and the squadron worked hard, averaging a "job" every couple of days. They went back to plaster the pens at Brest a couple of times and made several visits to similar targets at Lorient, Bordeaux and La Pallice.

On most of these raids the bombers took off independently to rendezvous over Hastings and form up into their "gaggle" at about 18,000 feet. "Baby-face" Willsher had been living there peacefully a year or so before and used to pick out his mother's house, stand up in the cockpit and wave out of the window, yelling "Hi, Mum! Hullo, Mum!" His mother must have seen them go over a dozen times, blissfully unaware that her favourite young man was on his way to the flak and fighters.

They lost two or three on the raids but morale was high. Some old crews went (or, rather, were sent) on rest; new crews came in, and between raids they all practised hard with the S.A.B.S. on the bombing range.

Sometimes there were not enough "tallboys" and they carried 2,000-lb. armour-piercing bombs, but these hardly chipped the pens. Sir Arthur Harris was constantly demanding more "tallboys," sending for his armament staff officer and saying to him: "Can you scrape up enough 'tallboys' by tomorrow for a go at Brest?" (Or Lorient, or La Pallice, or wherever it might happen to be.)

The answer too often was: "No. I'm afraid not, sir."

"That's no damn good to me. Go and see Freeman."

Off the armament officer would go to Sir Wilfred Freeman, who would usually end up by saying, "Tell Bert he can't have the moon." Back he would go and deliver the message in diplomatic language, to which Harris would reply with a ferocious grunt.

For one of the raids on La Pallice they could scrape up only seven "tallboys," and the squadron lobbed six of them as direct hits on the pens, getting more congratulations from Cochrane, who said, "You've broken all records."

Wallis had not designed the "tallboy" to go through thick ferro-concrete, but it was such an extraordinary weapon that time and again it did so, even though it never had time to reach its prescribed speed. They usually dropped it from around 18,000 feet instead of 40,000 because the Lancasters could not carry it higher.

The Brest pens had concrete roofs 16 feet thick. One or two of the "tallboys" split on them, but the rest penetrated deep and exploded the rest of the way through, creating chaos in the shelters. After the first raid the Germans tried to repair and strengthen them but a couple more raids taught them that it was no good. The "impregnable" concrete monsters were vulnerable, and that made their French ports too hot for U-boats. Agents sent word to Britain that the U-boats were fleeing from these ports and were not expected back.

The agents also suspected that the Germans planned to sink the old battleship hulk *Gueydon* in the mouth of Brest Harbour so the Allies could never use the port. 617 flew over and dropped 1,000-pounders on her at her old anchorage from three miles up and by evening the old battleship was many fathoms deep.

Wallis's new 10-tonner was coming along as fast as possible, but that was not very fast because it was a far more complicated job, even, than the "tallboy." Freeman had christened it with the name of "Grand Slam" and delivery date for the first one was roughly February, 1945. Meantime the Americans were starting to produce "tallboys" and were evolving a new (and very efficient) method of making "grand slams."

18

TO RUSSIA

It might be said that the fate of the battleship was finally sealed in the bath of Air Vice-Marshal the Hon. Ralph Cochrane. In his waking moments work was rarely absent from his mind; he had been thinking of the *Tirpitz* for a long time, and it was in his bath one morning that he finally made up his mind to get permission for 617 to sink her. He climbed out, dried, dressed and flew down to see Harris, and Harris said yes.

Tirpitz was still in Alten Fiord. in the Arctic Circle, by the northern tip of Norway. Merely lying inside her girdle of torpedo nets she forced the Allies to divert three battleships, badly needed elsewhere, to guard the Russian convoys. The Allies had been trying to "get" her for over two years. First a Russian submarine damaged her; then British midget submarines put her out of action for six months. Next the Fleet Air Arm hit her, but now she was ready for sea again.

Cochrane flew to Woodhall. "Tait," he said (typical of the man), "you're going to sink the *Tirpitz*." For a while they discussed ways and means. One problem, Cochrane warned, would be the smoke screen round the ship. The Germans had run a pipeline round the shores of the narrow fiord and could pour out smoke by turning a tap. Also there were scores of smoke pots round the ship, and they could smother the fiord under smoke in eight minutes. There would be no time to waste manoeuvring for a bomb run. Tait went over to the mess to have a glass of beer and think about it.

He spread maps on his office floor and measured the distance there and back. It was formidable; something like 3,000 miles . . . probably beyond range. He loaded three Lancasters with bombs and full petrol and sent off three of the youngest crews (because the maximum range is what the least experienced can do) to fly round England a distance equal to the distance to the target. He sent another plane with half petrol to fly similarly, representing the distance back with a lighter load. When they landed he measured the petrol they had used, and the two ends of the string did not meet. He reported to Cochrane that the *Tirpitz* was just outside their range.

Two days later Cochrane flew over and said, "You can do it from Russia." He put a finger on the map. . . . "Here. Yagodnik." Yagodnik was a Russian airfield on an island in the Dvina River, about twenty miles from Archangel . . . . only 600 miles from Alten Fiord. "Fly to Yagodnik from northern Scotland with your bombs," Cochrane said. "Refuel there, do the job, return to Yagodnik to refuel again and come home."

He said there were enough "tallboys" now to send 9 Squadron with them. 9 Squadron could not use the S.A.B.S. but had become nearly as accurate with the Mark XIV bomb sight. Two Liberators would carry ground crews and spares.

The planners worked fast, and three days later, on a good weather report, the squadron (carrying their "tallboys") flew to Lossiemouth, refuelled and in bright sunshine on September 10 took off heavily on the long haul to Russia, laden a ton overweight with petrol and bombs.

At dusk they crossed the Norwegian coast, and as they droned steadily north, nearer the Pole, the magnetic compasses started to play tricks, but luckily the night stayed clear and they were able to pin-point themselves over the fiords and check with the sextants. They crossed the Gulf of Finland and flew on through the night till, in the half-light of an Arctic dawn, they turned east for Yagodnik.

Long separated from the others in the night, each plane found itself drifting alone through pale grey

cloud. Some Russian had said the cloud had never been below 1,000 feet in twenty-five years, but Tait was at 1,000 feet and could see nothing.

He eased her down gently, but at 500 feet still saw nothing but greyness. They should be over the steppes now; if so the ground would be flat with no treacherous hills rising in their path. He hoped they were over the steppes.

At 400 feet they saw trees like ghosts through the drifts and some of the strain lifted from the little huddle in the cockpit. They had been sitting there ten hours, silent in the glow of the instruments.

On and on they flew over a flat sea of trees, endless, desolate and remote; no roads, no towns, not even a track, here and there a small pool of grey water. Otherwise only trees with mist twisting round their trunks. Drizzle blurred the windscreen; they were flitting in and out of cloud even at 300 feet, and Arthur Ward, the wireless operator, could not raise the Yagodnik radio beacon (none of the others raised it either. It was the wrong kind of beacon).

E.T.A. was up. They should be there now, but still only the trees and less than an hour's petrol. Tait turned south to search. Knowing the compasses and weather might play tricks, they had been relying on that beacon. Worry was hammering at him; not so much on his own account but for all his other aircraft.

Daniels, the bomb aimer, suddenly shouted that he could see a river through a break in the cloud and Tait slanted the nose down; they broke into clear air and below was an airfield with a Lancaster landing and two more circling. Five minutes later they were thankfully on the ground and found that only a handful of aircraft had arrived. Including 9 Squadron, there were over twenty more to account for. They walked over to a ramshackle hut on the field, Tait feeling the dread rising in him. None of the missing planes could have more than half-an-hour's petrol. It looked like disaster.

In the next half-hour seven more Lancasters and the two Liberators arrived, the crews dog-tired after twelve hours in the air and marvelling at having made it safely after the past hours of taut nerves.

The moment came when none of the aircraft could still be in the air, and thirteen were still missing. A Russian interpreter came over and said that a Lancaster had landed on an airfield on another island in the river. Five minutes later he reported that four Lancasters were safely there. Then word started coming in from all over the place of Lancasters in various fields a hundred miles around, and in three hours they knew the location of every aircraft.

It was unbelievable. In the wilderness the Russians had traced the aircraft as fast as could be done in England and dropped parachute medical teams and guides to isolated ones. (One parachute guide reached a stranded crew all right, but it was a case of the blind leading the blind because the guide himself got lost for twenty-four hours!) It was equally incredible that there were no casualties, though two 617 aircraft and four of 9 Squadron were written off because they were irretrievable in marshes.

Knilans had been getting ready to crash-land when he came to a small field, and the petrol gauges were on "Zero" when he dropped the plane low over a fence and, with brakes hard on, pulled up inches short of the trees. Minutes later Iveson droned into sight and landed safely in the same field. Wyness and Ross crash-landed in marshland. Flak hit Carey's plane badly over Finland, but Gerry Witherick nailed one of the gunners before they were out of range and they reached Yagodnik, where they riveted patches over the holes.

The Russians lodged all the sergeants in underground huts and escorted the officers over a gangplank to a houseboat where a banner flapped, bearing the words, "Welcome to the glorious flyers of the R.A.F." "Cor," said Witherick, "what a line!" Otherwise there were no social distinctions. Both huts and houseboat crawled with bugs and had the same musty smell of drains and lavatories. While the well-warned crews sprayed their quarters with Keating's and tried to prise the windows open, Tait stood by to fly to Iveson and Knilans. A Russian pilot took him to an antique bi-plane, and Tait flinched when he saw two mongoloid Russians hitting the engine with a hammer; they stopped, he climbed reluctantly in and the cabin lid closed over him like a coffin top.

To his faint surprise, the Thing flew and half an hour later the Russian pilot landed next to the two Lancasters. Tait found his two crews held in a tumble-down wooden house set in a sea of mud. The Russians had fed them well but were not allowing them out. Some Russian girls were there but the crews were be-having impeccably, not even ogling the girls, partly because the girls were not attractive and partly because one of them had entertained them by lifting a burly Russian guard off the floor with one hand. Paddy Blanche, Knilans' gunner, was recovering. He hadn't been injured, but at lunchtime they had set a tumbler of vodka in front of him, and he had thought it was water and drunk it straight off before his face had turned white then crimson and purple as he fought for breath.

Iveson had just enough petrol to get to Yagodnik and took off at full throttle, barely clearing the trees. The Russians brought more petrol for Knilans; he roared over the grass to take-off but his spark plugs were fouled and the engines were sluggish. Feeling the power lacking (she would have lifted easily enough but for the 6-ton bomb), Knilans shoved the throttles through the "gate," hauled her off the ground and she lunged into the tree-tops and cut a swathe through the fo-liage for a hundred yards. Boughs shot up all round, twigs and leaves scooped into the radiators, a lopped branch knifed through the nose and shot into the cock-pit beside Knilans, and then the engines hauled her clear. Wind howled through the smashed nose into Kni-lans' face so that he could hardly see and flew with a hand over his face, peeking between two fingers. One engine cut out because of overheating from the blocked radiator, but they made it safely to Yagodnik and the ground crews set about repairs.

Rain poured on Yagodnik and for three days they waited for it to lift. Friendly Russians tried hard to amuse them, but outside the huts lay a sea of mud and the crews relaxed indoors, chasing bugs and eating sour black bread, borscht and half-cooked bacon . . . when the last of the breakfasters rose the head of the lunch queue sat down. They washed it down with vodka, which (said Willie Tait) was the secret of Russian survival in that climate. His opinion was respected because he was the only one the bugs refused to bite. Tait claimed it was because they were capitalist bugs and respected his rank, but Witherick said that even Russian bugs had to draw the line somewhere.

A Russian interpreter, who grinned all the time (showing steel false teeth) and smelled of perfume, took them at night to an underground cellar to see an unnerving film that went on for hours, all about battles . . . mostly Russian tanks, planes and cheering soldiers rushing forward in a continuous pandemonium of crashing explosions . . . dead Germans everywhere.

Next day a team of bullet-headed little men (imported for the occasion) played them football. Whenever Russian players tired they went off and on came reserves, among them the local Russian commander and the airfield commander, who were fed assiduously with passes by their men until a glancing blow off the senior man's knee went into the goal, whereupon the band struck up triumphantly and the rest of the team, duty done, went back to playing normally. The Russians won easily, 7—0.

On September 15, the sun crawled out of the horizon low to the south and shone in a clear sky. The crews were out in their aircraft, running up the engines hopefully, when the weather plane darted over the airfield like a blue kingfisher and landed with the report that the sky over Alten Fiord was clear. Minutes later twenty-eight Lancasters of the two squadrons were lifting off the bumpy grass and turning west. Tait flew slowly, the rest of his squadron picking up station behind till they were in their gaggle low over the White

Sea, and on strict radio silence to delay detection. Grey water close below muffled the thunder of the engines till they crossed the barren shore of Lapland and the echoes came up from the ice-worn rocks. The land was lifeless but for odd stunted trees; it rose a little and the aircraft lifted their noses gently over the contours.

Tait had an engine running rough, shaking the plane like a rolling-mill, but he headed on worrying about having enough power for the bombing climb. Ninety miles from Alten Fiord the mountains reared ahead and, on full throttle and revs., Tait's rough engine cleared and he climbed easily over the last ridge. They were dead on track.

Ahead Alten Fiord lay quietly in the sun like a map; they raced for it at 11,000 feet to beat the smoke screen, but as they picked out the black shape at her anchorage under the cliff, white plumes started vomiting out of the smoke pots and streaming across the water.

The bombers were quivering on full power five minutes from bombing point as the white veils started wreathing her. There must have been a hundred pots pouring smoke. Flak was firing from the heights now; the gaggle ran steadily through the black puffs, and then the *Tirpitz's* guns opened up. Two minutes from release point the drifting veils were fast smothering her. Daniels, in the nose of Tait's aircraft, took a long bead and called, "Bomb sight on!"

The black hull finally vanished in its shroud but the mast-tops stood clear a few seconds later, and then they too were gone. Daniels tried to hold his graticule on the spot but found no mark in the drifting smoke and guessed as the seconds dragged that he must be wandering off. The Lancaster leapt as the bomb clattered away and Tait swung the wheel hard over, swerving out of the flak.

Behind him the others had all lost their mark in that agonising last minute. Howard, Watts and Sanders bombed on dim gun-flashes through the smoke. Kell and Knilans bombed on the spot last seen, and the others, in frustration, did not bomb at all. Pale flickers in the smoke showed bombs exploding, and after one of them a plume of black smoke spurted through the whiteness. Tait felt a moment of hope but judged it was only a "tallboy" striking the shore. Some of the Lancasters swung back through the flak for a second run, but the screen was thicker than ever and they turned for Yagodnik.

When they landed, Woods, one of the bomb aimers, said he had seen Daniels' "tallboy" hit the ship but no one believed him. The Russians did not try to hide their displeasure at the failure. Some of the bombers still had their "tallboys" and they wanted to go back and try again, but the weather broke once more, rain drizzled down, winter's cloud hung over the north, and disconsolately they gave up the idea and took off for home. Levy's aircraft never arrived. Somewhere over Norway they wandered off track—probably through a flabby compass—and flew into the mountains. They were an all-Jewish crew, a quiet, unobtrusive team, utterly reliable. With Levy were four of Wyness's crew.

It was the nearness to success that hurt Cochrane most. He said wryly, "Another minute's sight and you'd have got her. I was afraid those smoke pots might balk you." He did not tell Tait at the time but he had no intention of leaving the *Tirpitz* in peace.

A couple of nights later the squadron joined 5 Group to bomb the Dortmund–Ems Canal, scene, a year earlier, of 617's blackest night. Mosquitoes marked at low level in the way they had learned from Cheshire and the bombs that followed split the canal embankment. The group bombed more accurately now than a year earlier. After his experiment with 617, Cochrane had seen that the rest of his squadrons trained hard in the same direction.

Tait had lost an engine on take-off that night but had feathered and kept going hard on the other three; slower, of course. He came out of cloud over the target and saw the water that was the artery of Germany's northern transport system pouring through the gaps into the countryside. There was a price on it that night; fighters got among the returning bomber stream, and Tait saw the path back littered with burning Lancasters. 617 was lucky and lost only one. Stout's plane went down somewhere; they never found out where.

The canal had a bad time after that. The water drained for miles between lock gates, and scores of barges were stranded on the mud with coal, prefabricated U-boats and other essentials. Hitler drove 4,000 slaves to rebuild the breached walls, and when they had nearly finished, 5 Group knocked them down again. Back to work went the reluctant slaves, and this time they finished it. The Germans opened the lock gates to let the water through again, and two hours later the Lancasters were over and away went the walls again. They never did get the canal working again.

Knilans was told he had "finished." After two straight tours without rest he had "operational fatigue"; his mind still registered mistakes in the air but his muscles would not respond. He had another disappointment too. His D.S.O. medal arrived—in the post. Knilans had set his heart on having it pinned on at an investiture.

Humphries kept it for him in the squadron safe while Knilans miserably waited for his posting, and whenever the inactivity got a little too much for him he used to wander down to the squadron office, moon around bashfully for a while and then say, "Hump, can I have a look at my medal?" Humphries would solemnly take it out of the safe and Knilans would hold it in his hand and sigh, "Heck, I guess that King never will get to meet me now."

He was entitled to several medal ribbons, including some American ones, but for a long time the only one he would wear was the D.S.O. ribbon. (Later he added to it when his D.F.C. came through.)

Recce aircraft reported the *Tirpitz* was missing from Alten Fiord and there was a great "flap" (particularly among the nautical people) till a message came through from a Mr. Egil Lindberg. Lindberg was a Norwegian who operated a secret transmitter from a room above the morgue in Tromsö. The *Tirpitz* had arrived in Tromsö, he reported, with a great hole in her for'ard deck. She had been hit by a very heavy bomb

(Daniels' "tallboy" *had* hit the ship. He was probably the most "hawk-eyed" bomb aimer of the war). Lindberg thought the *Tirpitz* had come to Tromsö because the repair facilities were better there. Cochrane got the news and did not care a hoot about the repair facilities. The important thing to him was that Tromsö was 200 miles south of Alten Fiord—it shortened the return trip by 400 miles . . . and that put the *Tirpitz* just within range of Lossiemouth.

He called Wing Commander Brown, his engineering staff officer, and said, "Brown, we've got to get three hundred more gallons in 617's Lancasters."

"Yes, sir. We can fit overload tanks in the bomb bays."

"No, we shall want the 'tallboys' there. Come on, come on, you're versatile. Is there anything in the depots that would do? We haven't time to get anything made."

Brown was miserably without a glimmer of an idea till he remembered some Wellingtons had once carried long pencil-shaped overload tanks. If they could find some of those they could slide them into the Lancaster fuselages. Cochrane grunted approval, and Brown scoured England by telephone, locating tanks one by one and sending trucks to collect them.

A new consideration interrupted Cochrane's *Tirpitz* plans. The right flank of the American dash across France into Germany had been halted at the Belfort Gap; ahead the Rhine barred the way into Germany, and on the Rhine by the Swiss frontier lay the Kembs Dam. It was obvious that when the Americans stormed the river the Germans would blow up the flood-gates, releasing a massive head of water that would sweep the assault forces to destruction in mid-river or isolate those who got across. There was only one way out— smash the flood-gates first, let the water spend itself and then drive at the river. Only a heavy charge, deep in the water and pressed against the sluice-gates, would burst them; the ideal target for the freak bomb 617 had used on the Moehne and Eder but the modified aircraft to carry that bomb had long been re-modified

to normality. It would take weeks to adapt more aircraft for the bomb and train the crews in the delicate
technique; more weeks than they could afford.

It was no good trying to bomb it from high level.
The chance of a heavy bomb landing in exactly the
right spot, within a foot of the dam wall on the up-
stream side, was far too slim. A direct hit on the top
would do no good. There was only one way . . . Cochrane decided that a "tallboy" dropped low over the
water just short of the flood-gates would slide cleanly
into the water till it hit a gate and stick in the concrete.
They would give it a delayed fuse so the low-flying
bombers would not be blown up as well.

It would have to be done very accurately; that meant
doing it in full daylight, and the dam was circled with
guns. The bombers would have to fly very low, straight
and level, and run the gauntlet. No question as to who
should do it!

Cochrane planned it craftily. They would split in two
formations; one would come in and bomb from the
west at 8,000 feet, drawing the flak; and in the precise
moment their bombs were hitting, six Lancasters would
sneak in low from the east for the real assault. At the
same instant a Mustang squadron would dive on the
flak-pits with guns and rockets so the flak might not
notice the low-level force, at least till the bombs were
gone. It was going to need split-second timing, and 617
practised every day for a week till their final rehearsal
over Wainfleet went perfectly. Tait was insisting on
leading the low-level force.

They knew, or sensed, that the Kembs might be a
"shaky do," though that did not much affect their thinking or living. They were used to it and the mind makes
its own defences. After battle they always flew home to
the island fortress and lived among fields and placid
villages, which rather insulated them in the mess
from the sharper realities of battle, just enough to take
some of the edge off the fear that lived in them like a
raw little nerve.

617's mess at Woodhall was in the Petwood Hotel,

for instance; stockbroker's Tudor if you like but a pleasant place, agreeably panelled and set in gardens. The beer was good, W.A.A.F.'s in white coats served your meals and you slept in a bed with sheets, remote from battle. You lived like a normal human and it fortified that deceitful little thought, "It can't happen to me," until the weather cleared and you got a time on target: then the transition was always brutally swift —four hours later you would be a few hundred miles away, tight-lipped and sweating it out in the noise, the ugliness, the fear and the death.

Sometimes, if the time on target were a few hours away, some of the insulation stayed a while round the little nerve, as on October 7, the day of the Kembs raid. Take-off was in the afternoon, and after morning briefing and testing the planes the crews read in the mess or walked in the garden, and two of the flight commanders, Tony Iveson and "Duke" Wyness, even went over to a nearby Army mess to lunch with their friend the lieutenant-colonel, commander of the local regiment.

Among the waiters, white linen and conversation the war shrank; it was not forgotten but you observed it through the wrong end of a telescope and talked of it as if it were almost abstract. Wyness, for instance, talked during lunch not of the raid but in philosophical terms of courage and cowardice in the face of the enemy, saying with the earnest assurance of twenty-three years that a man's duty lay along the path of the utmost endurance in the face of the enemy's efforts.

That very neatly expressed the distinctive quality of the squadron and it was apt enough coming from Wyness because he himself was quite typical of the new types who made the squadron. He already had a D.F.C. when he came to 617 and a reputation as a "press on" type, a handsome young man, a six-footer, slim, with blue eyes, a somewhat classical nose and really golden, curly hair.

One of the pilots under him was Kit Howard, and the orderly room had a story that Wyness came from the estate of Howard's family, though neither Howard nor Wyness seemed to notice it. In both of them, as in Tait, Iveson and the others, was the continuity of the early, chosen types like Gibson, Cheshire, Martin and Shannon. They maintained the quality and buttressed the tradition.

And then, after lunch, they accepted the transition and went to battle. The colonel drove them to their planes in his jeep, asked them both to dine with him that evening when they got back, and waved them off.

They all took off into light haze and ran into a pall of cloud over Manston, where they were to meet the fighters. It is dangerous to break radio silence on the outward journey but this time it was less of a risk than missing the fighter escort, so Tait made two short transmissions; the first to 617: "Four thousand feet. Don't acknowledge." They recognised his voice, climbed blind through the cloud and at 4,000 feet came into the sunshine. Tait called the fighter leader and told him they were overhead; two minutes later the Mustangs lifted out of the white carpet, shook themselves into formation and they were on their way.

It was clear over France, and strange to be flying peacefully over the land that had been hostile so recently. Bomb craters still studded the fields but the scars were already softening as rain and sun mellowed the torn earth and the grass crept in.

The scars vanished over Champagne and they flew over green and yellow meadows and towns by gleaming rivers. Tait, for the first time, felt an intruder, finding it hard, this day, to adjust himself to the sharp transition. Raiding at night they were alone in darkness filled with unknown danger, and inside the cockpit it was tense and appropriate to war, but this peaceful sunshine made it somehow unreal and the task ahead repugnant. He found himself thinking of wine and clear river water, lost in introspection, while a separate part of his brain and his arms and feet were part of the aeroplane, flying on undeviatingly.

Patches of cloud brought him back to reality. Cloud

over the Rhine would hide the high force and leave him and the "suicide squad" open to the flak. The cloud thinned again; the high force swung behind Fawke and started climbing; Tait slid to the right and nosed down till he was hugging the ground under the radar waves, and the other five Lancasters trailed after him. They skirted the Swiss frontier, clearly marked with red and white crosses on the ground, but Watts must have swung his plane a shade too close and the Swiss flak opened up on him, smashing his starboard outer engine. He feathered quickly, hauled over to the left and kept going. From a rear turret a voice said, "It's O.K. I'm here." Gerry Witherick was riding with Watts this day, and everyone knew he always got back unscratched.

They slid past Basle on the right and turned down the river, opening bomb doors. Three miles ahead Tait saw flashes round the low parapet of the Kembs, but the guns were aiming high at Fawke's formation. Great flashes and columns of spray rushed up round the dam; the timing of the high-force bombs was perfect. Tait's aeroplane was rock-steady on course and no word was spoken, except once, a terse "O.K." from Daniels. They were committed to it now, sliding over the smooth water with taut nerves and dry mouths. Tait saw Mustangs diving out of the sun over the dam and dared to hope the flak would not see him, but abruptly the white-hot balls came darting at them. He felt the plane jump as the bomb slid away, slammed the throttles on, did not see the bomb knife cleanly into the water 10 yards from the right-hand sluice-gate, but heard the vibrant rattle as the rear gunner opened up and they hurtled over the dam.

Behind him Castagnola's plane lurched in Tait's slipstream and threw the bomb wide. Tait hauled hard over to the right for the shelter of the hills, climbing on full power, engines blaring in fine pitch as they dragged her up. He turned abeam and saw a Lancaster rocking over the dam on fire, flame and smoke streaming in her wake. She dropped a wing and plunged into the river bank, rolling over in a ball of fire. When it is quick it is a good way to die.

Tait heard a voice in his earphones—Howard's, he thought—saying, "Had a hang-up. Going round again." Howard, of the noble family, was rather a formal boy, but brave. Perhaps foolhardy. This time the gunners were wary, not distracted. Howard came alone down the river and all the guns saw him. They got him a long way back and he blew up in mid-air with the bomb on board.

The surviving bombers turned for home; in five minutes the sound of their engines had died away and the dam lay quietly in the sun as though nothing had happened, except for the two columns of greasy smoke pouring from the spots where Howard and Wyness and their crews had died.

There had been half-hour delay fuses on the low-force "tallboys." Twenty minutes after the raid a Mosquito droned high over the dam and circled it, the pilot watching till he saw the water beside the right-hand sluice-gate burst and mushroom into the air. A massive torrent plunged through the gate, and in twenty-four hours the banked head-waters of the Rhine had dropped so much that barges far into Switzerland grounded on the mud.

Tait had made a "dicy" landing with a flak shell in one wing-root and a tyre shot away. Several of the others were badly holed. Iveson, without changing, walked over to the Army mess to tell the colonel that his other dinner guest, the boy who had lunched with him, was lying several hundred miles away in another country, cremated in his plane. He found the colonel (who was a Scottish rugby international) in the bar, took him aside and they sat on the stairs while Iveson told him about it. The hurt was gathering in the colonel's face and then, very quietly, he was crying: you could, I suppose, call it crying; no noise, no sobs, no shaking shoulders but the tears starting to glisten in his eyes till they spilled and kept wetting his cheeks.

When he was able to, he said, a little unsteadily and

with humility, how futile he felt his own efforts were
in comparison to the Air Force. He said he had never
had much chance for action but now he felt the impact
of the war more than ever before.

So did Iveson when he saw the tears. They had got
so used to seeing planes beside them with their friends
fall smoking out of the sky that the familiar expression
they all used, "got the chop," had almost a humorous
quality about it, but that was just part of the insulation,
the old mental defence mechanism.

(Three weeks later, in the landing on Walcheren,
the colonel won a D.S.O. for some act of inspired
bravery.)

The squadron never knew for certain whether the
raid helped the advance, whether their fourteen room-
mates died in saving hundreds or whether it was just one
of the premiums paid in war, a precaution which, after
all, was not needed. So many valiant deeds in war are
sterile. The monstrous rocket sites they bombed in the
Pas de Calais may never have been finished in time,
whether they had bombed them or not. It was a part of
war. Tait was well aware that most of the effort
of war was spent against an enemy who was not there;
that for every shell which hit a target, hundreds were
fired that missed, and for every bullet, thousands.

The next days were a fever of activity getting ready
for the *Tirpitz*. The brunt of it fell on Cochrane, Tait,
Brown and the ground crews. With tests and graphs
Tait worked it out that from Lossiemouth they could
just reach the *Tirpitz* in Tromsö with a bare—a very
bare—safety margin in case of adverse winds, but it
meant loading in so much petrol they would be taking
off nearly 2 tons over the maximum permissible weight.
He agreed to try that if they could have Merlin 24
engines . . . they were more powerful than the engines
in the 617 Lancasters. There were some of these engines
in 5 Group, scattered among odd aircraft in various
squadrons at other airfields. For three days and nights
the ground crews worked non-stop in shifts, taking the
Merlin 24s out of aircraft all over Lincolnshire, bringing

them back to Woodhall, taking out the 617 engines,
putting in the new ones and taking the 617 engines to
be put into the other aircraft they had "robbed." It
would have been so simple if they could merely have
exchanged planes, but only the 617 Lancasters had the
specially big bomb bays to carry the "tallboys." The
weather was dense fog continuously, and at night
the bright hangar lights gleamed like will-o'-the-wisps
across the streaming tarmac.

Brown had collected the long, thin overload tanks
from all over England. The erks had to take the rear
turrets off every plane to slide the tanks in, then put
the turrets back on again. They took the mid-upper
turrets off completely, also the pilot's armour plate and
any equipment not vitally necessary, so as to save
weight. —

(The same things were done on 9 Squadron aircraft
too. Cochrane was sending them as well.)

That done they waited on the weather, and that was
the worst time of all. In October and November a pre-
vailing westerly blows continuous stratus cloud from
the sea over Tromsö . . . except for perhaps three days a
month, when the wind briefly changes to the east and
the sky is clear for a few hours. They would have to
be in position at Lossiemouth to take off when one of
these clear periods existed, and hope it would last till
they got there. But neither Harris nor Cochrane could
let them stay at Lossiemouth indefinitely "on spec."
They needed them down south in case of emergency
targets. The only way was for the squadron to fly to
Lossiemouth when a break seemed possible. At the
most they had six weeks left for the attack. After November 26 the sun does not rise above the horizon at
Tromsö, though for a few days after that there would
be just enough twilight at midday for bombing. After
that no light till spring. A nice problem in long-range
weather forecasting.

The word came on October 28, and thirty-six Lancasters of 617 and 9 Squadrons flew north to a bleak
field near Lossiemouth. At midnight a Mosquito over
Tromsö radioed that the wind was veering to the east,

and in drizzling rain at the deathly hour of 1 a.m. the Merlin 24s, straining on emergency power, dragged the overburdened Lancasters off the ground.

They flew low as usual, in sight of the caps on the dark water; hours later crossed the Norwegian coast and turned inland towards Sweden to keep the mountains between them and the Tromsö radar. They wheeled left in a long climb, topped the ridges and saw Tromsö Fiord and the ship . . . and saw in the same moment, moving in from the sea, towering drifts of cloud. The wind had changed.

It was a race again, like those sickening moments over Alten Fiord, but this time the white screens were higher and thicker. At 230 m.p.h. the bombers charged towards the ship and the cloud. A minute from release point they still saw the ship, but with thirty seconds to go the cloud slid between them!

They couldn't dive under it to bomb; lower down the "tallboys" would not have penetrated the armoured decks. Daniels tried to keep his bomb sight on the spot where he last saw the ship. Flak was bursting through the cloud among them now. Daniels called "Bombs gone!" and Tait dived into the cloud to try and see where it fell. Fawke, Iveson, Knights and one or two more bombed on vague glimpses and dived too. Others swung away to try another run. Through gaps in the cloud at about 13,000 feet Tait saw flashes as bombs exploded in the water round the ship. One or two others said they thought they saw a direct hit or near miss. Martin (a different Martin) made two more runs, got a glimpse on the third run and bombed half blindly. Gumbley made four runs but got no sight at all.

Carey's Lancaster had been hit by flak on the first run; the starboard outer engine stopped and petrol streamed out of a riven tank, luckily without catching fire. He turned back on three engines for another run and the cloud foiled him. He tried again and again, ploughing steadfastly through the flak till, on the sixth run, an almost desperate bomb aimer let his "tallboy" go with faint hope.

Tait had ordered everyone to dive to 1,000 feet to pick up speed and steer for home. As Carey screamed down he passed over a small island; a single gun on it pumped a shell into another engine, which died instantly; petrol was streaming out of another burst tank (miraculously no fire again), and then the hydraulics burst and the bomb doors and undercarriage flopped down. The two good engines on full power just held her in the air against the drag; the engineer thumbed his gauges, scribbled a few calculations and said, "Sorry, Skip. Not enough gas to get home."

From the rear turret came a protesting, grimly flippant voice: "Hell, this can't happen to me." Witherick was flying with Carey this time. He had a habit of switching crews.

"Christ!" said Carey. "Can't it? You watch!"

He turned the winged plane back towards the land and, staggering through the air a few hundred feet up, they threaded through a mountain pass and slowly crossed the barren country. Half an hour later the navigator said they were over Sweden. The two engines were dangerously hot and Carey crash-landed in a bog near Porjus. The Lancaster tilted frighteningly on her nose, poised a moment and settled back, and they climbed out.

The rest of the squadron landed at Lossiemouth and heard that a recce plane radioed that the *Tirpitz* was untouched. They flew down to Woodhall, where Tait found a message from Cochrane: "Congratulations on your splendid flight and perseverance. The luck won't always favour the *Tirpitz*. One day you'll get her."

On November 4 they flew up to Lossiemouth again. A gale warning came through that night and in the morning the weather was dreadful. It stayed dreadful; they flew back to Woodhall and waited, practising bombing whenever they could. Five days later they were still getting gale and frost warnings and time was getting short.

Arthur Kell's bomb aimer tripped on the stairs and fractured his skull, and Tait told Kell he would have to miss the next *Tirpitz* trip unless he could find a

S.A.B.S.-experienced bomb aimer. Kell rang Astbury, now twice tour-expired, waiting at Brighton for a ship home to Australia. Astbury went A.W.L. from his draft and turned up at Woodhall, a misdemeanour on which Tait turned a blandly Nelsonian blind eye.

19

THE NAKED BATTLESHIP

A new complication jolted Cochrane. Intelligence reported that twenty to thirty German fighters had moved in to Bardufoss airfield, 30 miles from Tromsö. No doubting why! Two strong attacks had been made on the *Tirpitz*; the Germans would give the next one a lethal reception. For accuracy the squadron would have to bomb by day spread out in the gaggle so they could not give each other protection, and the R.A.F.'s .303 guns were no match for the cannon of fighters. If the fighters fell on them—and that seemed likely—there was every chance of slaughter. Few bombers, if any, would return.

Cochrane found himself in the old position of the commander forced to stay at his desk and decide whether to send his men into an ambush. Some commanders grow too detached to be particularly conscious of the problem. Cochrane was acutely conscious of it. There had been two unlucky failures, and he spent troubled hours trying to equate the chance of a "third time lucky" success with the probable losses. For all his coldness there was a personal factor this time that he tried to eliminate. 617 never knew (and would never have guessed) that they were the apple of his eye; he had a respect for them amounting to affection.

But it was an operational war. That was the clinching factor. He decided they would have to go if the cloud let them.

Next day the weather was improving. Tait was playing football with his crews on the airfield, surrounded by the circle of silent cloaked Lancasters, when he was summoned to the operations room, and there, still in striped jersey and studded boots, he got his orders. In a few hours they were flying up to Northern Scotland.

That was about the afternoon a paper was dumped in an "In" tray in Whitehall, and a senior officer with a lot of braid round his sleeve picked it out and groaned when he read the rather peremptory suggestion from High Circles that instead of "tallboys" on the *Tirpitz* raid they should drop 2,000-lb. armour-piercing bombs. In the room at the time was an airman who had done a lot of work in developing the "tallboy." "Oh God," he said, "the two-thousand-pounders'll never do it! What do we do now?" The high officer pondered, his fingers relaxed and the slip of paper floated back into the "In" tray. "Have lunch," he said, and added a moment later, piously, "I'll look into this tomorrow. I *do* hope I'm in time."

Some time after midnight the weather Mosquito, sliding through darkness on the way back from Tromsö, reported fog in the fiords and cloud half-way up Norway. There was a possibility Tromsö might be clear by dawn, but there were distinct icing conditions (a real bogy for heavy-laden aircraft). It was not encouraging. Tait discussed it with the Met. men, and at the end he said, "All right. We'll give it a go."

Over Lossiemouth stars were glinting in a clear sky and the air was frosty. Tait drove out to his aeroplane and found the dangerous rime ice already forming on his wings in spite of the glycol the ground crew had poured on the leading edge. One by one round the field the engines were whining and coughing explosively, bringing the big bombers to quivering life. When Tait started his starboard inner it let out a high-pitched scream as the starter motor stuck in engagement. He hoped it would clear before the engine seized—in much the same way as he hoped the rime ice would clear. With 7 tons of fuel and 6 tons of bomb, each plane was grossly overweight at 32 tons. No margin for any trouble on take-off.

At 3 a.m. the straining engines dragged them into the air, the great wheels slowly retracted and locked, the engines relaxed and they turned slowly on course at 1,000 feet. (Tait's engine chewed the gears off the starter motor and was all right. He was flying his own aircraft again, "D Dog," for the first time since she was crippled over the Kembs Dam. He always had luck in her.)

They flew slowly to save petrol, flame floats bobbing on the water in their wake as they checked for drift. Tait had slipped in the automatic pilot and tried to doze, as he always did on outward trips over water; he believed in taking sleep when he could get it, but seldom got it.

The sky was paling in the east as they reached the Norwegian coast, turned right, climbed over the mountains and dipped into the inland valleys. The sun lifted over the horizon and the valleys lay soft under snow, flecked with bare rocks. Snow crests surrounded them, tops laced with pink like vast wedding cakes, except to the south, where the sun splintered on the ice-peaks and sparkled with the colours of the spectrum like a diamond necklace, radiantly lovely. Fog-filled lakes passed slowly below but there was no cloud. Rendezvous was a narrow lake cradled between steep hills a hundred miles southeast of Tromsö, and Tait flew slowly towards it, saw no water but recognised it as a long pool of fog in the trough and over it saw aircraft circling like black flies.

He flew across it firing Véry lights to draw them, and they turned in behind and started the climb towards Tromsö. That was the moment the radar picked them up, and within a minute the fighter operations room at Bardufoss knew that enemy bombers were closing on the *Tirpitz*. At 14,000 feet the bombers were all at battle stations. One last mountain shouldered up, and as they lifted over the peak it lowered like a screen and there again, folded in the cliffs, lay Tromsö Fiord and the black ship, squat in the distance, like a spider in her web of torpedo nets. It was like looking down from the "gods" on a Wagnerian stage, a beetle in green water cupped in the snowy hills, all coral and flame. There was no cloud. And no smoke screen. *Tirpitz* lay naked to the bomb sights.

Even the air was still. On the flanks of the gaggle Tait saw the front rank riding steadily. They seemed suspended; motionless but for the sublime hills falling slowly behind, immaculate and glowing with the beauty of sunrise and the indifference of a million years to the ugliness of the intrusion. So must many an Arctic coast burn unseen.

Far below the basin seemed to sleep in the shadow, but *Tirpitz* broke the spell with a salvo, sparkling from stem to stern with flashes as billows of smoke from the guns wreathed her and drifted up. Her captain had just radioed urgently to Bardufoss to hurry the fighters.

Tait opened the bomb doors and slid the pitch levers up to high revs.; the engines bellowed and the exhausts glowed even in that cold light. Black puffs stained the sky among the gaggle as the flak reached them, and then the guns round the fiord opened fire. Tait watched anxiously for the smoke pots, but the smoke never came (the pots were there all right, just brought down from Alten, but the Germans had not yet primed them). The bomb sight was on and the ship drawing nearer while the gunners in the rear turrets watched the ridges anxiously for the first fighters. It was all up to the rear gunners when the fighters came; there were no mid-upper gunners.

Now it was water, far below, sliding under the nose. Tait felt his hands on the wheel were clammy, and Daniels' breathing rasped over the intercom. The bomber was unswerving, shaking in the engines' thunder, and out of the cockpit Tait could see the bomb doors quivering as the airflow battered at them. The red light came on—ten seconds to go . . . seconds that dragged till "D Dog" leapt as the grips snapped back and the bomb lurched away. Tait hauled hard over to the left and on either side saw others on the front rank doing likewise.

One by one the gaggle wheeled as the bombs went. They watched, wordless, through the perspex for thirty

seconds till a great yellow flash burst on the battleship's
foredeck. From 14,000 feet they saw her tremble. Another bomb hit the shore; two more in close succession
hit the ship, one on the starboard side, by the bridge,
and another abaft the funnel (one of them was Astbury's). Another one split the sea 5 feet from her bows,
and then the smoke pall covered her and only dimly
through it they saw the other bursts all inside the crino-
line of nets.

One constant glare shone through the smoke. She
was burning. There came another flash and a plume of
steam jetted 500 feet into the air through the smoke as
a magazine went up.

Three minutes later 9 Squadron bombed the dark
shroud over her, and then the black flies crawling in the
sky turned south-west and curved down towards the
sea, picking up speed for the run home. They never saw
a fighter. The last thing they saw as the smoke lifted
was the *Tirpitz* starting to list.

The cloud they had feared closed in on the long slog
home, and Tait was driving blindly through it when his
artificial horizon collapsed in a mess of ball bearings and
mechanism. After eleven hours in the air his eyes felt
like hot coals as he focused rigidly on the other instruments; then the aerial iced up and they could not get a
homing for a long time, and when they did it was a
diversion. Lossiemouth was cloaked in rain, and Tait
turned east and found a small Coastal Command field,
where he touched down smoothly.

At the control tower a young pilot officer asked if
they had been on a cross-country, and Tait primly
pursed his mouth, looked in aloof shyness at the ground
and said, "Yes." A torpedo-bomber squadron lived on
the field, and later he told the C.O. where they had
been.

"Did you get her?" the C.O. asked.

"I think so. Gave her a hell of a nudge anyway."

"Thanks," the C.O. said. *"We* might have had to do
it. Low level. I shouldn't have liked it."

They drove over to Lossiemouth, where they met the
rest of the squadron, and were drinking in the bar when

the recce plane radioed that *Tirpitz* was upside down in Tramsö Fiord, her bottom humped over the water like a stranded whale.

In his room in Tromsö, Lindberg, the Norwegian agent, was tapping out the Morse signals that confirmed it. Under his floor, in the morgue, the Germans were laying out their dead.

Not all of the dead. A thousand men were trapped below when she rolled over. The Germans tried to cut holes in the hull to reach them but did not get any out. They had spent the war miserably, lying in the bleak fiords of Norway, never venturing out. They fought the ship to the last, died without honour when the war was nearly over, and after the war still lay rotting in her hull.

The fighter commander at Bardufoss was facing court martial. Radar had warned him forty-five minutes before the bombers reached the ship, and all that time the *Tirpitz*'s captain had been sending him urgent messages. He was still asking for the fighters when the bombs blotted out his radio, but the fighters never came.

Just after *Tirpitz* saw the bombers come over the mountain, a message came from Bardufoss that an enemy formation was over the airfield and the fighters could not take off, but there were no Allied fighters for a thousand miles. No one seems to know quite what happened. Some of the fighters are said to have taken off, but by some miracle they did not intercept.

The squadron flew back to Woodhall and were greeted outside the control by an Army band playing "See the conquering heroes come." In the mess they found messages from the King, War Cabinet, Harris, Cochrane, Wallis, the Navy, Prince Olav of Norway, and even one from the Russians, congratulating them.

(It was not till after the war they found it had all been unnecessary. The bomb Tait and Daniels had dropped six weeks earlier at Alten Fiord had damaged *Tirpitz* beyond repair.) The Germans towed her to Tromsö, not to repair her but to moor her in shallow water as an unsinkable fortress. Powerful German forces in Northern Norway meant to hold out there. They blundered and moored her in 50 feet of water and tried to repair the mistake by filling in the sea-bed beneath her with dredges, but did not have time. There was still enough water below to let her down.

Someone at the Admiralty apparently did not *quite* agree and said (a little huffily, according to the story) that they could not mark her as definitely sunk because her bottom was still showing; but that did not deter a certain dynamic personality at Bomber Command from grunting with deep satisfaction to one of his subordinates when he heard the *Tirpitz* was sunk, "That's one in the eye for the Nautics!"

The incredible Cochrane took it all in his stride. At least on the surface. They held a conference every morning at 5 Group to discuss the previous night's operations, and the coming night's plans. Cochrane presided over them, looking flintily over his half-moon glasses like Harris, and the morning after the raid, when he sat down, his staff officers thought that this time they would see a break in the iron exterior. Cochrane glanced at his minutes and said, "Er . . . last night's raid. . . . Successful! *Tirpitz* sunk! Now, about to-night's operations. . . ."

20

BACK FROM THE DEAD

After the excitement of the *Tirpitz* came anti-climax. Unbroken cloud lay over Europe for weeks, making high precision bombing impossible. 617 stood by constantly, were briefed hopefully a dozen times and then the cancellations came. Once they got into the air but were recalled.

Carey, Witherick and company arrived back, gloating over their taste of peacetime flesh-pots in Sweden but furious at missing the end of the *Tirpitz*. "You might have waited for us, sir," Witherick said aggrievedly to Tait. "You *know* I always come back."

Increasing sea losses testified to the fact that Germany's fleet of "Schnorkel" U-boats was increasing. For all the main force bombing, the U-boats found shelter in the massive pens and Cochrane switched 617 on to them again. They battered the pens at Ijmuiden (the port of Amsterdam) with six direct hits. Calder's Lancaster was badly hit by flak and he made an emergency landing at a nearer base. A fair-haired, keen-faced young Englishman, Calder was making a name for himself as a determined pilot. Joplin was hit in Knilans' old "R Roger," struggled back to England but crashed near Woodhall, killing two of the crew. Calder led them on the next trip and they slammed some more "tallboys" on top of the Ijmuiden pens, leaving a huge hole in the massive concrete roof.

Cochrane decided that Tait had done enough. Tait had four D.S.O.s now and two D.F.C.s—a record—and Cochrane did not want him to strain his luck too far. Shopping round for a new commander, he found no one with all the qualities he wanted till an air commodore heard the position was vacant and asked to be dropped in rank and given the job—a laudable request, as it meant stepping down from a highly-prized rank. This was Johnnie Fauquier, a Canadian, and a tough one, a thick-set, ex-bush-pilot, who did not smile much (nor say much. With his curt voice he did not have to say much). Ten years older than most of them, he was as forceful as a steam-roller. The night he arrived there was a party to farewell the revered Tait and welcome the new man.

To put it mildly, 617's welcome to a new commander was exacting. They were, perhaps, a little above themselves, conscious of their lustre and jealous of trespass on it. It is a trait common to an elect corps, an inseparable if less tractable facet of the unique ardour that leads men to the corps and drives them on to the heights. It is the hand-maiden of achievement and often the mainspring of it. You find it among commandos, business tycoons, geniuses, and sometimes in child delinquents. It is invaluable in a soldier and sometimes indecorous in a civilian. 617 had it. That was the first thing Fauquier found out.

Someone said, "Sing a song or take your pants off" . . . their favourite way of puncturing the dignity of a high officer. Fauquier unhitched his pants imperturbably, and Witherick, secure in the legend of his immortality, cooled him off with a can of beer strategically aimed from the rear. Fauquier philosophically hitched up his pants and thus passed the test.

He had his revenge. Cochrane had told him when he took over, "You've got to see 617 is kept up to the mark and stays as good as ever." Fauquier saw to that. Feeling that the war was almost over, the crews had been in a mood to relax and were scandalised when Fauquier got them out of bed in the frosty early mornings for P.T. Storms were sweeping over Europe and the runways were snowed up, so there was no flying. Fauquier gave them lectures instead, and then made them shovel snow off the runways.

On the last day of the year the weather eased and he

led them on more serious work. Convoys had been streaming out of Oslo under cover of night as the Germans tried to move troops back from Norway to reinforce the crumbling fronts. Cochrane told them to unmask a convoy with flares and set about it. It was a bleak, black night, but they found the convoy and, lit by the floating flares, the convoy fanned out and scattered. The bombers chased them, but the ships zigzagged all over the sea. 617 had never dealt with mobile targets before and cursed eloquently as they found they had not mastered the technique of position the flares. Fauquier and a couple of others found a cruiser and hunted her, only to see their bombs fall just too wide to be effective. The others all missed too and flew home in chastened mood, but cheered up considerably when they heard that the cruiser in her efforts to dodge the bombs had run on the rocks.

More days waiting for weather; more briefings, more cancellations, till January 12, when they went to Bergen, in Norway, on the old campaign against U-boats. For the first time Fauquier flew a Mosquito to direct them and for the first time in months German fighters fell on them like a swarm of hornets. They got Pryor on their first strike and he went straight into the sea. Three of them lunged at Nicky Ross on the flank of the gaggle. Watts, next to him, saw the tracer flicking into the Lancaster and lumps flying off her. He wheeled to help him, but Ross was going down, slewing into a spiral with three engines smashed. Near the water he seemed to recover; the spiral stopped, the mad dive eased and the plane had almost flattened out when it abruptly vanished in a sheet of spray.

The fighters hammered Iveson too, set his port inner on fire and riddled his tailplane and rudder so that he had almost no fore-and-aft control. He was fighting to keep her flying, while his two gunners and the wireless operator baled out, and suddenly the fighters broke off the attack and vanished. They were not very resolute.

Heavy flak over Bergen crippled Castagnola and he had to jettison and turn for home. The rest took vengeance. Someone put a "tallboy" squarely on the stern of a large ship and in two minutes she had blown up, rolled over and sunk. The rest got several direct hits on the pens.

Next morning Chiefy Powell was sadly typing out the casualty report on Nicky Ross (who had been on the squadron nearly a year—longer than any other pilot) when the door swung open and in walked Ross himself.

Powell gaped.

"Wotcher, Chiefy," quoth the ghost. "Home again!"

"Good God, sir! Where've you come from?"

"Air-sea rescue picked us up. Bloody cold in that dinghy." He sat on a corner of the desk and rattled on amiably about the details.

After some splutters Powell found speech. "D'you know what I was doing when you walked in, sir? Typing your death notice!"

"Ar, hold it for a while, Chiefy," said the cheerful Ross. "You're a bit premature."

Bad weather again. Weeks of it, with stand-by, briefings, cancellations, training and more training—and P.T.

Meantime the first "grand slam" was nearly ready. A thousand craftsmen had been working for months on the top-secret project and only a bare dozen of them knew what it was all about. In Sheffield the English Steel Corporation had spent weeks trying to find a steel that would stand up to the shock. They forged shells from all the steels they knew and fired them into concrete and steel till they found one that stood up to it, a secret formula of their own. Two firms in the country could cast the complicated casing, and for each bomb they had to build an individual concrete-covered core to the most precise ten-thousandth of an inch, position it meticulously inside a sand-surfaced mould, pour the molten steel in and wait two days for it to cool before they could chip the core away. The 10-ton casting travelled then a hundred miles for machining.

It puzzled the workmen. One man watching the shining brute said he thought it was a midget submarine. The executives labelled it officially as a "boiler" but that fooled no one. Around the Sheffield pubs the men

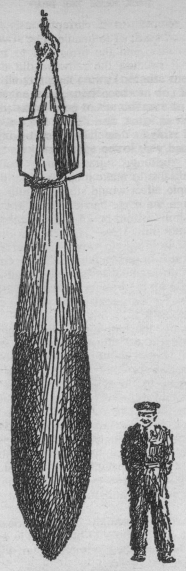

Grand Slam

sometimes referred to it surreptitiously as "the big bastard." It was a devil to handle. The Army had nearly all the cranes, and the firms had to make special trailers for it because the railways did not have the facilities to handle it. At the filling factory they built a special cradle for it, stood it inside on its nose and built a high platform so they could pour in the tons of explosive a bucketful at a time. They tried thirty different types of fuse before they picked on one they thought would stand up to the shock of impact.

Like the "tallboy," "grand slam's" tail had offset aero-dynamic fins to make it spin so fast in falling that the gyroscopic effect would stop it toppling as it shuddered through the sonic barrier. When the tail was put on "grand slam" would be 25 feet 6 inches long. At its thickest part it was 3 feet 10 inches in diameter, and the finished bomb was to weigh just over 22,000 lb. It was such a difficult undertaking that they could produce no dummies for normal tests; they hoped to have one prototype to drop before they used it on business.

But that was a few weeks ahead yet.

The German fighter force was nearly spent now, making it possible for 617's inadequately armed Lancasters to penetrate deeper and deeper against the enemy by day. They carried on with "tallboys" against the U-boat pens, slathering the concrete strongholds at Poortershaven, Ijmuiden, Hamburg and the monster at Farge, near Bremen, losing two or three crews but getting literally dozens of direct hits on the massive roofs.

Designed for earth penetration and dropped from less than half the prescribed height, the "tallboys" never did quite penetrate the thickest of the concrete before exploding, but did almost as well. As on the Brest pens, they knifed deeply in and then blew right through the ceiling.

At Hamburg they brought down a thousand tons of concrete that crushed two U-boats inside and crippled six others. They smashed servicing gear, killed dozens of men and created panic.

At Ijmuiden they brought down 13,000 tons of concrete over hundreds of feet of roof and wall (near misses did a lot of that by shock wave). Much the same things happened at Bergen and Poortershaven. At Bergen a near miss sank two U-boats and lofted another one on to the dock wall.

Congestion in these ports and pens had been growing steadily worse as the Allies overran Germany's other bases. Now, after the bombing, it was lapsing into chaos, U-boat raids were dwindling and the morale of the men who built, serviced and sailed them was decaying.

His armies poised for the jump over the Rhine, Eisenhower asked the Air Forces for an all-out assault on German communications to sever the front from the rest of Germany. Now that the Dortmund–Ems Canal was permanently drained the vulnerable points were the railway bridges, the most vital of these was the Bielefeld Viaduct, not far from Bremen, main link between the Wehrmacht defending the arsenal of the Ruhr and the great centres of north-west Germany. The idea was to starve the front of men and materials and split the country into "islands" that could be taken one by one.

Three thousand tons of bombs had already been aimed at the Bielefeld Viaduct; the earth for a mile around it was torn into overlapping craters, but the 75-foot arches of the viaduct still firmly bridged the marshes for the trains running south. The light-case bombs of the main bomber forces were not powerful enough to do more than chip it. Cochrane turned 617 on to it, and so began the battle of Bielefeld.

They took off with their "tallboys" one morning, but found the viaduct under ten-tenths cloud and brought them back. Next day they tried once more but again found unbroken cloud. Days later the cloud had cleared; they flew back to Bielefeld, found it reasonably clear and a few minutes later the viaduct was hidden under smoke as the "tallboys" crashed round it. Half an hour later, when the smoke lifted, a recce aircraft found the viaduct still there. "Tallboy" craters lay in its shadow, but the viaduct was no rotund target like a bull's-eye or a U-boat pen. From 18,000 feet it was

The Bielefeld Viaduct

almost indistinguishably threadlike. It was like trying to stick a dart in a line.

They waited on the weather and tried again a few days later, but once more found it under cloud. Doggedly they went back a fifth time and turned away in fuming frustration once more. There seemed to be something diabolical about the persistence of the cloud that shielded it.

That night two heavy trailers rolled round the perimeter track to the bomb dump carrying the first two "grand slams." In the morning armourers trolleyed them out and slowly winched them up into Fauquier's and Calder's Lancasters, specially modified in readiness for this day. They had the most powerful Merlin engines, the fuselages, undercarriages and main beams of the bomb bays had been strengthened and the bomb doors taken off (they could not have closed round the great girth of "Grand Slam").

"Grand Slam" had never been tested. There had not been time. Only one other "grand slam" existed, and that very morning a Lancaster was going to drop it over the range in the New Forest. Group was waiting for that, and also for the cloud to clear.

Just before noon Met. reported the cloud over Germany rolling away. As Fauquier was briefing his crews a phone message reached Group from the New Forest: "The beast went off all right!"

21

"GRAND SLAM"

At one o'clock 617's engines were bursting into life round the field. Fauquier was running up his engines, testing his magnetos, when there was a crash from the starboard inner and the propeller jerked to a grinding halt as it seized. Fauquier, muttering with frustration, knew the aircraft would never get off the ground on three engines. There was only one thing to do . . . borrow Calder's aircraft. The fact that he might then be shot down instead of Calder never even occurred to him, and would not have worried him if it had. He scuttled out of his plane and went haring across the field.

Calder saw the running figure, shouting and waving hands in urgent signals, guessed what had happened and cracked his throttles open. The Lancaster lurched forward and, with the small figure sprinting despairingly in the rear, rolled thunderously down the runway, picking up speed till it lifted heavily over the far fence on the way to drop the world's biggest bomb.

The "tallboy"-armed gaggle fell in behind, watching Calder's wings in wonder and alarm. On the ground a Lancaster has no perceptible dihedral, the wings spread in a flat, straight line, but Calder's wings now were a graceful arc, curving up at the tips as they took the strain of the 10-tonner. Those underneath could see the great missile hanging in the bomb bays where the bomb doors used to be.

The sky was clear of cloud; they skirted the flak at Bremen and ten minutes later picked up the line of the viaduct threading across the marshes. Calder headed

in, the laden bomber thrusting smoothly through the
bumps till Calder felt her bound up as the "grand slam"
slipped away from the grips.

Wheeling away, they watched it drop like a silver
shark, slowly starting to spin as its nose dipped lower
and it picked up speed, lunging towards the viaduct. It
fell for some thirty-five seconds and from far above
the sharpest eyes picked up the squirt of mud as it
speared into the marsh 30 yards from the foot of one of
the arches.

Eleven seconds later the marsh seemed to split and
a vast core of mud and smoke vomited up, blotting
out 500 feet of the viaduct. In the next seconds "tallboy" explosions erupted along both sides of the viaduct.
Calder peeled off to try and see what had happened;
slowly the mud settled, the wind wafted the smoke
away, and as the target appeared through the veils
Calder saw that the viaduct looked like a Roman ruin.
Seven massive arches over a hundred yards were missing.

He could see almost no collapsed masonry underneath and thought for a moment that the bomb had
blasted the arches into dust, but could not believe that
possible.

Later they found that the one "grand slam" had
completely vindicated Barnes Wallis's theory that a
near miss could be more effective than a direct hit. It
had penetrated about a hundred feet, and the shock
wave had shivered the arches to cracking point; the
explosion had produced a near "camouflet," blasting
an enormous subterranean cavity underneath, and,
robbed of their foundation in the mud, the weakened
arches had collapsed into the abyss. It was the perfect
trapdoor effect, the "hangman's drop" that Wallis had
planned in 1939.

A recce photograph showed an enormous crater
which Wallis described as "exquisite." Cochrane wired
617: "You certainly made a proper mess of it this
time and incidentally added another page to your history
by being the first squadron to drop the biggest bomb on
Germany. Good work. Keep up the training. We can't
afford to put them in the wrong place."

In the next few days trailers delivered several more "grand slams" to the bomb dump, and on March 19 Fauquier got his delayed chance to drop one. The target was in historic territory for 617, the Arnsberg Bridge, a long masonry viaduct a few miles north of the Moehne Dam. Five Lancasters carried "grand slams," and the other fourteen had "tallboys." The first bomb was a direct hit on the viaduct, and the rest, including Fauquier's "grand slam," went down into the centre of the smoke that gushed up. When the smoke lifted, the central spans were a pile of rubble in the river bed.

Two days later they went to the Arbergen Bridge, near Bremen. Flak got a direct hit on Gumbley's aircraft on the run-up and he went straight down in flames. Price had to swerve out of the way of the falling aircraft, marring his bombing run, but he straightened up and his bomb aimer, Pilot Officer Chance—by a very good chance indeed—lobbed his "tallboy" a direct hit on the viaduct. There was one more direct hit and a lot of near misses. Two piers collapsed, another one was thrown 15 feet out of alignment and earthquake shock threw a span off another pier. Target destroyed.

Next day they went to the Nienburg Bridge, near Bremen, over which the Germans were taking oil to the front. It was not heavily defended, so Fauquier evolved a new plan to try and save some of the precious earthquake bombs. On the way up to the target he ordered four aircraft to start their bombing runs and told the others to circle nearby and wait for orders in case the first four missed. It was an unprecedented idea, and the very fact that Fauquier considered it possible speaks eloquently of their phenomenal accuracy. He himself dived low to one side of the target to watch.

The results were fantastic. The four Lancasters made a steady run in loose formation and bombed almost in the same second. Fauquier saw the first two bombs hit simultaneously (one of them a "grand slam") on each end of the bridge. The bridge span lifted bodily and still intact into the air, seemed to hang there a second, and in that very moment a third bomb hit it fair and square in the middle. When the smoke had cleared there was no visible sign of the bridge whatsoever and the squadron turned for home, taking their fifteen remaining bombs with them.

Fauquier said when he landed, "Hell, I'd hate to have to do *that* again to prove it."

The Germans had one last railway bridge still serving the Ruhr; it was also near Bremen, and 617 went there early next morning. The first three bombs (from 16,000 feet) hit almost in the same second, all direct hits (including Fauquier's and Calder's "grand slams"). The next two were very near misses, followed by what seemed to be one more direct hit before smoke smothered the ruins.

(Kehrl, head of the German planning office, said later that chaotic communications were responsible for 90 per cent of the decline in German war production in the last three months of the war.)

If Wallis's big bombs had been available earlier (with the aircraft to carry them) the Germans would probably not have lasted as long as they did. Their industry and transport would have been disrupted earlier, just as Wallis had forecast in 1939, though the R.A.F. might have suffered sore losses battling through the fighters by day deep into Germany in the earlier stages, as the Americans did.

As there were no worthwhile bridges left, 617 went back on the U-boat pens. At Farge, near Bremen, 7,000 slaves had sweated for two years to build the biggest concrete structure in the world, 1,450 feet long, over 300 feet wide and 75 feet high, a staggering monument to Hitler's ruthless obstinacy. The first design was for a roof 16 feet thick, but after 617 had visited the Brest pens Hitler had put on another thousand slaves, and in March, 1945, the roof was 23 feet of solid reinforced concrete and the pens were just ready for use.

617 paid their call on March 27 and sank two "grand slams" deep in the roof which exploded right through, making holes 20 feet across and bringing down thousands of tons of concrete. Several "tallboys," di-

rect hits and near misses, cracked the monster and undermined it and the pens were never used.

It was hard to find good targets now till a recce plane brought a report that Germany's last pocket battleship, the *Lützow,* was sheltering in Swinemünde, in the Baltic, deep into enemy territory towards the Russian Front, where fighters could be expected. 617 slogged up there on April 13 (not an encouraging date) only to find it smothered under cloud. They went back two days later; ten-tenths cloud again. By this time it was obvious they were after the *Lützow.* Fauquier guessed the German fighters would be alerted and he asked for, and got, an escort of long-range fighters. Next day they went back with the fighters and found the target clear but the flak waiting for them.

They picked out the *Lützow* far below, a microbe on the water beside the quay, and as they turned on her the flak burst among them savagely, predicting deadly accurately on the unwavering formation. Clusters of puffs blotched the patch of sky in which they moved, so that nearly every one of the eighteen bombers was hit and holes opened in wings and fuselages as shrapnel ripped through. Gordon and Gavin both lost engines and started to lag. A heavy shell got a direct hit on Powell; his port wing folded up and the big plane spun down dragging a tail of flame like a comet. One parachute came out.

Then the gaggle was peeling off out of the flak as the bombs went down. Three bombs hit close together, straddling the ship, one in the alley between the bows and the quay. Other bombs vanished into the spray and smoke that enveloped her.

They flew back unmolested and next morning were stood down completely. After the flak only two of their aircraft were serviceable, and the ground crews were toiling over the others, riveting on patches. The aircrews were content to relax and await news of the *Lützow.* The recce aircraft landed with photographs, and such was the squadron's self-confidence that a howl of incredulity went up as they saw the *Lützow* still by the quay, apparently untouched. The recce pilot swore there was no mistake. He had flown right over her, and there, indubitably, she lay, decks clearly visible.

It was another two days before they found out that *Lützow* had sunk as far as the sea-bed would let her. The near miss by the bows had torn out her bottom; the dock was not very deep, but *Lützow* was finished, lying on the mud.

(Someone in the Navy claimed she was not *really* sunk because her decks were still above water.)

As soon as their aircraft were repaired 617 took some "grand slams" and "tallboys" to Heligoland and plastered half the island fortress's big guns. Next day they went back and plastered the other half, ending Germany's mastery of the approaches to the north-west ports.

Cochrane went to take over Transport Command, which, now the shooting was nearly over, was coming into its own. The new 5 Group A.O.C. told Fauquier he was grounded because he did not want him killed in the last moments. The tough Canadian had just finished his third tour and had won three D.S.O.s and a D.F.C.

The remnants of the Wehrmacht were said to be pulling back into Hitler's "Southern Redoubt" in Bavaria, where Berchtesgaden lay. It seemed that there was no more work for 617 till someone remembered that Hitler had recently told his Party chiefs, "I have read these days in the British Press that they intend to destroy my country house. I almost regret that this has not been done, for what I call my own is not more valuable than my compatriots possess."

Eager to ease his conscience, 617 flew to Berchtesgaden, hoping that if Hitler was there they might bury him in his house. As the world knows, Hitler was in Berlin, but it made no difference because the land was deep under snow and Berchtesgaden merged with the white hills and low cloud so that the squadron could not pick it out. However, they identified the nearby S.S. barracks, home of Hitler's bodyguard, and flat-

tened them with four "tallboys" and a selection of
1,000-pounders, and that, with Hitler away, was probably more useful than laying their eggs on the Eagle's
Nest.

That was 617's last operation, or perhaps not quite
the last. Fauquier went to Germany on his own and by
chance received from a beaten enemy a somehow sym-
bolic surrender in the name of the squadron.

The Admiralty, while admitting 617's accuracy on
the U-boat pens, would not believe that their big
bombs had gone through the concrete roofs. Harris told
Fauquier to go over and see, and he flew to a Tactical
Air Force base just south of Hamburg. In the morning,
with another group captain and an interpreter, he drove
off in a jeep for the Hamburg dock area on the understanding that Hamburg was to surrender at ten o'clock
that morning.

Driving through Hamburg they wondered why they
saw no signs of Allied troops and why German soldiers
stared at them, but it never occurred to them that
Hamburg had not, in fact, surrendered and no British
troops, apart from themselves, had reached the city.

They pulled up in the shadow of the great pens,
walked through a side door and stood fascinated by
the cavernous ruin inside. Several of the big bombs had
punched through the roof, and twisted metal and the
rubble of fallen concrete littered the place. They were
looking soberly down on two crushed U-boats sunk in
one of the docks when they became aware that they
were not alone. A Nazi sailor stood behind them. He
saluted. Would the officers be good enough to come and
see his commanding officer? They followed him to the
other side of the pens and stopped in surprise to see
200 German sailors lined up. Their commanding officer marched up, clicked his heels and saluted. He
would like, he said, to surrender the Hamburg dock area.

Fauquier was most embarrassed. He still did not
know that Hamburg was still in German hands. Neither, as it happened, did the German officer. The pens
were out of touch by phone with Hamburg city, and

that is the only reason he was surrendering to Fauquier instead of Fauquier to him.

The interpreter rather tactlessly told the German that Fauquier had led the raid which had smashed the pens, a most disconcerting *gaffe*. Fauquier waited warily for the avenging wrath and was astonished when the German clicked his heels, bowed to him and said cordially, "My congratulations on a very good raid."

Fauquier, not knowing quite what to do, clicked his own heels, bowed back and said, "Thank you."

The German said that he had been in the pens at the time with a lot of his men and everyone had been killed except him. He was the sole survivor because he had happened to be in the steel-enclosed overhead crane. He invited them to lunch in his mess. The mess was a literal "mess" in a crazily-tilted cabin of a half-sunken cargo ship. They followed him on board and lunched on dry biscuits spread with sausage meat while the German told them their bombs were rocket-propelled to break through the concrete roof of the pens. Fauquier did not enlighten him.

Totally unaware of the protocol of surrender, Fauquier got the Germans to pile all their small arms in the jeep and drove off back through the city.

And then on May 8 it was all over and the 150 pilots, navigators, bomb aimers, wireless operators, engineers, and gunners realised they were going to have the same chance as ordinary people of walking down the years to a more natural death.

But no. Not quite. 617 and one other squadron were detailed for "Tiger Force," to be the R.A.F.'s contribution to the strategic bombing of Japan. They were to fly from Okinawa and drop their "tallboys" and "grand slams" on the bridges connecting Kyushu to the main Japanese island of Honshu to cut off reinforcements when the Americans invaded Kyushu, as they planned, in January, 1946. They were all set to go when the two bombs so much deadlier than "Grand Slam" fell on Hiroshima and Nagasaki and Japan surrendered.

"Hell!" said the thwarted volunteers. "They must have heard we were coming."

EPILOGUE

617 is still flying, but all that is left of the old days now are the squadron number and the tradition. The men who won over 150 decorations and made the tradition are scattered, and many of them are dead.

Gibson is dead. When he came back from America he toyed with the idea of going into politics but soon perceived there is a little more to politics than wisdom and sincerity, so he politely declined the prospect of directorships and elected to stay in the R.A.F.

On July 11, 1944, he was disconsolately flying a desk when Micky Martin flew over in a Mosquito, and Gibson eyed the little plane wistfully. Martin took him up for a couple of circuits and then Gibson flew it himself; he said when he landed, "I'm fed up with sitting on my tail. I'm going back on ops." He worried his seniors till they reluctantly agreed, and a few weeks later Gibson took off in a Mosquito for one last raid to act as master bomber of 5 Group on a factory at Rheydt, near the Ruhr. He guided the bombing, and when it was over they heard his voice on the R/T saying, "O.K., chaps. That's fine. Now beat it home."

No one knows exactly what happened after that. They think Gibson may have been hit by flak. He crashed into a low hill in Holland 60 miles from Rheydt on the way home, and the Dutch buried him there.

The Moehne Dam has been repaired, the lake refilled, but the valley below is littered with twisted, rusted girders and lumps of concrete, and the earth still looks as though a giant's rake had scoured it. Where Himmelpforten stood the foundations still lie round the ruins of the church. Set among them is a rough wooden cross with neither name nor inscription. As far as 60 miles away the surviving villagers found the church's chalice, christening font, crucifix and some of the stones, and less than a mile away stands the new church of Porta Coeli built by the villagers. Around the altar is a Latin inscription, restrained and unmalicious: "The wreckage of the church of Himmelpforten, destroyed by flood in 1943, served six years later to build this new altar and his new Porta Coeli."

Martin distinguished himself as a night-fighter pilot, winning another bar to his D.F.C. After the war he shepherded the squadron of Vampires in the first jet flights across the Atlantic, nursing them skilfully through foul weather that nearly brought them to disaster. Then he broke the London–Capetown and return record in a Mosquito and added an A.F.C. to his two D.S.O.s and three D.F.C.s. That year he was awarded the Britannia Trophy, Britain's premier aviation award.

Cheshire's forecast about Martin and his potential came true. As I revise this in 1969, Micky Martin is now an Air Vice-Marshal in command of the R.A.F.'s biggest Group. But still not far under the brass hat and braid lies the same old blithe and mettlesome spirit. He had married the girl, Wendy, who was so reluctant to lunch with him after the dams raid, and under her tuition has become a very accomplished painter in oils. (At the dawn of 1971 Martin was promoted again and knighted, becoming Air Marshal Sir Harold Martin, K.C.B., D.S.O., D.F.C., A.F.C.)

Cochrane is now an Air Chief Marshal, three times knighted and second in command of the R.A.F. Now that the pressure of war is off his austerity has thawed, except when he finds inefficiency, and then he is his old incisive self, still probably the best brain in the Air Force.

Not far from Whitehall, Willie Tait has also been patiently decorating an R.A.F. desk. Usually he wears mufti and a bowler, and looks deceptively shy and neat until someone blunders; then the lips still tighten into that prim, pursed look that Cochrane once called his "mule face."

Fauquier retired with his old rank of air commodore

and is now head of a big company in Toronto. His business, oddly enough, is building concrete structures. A change from knocking them down.

Cheshire! Cheshire had a variety of ideas for after the war, most of them as original as himself. One was the "Modern *Mayflower*," to take picked comrades on a chartered ship and settle on an island. Another was to fly orchids from the Caribbean to New York, and another to grow mushrooms in disused tunnels. He had another scheme for forming a company with Martin, Shannon and Munro for experimental aviation. Cheshire said they might finish up flying to the moon, and they looked sideways at him, though it seems now that he was not looking impossibly far ahead after all.

Then the Prime Minister sent him to the Pacific, and he flew in an American plane as Attlee's personal representative to watch the atom bomb fall on Nagasaki. He came back, resigned from the Air Force and collected a band of unsettled ex-Servicemen to form a communal group which he called *"Vade in Pacem"* (May you walk in peace) in an old house in Hampshire left him by an aunt. Cheshire's health broke down; he went to Canada to recover, and for eight months in a forest hamlet in the Rockies the intellectual V.C. delivered groceries, cut wood and collected corpses for the local undertaker.

He sold his clothes to pay his fare back to England, arriving in Hampshire at Christmas, 1947, to find his settlement breaking up and £18,000 of debts on his head. He sold his furniture to pay his more pressing debts, and was sitting alone in the empty house when he heard of an old man dying of cancer nearby; he had put his age back fifteen years to join the R.A.F. in the war and now had no one to help him. Cheshire borrowed a bed and took him in, nursed him, cooked for him, scrubbed the floors, carried the bedpans, washed the old man's pyjamas and lived off the garden. He heard of a bedridden women of ninety-five with no one to help her, borrowed another bed and took her in.

The man was dying, and Cheshire was sitting with him in the middle of the night when he stopped breathing. There was a religious book on the bed, and Cheshire picked it up and started to read. When he had finished it he went to see the local Roman Catholic priest and four months later joined the Catholic Church.

Meantime, of its own volition, the house had grown into a hospital. Incurables kept knocking on the door and he took them in. The place had a strange spirit about it; bed-ridden patients helped by sewing and darning; a few who could walk put rags under their feet and shuffled over the floors to scrub them. Nurses and students came down to help in their spare time, and several men and women gave up their jobs for the privilege of living and working in the place. They had nearly forty patients and no money but somehow kept going.

Cheshire sold some cottages on the property, and some time about the middle of 1949 found he was free of debt. I've asked him several times how he paid it all off, and he always says, "I can't really explain it. Things just seemed to work out." He did, in fact, develop a fatalistic attitude that if he did not worry things would be all right. Peculiarly enough, they were.

A man called Cowie did his books, and one Wednesday he went to Cheshire and said, "Look, we're ten pounds short for our bills on Friday. We can't meet them."

"This isn't Friday," Cheshire said. "See me about it then. Something will turn up."

On Friday a letter arrived with £12 in notes from a woman in London. No one had been in touch with her.

Weeks later they were about £10 short again on the Wednesday. On the Friday a letter arrived from the same woman with another £12. Again no one had told her. The same thing happened once more a few weeks later.

Cowie, who has no faith (he is an agnostic), says that sort of thing kept happening. After a while, in spite of himself, he developed some of Cheshire's fatalism, and once, just before Christmas, when they had debts of £40 to pay and no money in the bank, Cowie went nervously to Cheshire and said: "I've sent off those cheques for the full amount. I only hope something turns up."

Next morning's post brought a cheque for £41.

The renown of the place spread until regular bene-factors shouldered the burden of paying some of the bills. That left Cheshire with time on his hands, and it was Sir Ralph Cochrane who found him a job. A singu-larly appropriate one—working for Barnes Wallis.

Later, Cheshire felt the call to go on with his Homes for the Needy and since then he has established them, with the help of the Church, in various quarters of the world. At last he has found his niche—a full and satis-fying one.

At Weybridge, Wallis stayed the white-haired pa-triarch, pink-faced, gentle and abstracted as ever, an old-fashioned doyen with new-fangled vision browsing over the same old drawing-board, still getting out-landish ideas which unaccountably work. Strange about Wallis. He designed and constructed the only successful British airship during the 'Thirties. Then he designed the Wellesley bomber which captured the world's long distance flight record. Then he designed the Wellington bomber, which was the early mainstay of the R.A.F. Bomber Command and was still operational into the fifties. When I was researching this book back in 1950, I can remember Barnes Wallis enthusiastically showing me his design for a "swing-wing" aircraft. It was turned down by the British Government but later taken up by the Americans and French! At this moment of revi-sion, 1969, he is working on a radical aircraft wing structure that will enable an aircraft to fly at 18,000 miles an hour. But the only official recognition he ever received was a C.B.E. after the dams raid. About as mean as one could get. In early 1969, some twenty-six years too late, the British Government belatedly offered him a knighthood. He accepted without much feeling one way or the other and the now Sir Barnes retains his same kindly and gentle attitude to the world.

After the war his friends urged him to claim a reward for his wartime inventions, but he said that if he did he would never touch such money for himself. I asked him why and he said, "My dear chap, go and read your Bible, turn up Samuel II, Chapter 23. You probably haven't got a Bible so I'll tell you this story about David.

"He was hiding in the cave of Adullam after the Philistines had seized Bethlehem, and in his anguish he said, 'O that one would give me a drink of water of the well of Bethlehem, which is by the gate!' Now the three mighty men who were his lieutenants were with him, and I'm dashed if they didn't fight their way through the Philistine lines and draw a goatskin of water out of the well by the gate. They fought their way back and took the water to David in the cave, but when they told him how they had got it he would not drink it. They asked him why, and he said:

"'Is not this the blood of the men that went in jeopardy of their lives?' "

(Just after this was written the Royal Commission on Awards to Inventors granted Barnes Wallis £10,000 for his wartime work. He immediately put it into a fund to help educate the sons and daughters of men who died serving with the Royal Air Force.)

BANTAM WAR BOOKS

Introducing a new series of carefully selected books that cover the full dramatic sweep of World War II heroism—viewed from all sides and in all branches of armed service, whether on land, sea or in the air. Most of the volumes are eye-witness accounts by men who fought in the conflict—true stories of brave men in action.

Each book in this series has a dramatic cover painting plus specially commissioned drawings, diagrams and maps to aid readers in a deeper understanding of the roles played by men and machines during the war.

FLY FOR YOUR LIFE by Larry Forrester
The glorious story of Robert Stanford Tuck, Britain's greatest air ace, credited with downing 29 enemy aircraft. Tuck was himself shot down 4 times and finally captured. However, he organized a fantastic escape that led him through Russia and back to England to marry the woman he loved.

THE FIRST AND THE LAST
by Adolf Galland
The top German air ace with over 70 kills, here is Galland's own story. He was commander of all fighter forces in the Luftwaffe, responsible only to Goëring and Hitler. A unique insight into the German side of the air war.

SAMURAI by Saburo Sakai with
Martin Caidin & Fred Saito
The true account of the legendary Japanese combat pilot. In his elusive Zero, Sakai was responsible for downing 64 Allied planes during the war. SAMURAI is a powerful portrait of a warrior fighting for his own cause. (May)

BRAZEN CHARIOTS by Robert Crisp

The vivid, stirring, day-by-day account of tank warfare in the African desert. Crisp was a British major, who in a lightweight Honey tank led the British forces into battle against the legendary Rommel on the sands of Egypt. (June)

REACH FOR THE SKY by Paul Brickhill

The inspiring true story of Douglas Bader. The famous RAF fighter pilot who had lost both legs, Bader returned to the service in World War II as a combat pilot and downed 22 planes in the Battle of Britain. Shot down, Bader survived the war in a German prison camp. (July)

COMPANY COMMANDER
by Charles B. MacDonald

The infantry classic of World War II. Twenty-two-year-old MacDonald, a U.S. infantry captain, led his men in combat through some of the toughest fighting in the war both in France and Germany. This book tells what it is really like to lead men into battle. (September)

Bantam War Books are available now unless otherwise noted. They may be obtained wherever paperbacks are sold.

THE SECOND WORLD WAR

The full drama of World War II is captured in this new series of books about a world on fire. In addition to paintings, there are maps and line drawings throughout the text at points where they are most informative.

☐ 11642 **FLY FOR YOUR LIFE** $1.95
by Larry Forester
Amazing story of R.R. Stanford Tuck, one of Britain's foremost air aces.

☐ 11709 **THE FIRST AND THE LAST** $1.95
by Adolf Galland
Unique view of German air war by commander of all fighter forces in the Luftwaffe.

☐ 12523 **SAMURAI by Sakai with Caidin** $2.25
and Saito
Sakai's own story by the Japanese combat pilot responsible for shooting down 64 allied planes.

☐ 11812 **BRAZEN CHARIOTS by Robert Crisp** $1.95
Vivid story of war, of fighting in tanks in the wide spaces of the Western Desert told by Major Robert Crisp.

These large format (8½ X 11), full-color art books capture the spirit of men and machines in action.

☐ 01063 **THE AVIATION ART OF KEITH FERRIS** $7.95
Canada $8.95
☐ 01049 **THE AVIATION ART OF FRANK WOOTON** $6.95
☐ 01004 **THE MARINE PAINTINGS OF CARL EVERS** $5.95
☐ 01029 **THE MARINE PAINTINGS OF CHRIS MAYGAR** $6.95

Buy them at your local bookstore or use this handy coupon for ordering:

Bantam Books, Inc., Dept. WW, 414 East Golf Road, Des Plaines, Ill. 60016

Please send me the books I have checked above. I am enclosing $_____
(please add 75¢ to cover postage and handling). Send check or money order —no cash or C.O.D.'s please.

Mr/Mrs/Miss _____

Address _____

City _____ State/Zip _____

WW—12/78

Please allow four weeks for delivery. This offer expires 5/79.

HOLOCAUST

"Those who cannot remember the past are condemned to repeat it."

George Santayana

The events leading up to, through and beyond the tragic years of persecution and resistance during World War II.

☐ 11877 **HOLOCAUST**
Gerald Green
$2.25

☐ 06407 **A BAG OF MARBLES**
Joseph Joffo
$1.75

☐ 11405 **THE HIDING PLACE**
Corrie ten Boom
$1.95

☐ 12510 **THE LAST OF THE JUST**
Andre Schwarz-Bart
$2.95

☐ 11968 **MISCHLING, SECOND DEGREE**
Ilse Koehn
$1.95

☐ 02858 **THE UPSTAIRS ROOM**
Johanna Reiss
$1.25

☐ 12492 **THE WAR AGAINST THE JEWS**
Lucy Dawidowitz
$2.95

☐ 11937 **MILA 18** Leon Uris
$2.50

☐ 11129 **THE MOON IS DOWN**
John Steinbeck
$1.50

Bantam Book Catalog

Here's your up-to-the-minute listing of ove
1,400 titles by your favorite authors.

This illustrated, large format catalog gives
description of each title. For your convenience
it is divided into categories in fiction and nor
fiction—gothics, science fiction, westerns, mys
teries, cookbooks, mysticism and occult, biogra
phies, history, family living, health, psychology
art.

So don't delay—take advantage of this specia
opportunity to increase your reading pleasure

Just send us your name and address and 50¢
(to help defray postage and handling costs).

BANTAM BOOKS, INC.
Dept. FC, 414 East Golf Road, Des Plaines, Ill. 60016

Mr./Mrs./Miss_____
(please print)

Address_____

City_____State_____Zip_____

Do you know someone who enjoys books? Just give us their names
and addresses and we'll send them a catalog too!

_____

Mr./Mrs./Miss_____

Address_____

City_____State_____Zip_____

_____

Mr./Mrs./Miss_____

Address_____

City_____State_____Zip_____